THE AUTHORITY TRAP

THE AUTHORITY TRAP

Strategic Choices of
International NGOs

**Sarah S. Stroup and
Wendy H. Wong**

CORNELL UNIVERSITY PRESS   ITHACA AND LONDON

First published 2017 by Cornell University Press

Printed in the United States of America

Library of Congress Cataloging-in-Publication Data

Names: Stroup, Sarah S. (Sarah Snip), 1978– author. | Wong, Wendy H., 1980– author.
Title: The authority trap : strategic choices of international NGOs / Sarah S. Stroup and Wendy H. Wong.
Description: Ithaca : Cornell University Press, 2017. | Includes bibliographical references and index.
Identifiers: LCCN 2017013877 | ISBN 9781501702143 (cloth : alk. paper) | ISBN 9781501702150 (pbk. : alk. paper) | ISBN 9781501709777 (pdf) | ISBN 9781501712418 (epub/mobi)
Subjects: LCSH: Non-governmental organizations—Political aspects. | Organizational behavior—Political aspects. | Organizational effectiveness— Political aspects. | Authority. | Reputation—Political aspects.
Classification: LCC JZ4841 .S78 2017 | DDC 352.3/421106—dc23
LC record available at https://lccn.loc.gov/2017013877

Cornell University Press strives to use environmentally responsible suppliers and materials to the fullest extent possible in the publishing of its books. Such materials include vegetable-based, low-VOC inks and acid-free papers that are recycled, totally chlorine-free, or partly composed of nonwood fibers. For further information, visit our website at cornellpress.cornell.edu.

Contents

Acknowledgments

This book began with many conversations about what scholars and practitioners know about international nongovernmental organizations. We have had scores of meandering Skype calls, working visits in Toronto and Middlebury, drinks, coffee dates, and conference presentations. We selected cases, took turns interviewing subjects, and debated our findings, finally landing on the idea of "the authority trap." Four years of collaboration have produced a great friendship and hopefully better scholarship.

Many people have given generous feedback on parts of the book, improving our argument and pointing out errors (we claim full responsibility for the remaining flaws). Thanks first to the participants in our book workshop held in Washington, DC, in September 2015. Martha Finnemore, Jennifer Hadden, Patrick Thaddeus Jackson, David Lake, Amanda Murdie, and Abraham Newman offered sharp critiques and priceless support, and we thank them for their generosity and insightfulness. We also shared chapter drafts in seminars at Dartmouth College, the University of Toronto, Claremont Graduate University, the University of Washington, the University of Southern California, and the University of Denver. We are grateful for the opportunities to get such a wealth of feedback, and we thank in particular Debbi Avant, Steven Bernstein, Mary Kay Gugerty, Patrick James, Lissa Rogers, and Brian Greenhill. We presented pieces of the book in progress at annual meetings of the American Political Science Association (in 2013, 2014, and 2016) and the International Studies Association (in 2014 and 2016); thank you to the wonderful panel participants. Our serious work on the book began after a workshop at the 2012 ISA annual conference that was convened by Hans Peter Schmitz and Beth Bloodgood.

We have floated our idea past many people and solicited suggestions shamelessly. We would like to thank in particular Clifford Bob, Anne Buffardi, Josh Busby, Sarah Bush, Charli Carpenter, Adam Dean, Lilach Gilady, Ben Graham, Duncan Green, Jessica Green, Seva Gunitsky, Laura Henry, Matt Hoffmann, Steve Hopgood, Jon Isham, Jonathan Jennings, Amme Kolovos, Randy Kritkausky, Sabine Lang, Ed Laurance, Charlie MacCormack, Mabrouka M'Barek, Bill McKibben, George Mitchell, Clementine Olivier, Darius Ornston, Aseem Prakash, Will Prichard, Paloma Raggo, Stephan Renckens, Steve Saideman, Wayne Sandholtz, Hans Schmitz, Anna Schrimpf, Michelle Shumate, Kathryn Sikkink, Jackie Smith, David Suarez, Lisa Sundstrom, Ann Swidler, Trevor Thrall, Nick Weller,

Scott Wilbur, Helen Yanacopulos, and Amy Yuen for their suggestions. David Lake has been an unflagging supporter of our work and helped us figure out which book we wanted to write. Michael Barnett offered early support for our ideas and led us to new and challenging literatures on global authority. Jeff Isaac helped guide our review essay to publication in *Perspectives on Politics*. Some of our findings feature in a volume on hierarchy edited by Ayse Zarakol, and we thank her, Alex Cooley, Janice Bially Mattern, Ann Towns, and the other participants of the workshops that took place in May 2014 at University of California, San Diego and June 2015 at the University of Cambridge. We could not have written the book without the diligence of our research assistants: Josh Berlowitz, Jack Clancy, Nick Delahanty, Olivia Heffernan, and Tom Yu at Middlebury, and Minah Ahn, Julia Chen, Jahaan Pittalwala, Kristen Pue, Noah Schouela, Takumi Shibaike, and David Zarnett at the University of Toronto. We also thank two anonymous reviewers for their thoughts in improving the book.

Roger Haydon made the prescient suggestion that we could and should write a book together, and his initial encouragement and supportive critiques have led to years of fruitful discussions and writing. We thank him for getting this project started. We gratefully acknowledge the generous support of our two institutions, Middlebury College and the University of Toronto, which made research and this collaboration possible. Thank you also to the Middlebury office in Washington, DC, for hosting our 2015 workshop.

We must thank our family and friends whose support makes our professional lives possible. Special thanks and much love to our patient partners, John and Rick, for enduring hours and hours of talk about the book and picking up the pieces when we disappeared to research or write. Madeleine and Henry Stroup were occasional participants in our many Skype calls and they offered welcome distractions, outdoor activities, and lots of hugs. We are grateful for both the space we received to think through our ideas, and the opportunities available when we needed to talk and do *anything* else.

Finally, we are grateful to the individuals who provided their time and frank reflections on our project. In the process of crafting this book, we have interviewed more than seventy people, sometimes multiple times, in various sectors and occupations. Though they are not personally acknowledged in the book, their thoughts are embedded firmly in these pages. The many INGOs and their state and corporate partners that we examine here affect global politics from different organizational, political, and economic positions. Our hope is that a clearer understanding of the authority trap proves a useful tool for them all.

Abbreviations

AC	INGO Accountability Charter
AI	Amnesty International
ATT	Arms Trade Treaty
ATTAC	Association pour la Taxation des Transactions financières et pour l'Action Citoyenne
BRAC	Bangladesh Rural Advancement Committee
CAC	Control Arms Campaign
CAFOD	Catholic Agency for Overseas Development
CARE	Cooperative for Assistance and Relief Everywhere
CICC	Coalition for an International Criminal Court
COP	Conference of the Parties [to the UN Framework Convention on Climate Change]
CRS	Catholic Relief Services
DFID	Department for International Development [United Kingdom]
ECOSOC	[United Nations] Economic and Social Council
EDF	Environmental Defense Fund
EU	European Union
FIDH	Fédération internationale des ligues des droits de l'Homme
FoE	Friends of the Earth
FSC	Forest Stewardship Council
FTT	financial transactions tax
G20	Group of 20
GRI	Global Reporting Initiative
HRW	Human Rights Watch
IANGO	International Advocacy NGO
IANSA	International Action Network on Small Arms
IATI	International Aid Transparency Initiative
ICBL	International Campaign to Ban Landmines
ICC	International Criminal Court
ICJ	International Commission of Jurists
ICRC	International Committee of the Red Cross
ICSC	International Civil Society Center
IGO	intergovernmental organization
IIED	International Institute for Environment and Development

IMF	International Monetary Fund
INGO	international nongovernmental organization
KPI	key performance indicator
LCA	life-cycle assessments
MSF	Médecins Sans Frontières
NGO	nongovernmental organization
NRA	National Rifle Association
SFI	Sustainable Forestry Initiative
TSC	The Sustainability Consortium
UIA	Union of International Associations
UN	United Nations
UNGC	United Nations Global Compact
USAID	United States Agency for International Development
WEED	World Economy, Ecology, and Development
WEF	World Economic Forum
WSF	World Social Forum
WWF	World Wildlife Fund/World Wide Fund for Nature

THE AUTHORITY TRAP

THE AUTHORITY TRAP

International nongovernment organizations (INGOs) seem to be everywhere in global politics, but they are not created equal. Kumi Naidoo knows a thing or two about running INGOs. He started out protesting South African apartheid and has since led both large and small INGOs, including Greenpeace International, where he was executive director from 2009 to 2015. At the gathering of powerful elites at the 2012 World Economic Forum (WEF) in Davos, Switzerland, Naidoo spoke to a journalist about his different INGO experiences:

> Naidoo had been to Davos eleven times, the first eight as the secretary-general of the Global Call to Action Against Poverty. "When I came in that capacity, I never could get a C.E.O. to talk to me," he told me later. "I used to follow them into the toilet. I met Bill Clinton in 2003, when we were standing next to each other at the urinals. When I came as Greenpeace, two years ago, I was amazed how keen they were to meet me. A C.E.O. told me, 'Some of my peers are eager to have you at their table so they won't be on your menu.'"[1]

States and corporations often claim to engage the concerns of INGOs in their decisions, but the specific INGOs that actually get access to decision makers are a very select group. Most of the time, INGOs are clamoring to have their voices heard, shouting in the street or cornering their targets in bathrooms and elevators.

Among the public and even many academics, the popular perception of INGOs is of a fairly homogeneous group of relatively powerless actors pushing for drastic social change. In fact, there are stark differences among INGOs in their power or, more precisely, in their authority. For all the sensational images of mass protests from events like the Battle in Seattle, the day-to-day reality is that of the tens of thousands of INGOs inhabiting the landscape of political action, exceedingly few have access to and deference from important audiences.

We call these very few groups *leading* INGOs, and they seem to have it all: their reports make international newspapers, they partner with powerful states, and corporations take their calls. In short, they receive deference from different audiences in global politics and therefore have *authority*. Their status as leading INGOs gives them a substantive role in the arena of global politics. But these leading INGOs face a cruel irony: their authority constrains their choices and activities. The central insight of this book is that more authority does not lead to more latitude. Leading INGOs have worked hard to achieve their rarefied status; the new measures of INGO authority that we present reveal how difficult it is for INGOs to receive deference from a single audience, much less several. Subsequently, maintaining that status requires that INGOs secure continued deference from multiple audiences that can be quite diverse in their preferences. In short, leading INGOs are caught in what we call *the authority trap*.

For leading INGOs, the authority trap pressures them to advance incrementalist proposals and prioritize organizational imperatives over larger—potentially unpalatable—demands to change the status quo. Their authority before multiple (and sometimes conflicting) audiences limits the content of what they say or do. They must moderate and curate their proposals and programs and fit them within the range of acceptable outcomes for *multiple* stakeholders. While they may push those targets to do things they might not otherwise do, pushing too hard or too far can threaten the deference they have received. Those with authority thus have both a megaphone and a muzzle; the more deference INGOs get from different audiences, the greater both effects. Escape from that trap is possible but it requires a defiance of organizational incentives, and as a result, a wealth of potential achievements is regularly left on the shelf. For the vast majority of INGOs, the ones we simply refer to as other INGOs, there is no muzzle. They can do and say what they want. But they are trapped in a different way: they lack authority and have low status. Their lack of authority gives them much greater latitude to pursue what they want, how they want, with few or no consequences. But they have no microphone, let alone a megaphone.

The authority trap operates by shaping the strategies of INGOs, depending on their authority. In their many interactions, INGOs choose among three broad strategic alternatives: collaboration, competition, and condemnation. In the chapters that follow, we show why and how authority shapes the strategies that INGOs employ as they target states, corporations, and their fellow INGOs.

Leading INGOs tend to be more collaborative with states and are favored as partners by corporations seeking to launch new private governance initiatives. Other INGOs have more freedom to condemn and compete with their targets, though they have little audience for their efforts.

Authority shapes the *strategic choices* of INGOs with particular audiences. First, authority affects how INGOs select state targets. Because leading INGOs need to show concrete outputs and claim credit to maintain their status, they tend to focus on friendly, middle-power states rather than target the most important states. In approaching private governance initiatives, by contrast, leading INGOs (like all INGOs) are divided on whether collaboration or condemnation of corporate practices is more desirable. Status still shapes the INGO-corporate relationship, however, as corporations prefer to launch new initiatives with leading INGOs. Leading INGOs thus help launch many private initiatives that later prove weak. Finally, leading INGOs are much less solicitous of other INGOs and must defend their status when engaging with their weaker peers. All INGOs collaborate and compete to offer specific but wildly different visions of what constitutes good practice for the INGO sector as a whole.

Second, across all audiences, leading INGOs will tend to employ strategies that yield "vanilla victories." These are policy changes that are widely palatable but yield only incremental improvements. Because of their status-maintenance concerns, the very INGOs invited in by states and corporations are the least likely to demand radical change. They may move the needle slightly, which these leading INGOs would argue is advancement. But their critics see these policy changes as vanilla victories, palatable to a wide array of audiences but unsatisfying reformist efforts.

Those who watch or work for INGOs are well aware of the diversity of the population. Many optimistic accounts celebrate this and suggest that a de facto division of labor might emerge. If some INGOs engage in quiet conversations or collaborative programming, others loudly demand action in the streets, and still others offer technical assistance on designing new human rights treaties or monitoring environmental initiatives, are not INGOs covering all the political bases? Our analysis suggests that this division of labor is unlikely. For one, only some of these efforts get heard by target audiences, and other strategies get ignored. In addition, status concerns interfere with either explicit coordination or implicit acceptance of this diversity. The need of leading INGOs to maintain their status can create heated disagreements among INGOs, and dysfunction and fragmentation frequently result.

This book also systematically evaluates the authority of INGOs across different sectors, before multiple audiences. For years, researchers have sought greater precision in explaining how INGOs influence politics. Many prominent studies of INGO influence have asserted that INGOs have power because they asked for and achieved a particular outcome on a single issue. This sort of work usefully justified the continued study of INGOs and established correlation between INGO demands and political outcomes. Yet what was missing was a systematic evaluation of what constitutes INGO authority across multiple cases. Our book, particularly chapter 3, presents a series of metrics that helps us score the overall authority of INGOs across a range of issue areas. These measures allow cross-sectoral comparisons of INGOs and offer a systematic way to articulate the differences in authority between leading INGOs and other INGOs.

This introductory chapter addresses four main concerns. We begin by exploring INGO authority. A few INGOs have become authoritative, but this is the exception rather than the rule. Next, we describe how the study of variations in INGO authority can offer new insights about INGO influence, global governance, and practical concerns about the limits of the authority trap. Third, we lay out the contours of our causal claim that status shapes collaboration, competition, and condemnation with INGO targets. Authority is not the only explanation for INGOs' strategic choices, but it is one that has received little attention because many studies have focused on simply showing that INGOs have power. We start from the point that INGOs *do* have power, as authority, and demonstrate how authority varies greatly among them. Finally, we outline the fundamental assumptions behind our argument.

A Full Picture of INGOs and Their Authority

INGOs are increasingly prominent players in world politics. Over the past three decades, a growing body of research has conclusively demonstrated that INGOs can be influential and has explored the conditions under which INGOs shape policies and social practices around the globe.[2] In public discourse, INGOs are often presented as part of a "David versus Goliath" narrative, where principled powerless agents in discouraging conditions triumph over giant, rigid, and inhumane interests (Lang 2013). To realize these triumphs, INGOs enjoy a form of potential influence. INGOs can set global agendas and frame issues, telling other actors what issues are important and how to think about them, often according to cosmopolitan principles. INGOs can also monitor and interpret the actions of others, condemning or congratulating. They might create new regulations and benchmarks to improve state and corporate practices. They might provide services to neglected populations, assist during man-made and natural disasters, and offer material solutions to problems that push on local sensibilities, such as providing menstrual pads to school-age girls. Finally, INGOs can represent societal interests as part of a large but disorganized global civil society. What unifies

INGOs is not what strategies they adopt or issues they address, but instead their position in global politics as nonstate actors that assert their principled commitments and expert capabilities.

Among the tens of thousands of INGOs, only a few have achieved the sort of influence described above. We identify a list of leading INGOs in chapter 3. The trajectories of those leading INGOs are complex but fairly well-known. What is less clear is how the distribution of authority among the entire INGO sector shapes the individual and collective influence they are able to realize.

The Path to Salience

A handful of factors help INGOs become politically salient players. First, charismatic and committed leaders have played key roles in the foundation of leading INGOs. David Brower and Julian Huxley respectively channeled their environmentalist sensibilities into Friends of the Earth (FoE) and World Wildlife Fund (WWF), Eglantyne Jebb founded and built a strong and international organization at Save the Children, and Lesley Kirkley of Oxfam was always first on the scene of a catastrophe (Mulley 2009; Penrose and Seaman 1996; Black 1992). Second, leading INGOs made early commitments to decidedly cosmopolitan principles such as the universality of human rights, a shared humanity, and a planetary ecosystem (Clark 2001; Wapner 1996). For example, World Vision was founded as an evangelical organization, but when its role as a relief and development organization conflicted with its religious mission, it scaled back the latter in favor of the former (Barnett 2011, 129–30). Over time, many of these purportedly cosmopolitan INGOs have been challenged to incorporate diverse viewpoints into their programming, and leading INGOs have reformed their organizational structures in response (Hopgood 2006; Commins 1997; Lindenberg and Bryant 2001; Stroup and Wong 2013).

Leading INGOs have also made three important choices. First, they developed a distinct identity or brand early on and promoted it (Finnemore 1996; Redfield 2013; Wapner 1996). For example, CARE's marketing acumen helped it move from being a loose association of civic associations to public prominence in the late 1940s (Campbell 1990), while Amnesty International's logo offered a powerful image of a candle behind barbed wire (Hopgood 2006). Second, leading INGOs successfully transitioned from being innovative idealists to professionalized bureaucrats. The transition may not have been that difficult for CARE, which had distinguished itself by its hard-nosed approach to aid (Linden 1976). At Greenpeace, the embodiment of "countercultural environmentalism," many national chapters were in disarray in its first decade, which opened the door for European chapters to consolidate their power and unify the global organization

(Brown and May 1991; Zelko 2013). Third, leading INGOs have developed a deep well of expertise. Groups like CARE, WWF, and the ICRC are leaders, respectively, in development programming, species preservation, and international humanitarian law (Stroup 2012; Banks 2010; Forsythe 2005). In 1972, the newly formed FoE published a useful daily newsletter at the UN Conference on the Human Environment in Stockholm (Doherty and Doyle 2013, 58). Médecins Sans Frontières (MSF or Doctors without Borders) disseminates its epidemiological research to public health and humanitarian professionals (Redfield 2013). Some expertise may be political, as with the training that Oxfam offers other NGOs on political campaigns (BOND 2005).

Finally, leading INGOs have successfully managed their external relations, although their performance has come under fire with advances in information and communication technologies (Yanacopulos 2015). They have carefully cultivated connections with other powerful actors. Those connections came early for some. Amnesty's Sean MacBride, for example, was an Irish diplomat also connected to the International Court of Justice, the United Nations, and the ICRC (Clark 2001, 7). INGOs have made themselves invaluable allies of many intergovernmental organizations (Weiss and Gordenker 1996). Early on, Oxfam linked itself closely to the UN's 1960 Freedom From Hunger campaign (Black 1992, 70). Leading INGOs have also cultivated financial independence. The heavy reliance on private members at Amnesty and FoE slowed the pace of organizational growth, but it also allowed the organization to define its own changing goals. Organizations like World Vision, CARE, WWF, and Save the Children take enormous sums from government agencies, but all have worked to create other sources of income or diversify the sources of "official" income (Lindenberg and Bryant 2001).

These factors—leadership, cosmopolitan principles, branding, professionalization, expertise, connectedness, and financial independence—are common characteristics of leading INGOs, but there is no clear, deterministic, or linear path to widespread authority. The rise of organizations like Oxfam and the International Committee of the Red Cross (ICRC) has proceeded in fits and starts.[3] For every group that successfully met a challenge, a dozen other NGOs disappeared or were simply absent from the public eye. Anti-Slavery International, for example, has fought its long decline but with limited success (Korey 1998; Wong 2011). Other INGOs have some mix of these factors and little authority. Consider the very different trajectories of two human rights groups, both founded in 1978 and funded by the Ford Foundation. Human Rights Watch (HRW) is a global human rights leader, wielding authority before many audiences. Global Rights was also committed to universal rights, and it had a professional structure and growing expertise (Stroup 2012), but it lacked a charismatic leader or diversified funding, and by 2014 it had closed all except for a few field offices.[4] Finally, the individual choices that INGOs make may be unsuccessful in the wrong environ-ment. INGOs must frame their claims in the context of existing social norms and work through specific institutional channels (Busby 2010; Keck and Sikkink 1998; Tarrow 2005).

The path to salience for a few INGOs is fascinating, and our understanding of this path is incomplete. Without denying the importance of those questions, however, one might alternately ask, "So what?" If the experience of Amnesty is exceptional, what is the norm, and what are the consequences? These are the concerns we address in this book.

An Incomplete Account

The stories of a handful of politically salient INGOs are valuable, but they are also insufficient. First, in fighting to demonstrate the importance of INGOs, sym-pathetic analysts may overstate the influence of these groups. Yes, INGOs are important global actors, but, like other actors, the power relations in which they are situated can constrain as well as enable (Barnett and Duvall 2005). In addi-tion, our familiarity with the stories of these leading INGOs, when combined with a dearth of accounts of the powerless, risks creating a fallacy of composition. Amnesty and its practices become equated with all human rights INGOs, rather than being understood as anomalous. The reality is that Amnesty and a handful of other INGOs are exceptional; they are not representative and do not fulfill all the potential roles that INGOs can serve. They enjoy an incredible amount of attention and deference from a wide range of audiences around the globe.

The subject of authority and power is an uncomfortable one within the INGO community (Stein 2008; Yanacopulos 2015). Even leading INGOs recog-nize that it is their image as powerless that gives them legitimacy and the resulting authority to act in the eyes of many audiences (Rubenstein 2014). For instance, in accepting the 1999 Nobel Peace Prize, the then-president of MSF International argued that "we exist relative to the state, to its institutions and its power. . . . Ours is not to displace the responsibility of the state. . . . If civil society identi-fies a problem, it is not theirs to provide a solution, but it is theirs to expect that states will translate this into concrete and just solutions."[5] Despite its well-known brand and substantial authority, MSF depicts itself as a righteous but weak advo-cate pleading for other actors to use their influence justly. This picture is at best partial and at worst disingenuous, as MSF is a leading INGO, not at all weak compared to other INGOs. Its statement reflects the *Fight Club* logic INGOs adopt when they think about their role in global politics. The first rule of *Fight Club* is not to talk about it; the first rule of being a leading INGO is that you do not talk publicly about being a leading INGO.

In the INGO community, as elsewhere, authority is concentrated in the hands of a few. In the following chapters, we demonstrate empirically that only some INGOs are authoritative and that most are not. Although such claims may make sympathizers of INGOs uncomfortable, or seem to offer too much ground to skeptics of nonstate actors, the evidence is strikingly clear. These differences in authority influence the strategies they adopt and, ultimately, the outcomes they demand.

Note that we use the concept of authority, rather than power, to discuss INGOs, as we wish to draw attention to social relations through which INGOs exert influence. In global affairs, a wide range of actors relate to one another on a crowded stage. In these relationships, INGOs enjoy more authority or less authority. Their capacity, principled commitments, and expertise must first become visible and then get evaluated by various audiences; occasionally, this translates into deference to an INGO that is then recognized as *an* authority. Conceptually, then, authority is not binary and it is not static. It can vary in level: for example, FoE gets mentioned in global print media almost ten times as frequently as the Rainforest Action Network. Authority can also vary over time as INGOs build and lose authority before audiences through their actions, which raises the importance of strategic choices. Authority can also be broad-based or narrow. CIVICUS is well-regarded by its INGO peers, but Oxfam is regarded as an authority by peers, ordinary citizens, media outlets, some corporations, and policymakers. INGOs struggle to establish authority with one audience, and reaching multiple audiences is an even more demanding task. Having succeeded, however, leading INGOs are not unfettered; they face "Gulliver's troubles" (Hoffmann 1968).[6]

Implications for Research and Practice

From the outset, our aim has been to provide a systematic way to study the authority of INGOs. By identifying the key audiences from which INGOs attain authority, we are able to measure to what extent INGOs are being heard by each of these audiences. This mapping exercise allows us to explore the effects of authority on INGO choice. Our conception of the authority trap should speak not just to analysts of international relations, but also to practitioners and activists in these INGOs. We offer an explanation for the gap between INGOs' lofty aspirations and their specific goals, giving support and ammunition to those that might try to narrow that gap.

Authority in Global Politics

Are INGOs influential? They do not invade countries or place economic sanctions on governments, as states can. They do not control what is bought and sold on the global market, as some corporations can. And yet decades of research have shown that INGOs can and do affect the actions of states, corporations, and one another, all the while shaping collective understandings of social problems.

We assume that INGOs enjoy authority based on criteria specific to them as a type of actor (see below), but that this varies substantially for individual INGOs. We move from this starting position to actual measures of INGO authority, which allows us to identify leading INGOs and other INGOs, and then explain how this shapes organizational strategies. We are inspired by scholarship on state power that has measured everything from military spending to state reputations and argued that these differences matter for state strategies and influence (Nye 2008; Krasner 1976; Mansfield 1993). Thus, for example, while we start from a radically different position from state-centric and materialist realists about the importance of nonstate actors and their social relationships, we are interested in many of the same questions that a scholar such as David Baldwin (2012) asks: Who has power with respect to which other actors and on which issues, and by what means is this power exercised?

Existing conceptions of authority offer a number of avenues for studying INGO strategies and influence. The study of authority raises questions of legitimacy (Hurd 1999), contracts between actors (Lake 2010, 2009), and the sources of authority (Avant, Finnemore, and Sell 2010), particularly the role of knowledge and expertise (Haas 1992; Sending 2015; Zürn et al. 2012). The various treatments of authority are all sympathetic to a conception of power more complex than simple material capacity (Barnett and Duvall 2005). We include but then move beyond agential choices and attributes to emphasize the external sources of authority. We take up a particular type of actor, INGOs, and explore the varied deference they receive from important audiences. These audiences confer authority to INGOs and listen to them when they identify relevant issues, criticize others, suggest useful tactics, and forward solutions to problems. The conferral of authority—from audience to INGO—allows INGOs to exercise authority within and outside of that relationship. INGOs have agency in the sense that they can make themselves more likely candidates for deference, but the efficacy of these strategies depends on how they are received. In short, their agency may be constrained by structural forces.

Relative to other actors like states and corporations, INGOs benefit from the presumption that their principled commitments make them different. Thus, broad studies of authority in global governance tend to distinguish INGOs as examples of moral or principled authority, while also noting their growing expertise. If we disaggregate the class of INGOs, however, and look at individual groups, the differences among them are marked. Moral or principled authority does not yield unfettered freedom to pursue those lofty aims. Instead, authority creates a new set of concerns for those that have it.

The authority trap reveals that the level and type of influence exercised by INGOs is less than transformative. That is not to deny either the diversity of INGO approaches or the actual influence they achieve, but rather to highlight that, as with other actors, authority can constrain as well as enable INGO choices. The broad-based authority of a few INGOs creates problems for those who hope for INGOs to represent the disenfranchised. Those INGOs that have achieved the widest deference promote cosmopolitan principles, but this expansive scope then challenges them to represent a multiplicity of groups, a task at which they almost necessarily fail given their limited resources and particular (and largely Western) values (Barnett 2011; Hopgood 2006).

To be clear, leading INGO status is not a necessary condition for INGO influence. The INGO Global Exchange, which describes itself as "small and feisty," has successfully pushed Starbucks Coffee to sell fair trade coffee, and Starbucks' long-standing partnership with the leading INGO CARE did not protect it from Global Exchange's critiques (Argenti 2004). But Global Exchange is the exception, rather than the rule; leading INGOs receive more frequent and more direct responses from their targets. Furthermore, as we discuss below, differences in levels of authority shape organizational strategies, and certain strategies may be more effective at yielding changes in behavior or ideas.

Global Civil Society

INGOs are often depicted as central nodes of global civil society, and many use INGOs as a proxy for evaluating trends among societal actors (Anheier, Kaldor, and Glasius 2012). INGOs, working within this broad group, are arguably the most likely actor to improve accountability, draw attention to new issues, or create better equity in global governance (Scholte 2002; Lipschutz 1992; Keck and Sikkink 1998; Price 1998). Of course, like INGOs, global civil society is politically diverse, which challenges the idea that these societal actors are a wellspring of progressive potential (Chambers and Kopstein 2001; Bob 2012; Amoore and Langley 2004; Dryzek and Niemeyer 2008). In addition, not all scholars of global civil society share this INGO-centric view. Some focus less on specific outputs and more on the deliberative process embodied in global civil society, a process that may be normatively desirable and a source of long-term transformation (Keane 2003; Anheier 2007; Dryzek 2012).

Our formal organizational focus does not fully capture the diversity of global civil society, but it does capture those groups that are often asked to stand in for the role. We articulate a systematic way to think about the multiplicity of INGOs that can get lumped into this catch-all category. Rather than separate INGOs by national origin, funding, or issue area, we look at INGOs by their attention from audiences and consequent authority. This perspective reinforces the diversity of global civil society actors, but it also suggests that there are two global civil societies. One group of societal actors regularly receives attention from powerful players and participates in global meetings and dialogue and another very large group does not.

Beyond Academia: Practical Applications

Outside of academic circles, INGO practitioners and the partners and targets of INGOs should also find this book useful; it confirms what many of them know and accept or rail against. The hundreds of INGO staffers we have interviewed for over more than a decade are all aware of the imbalances within the INGO community, but this truth is clouded by other concerns. Legally and culturally, INGOs are defined by their volunteer spirit, orientation toward some greater good, and roots in civil society rather than the state. Even if in actual practice all these are routinely violated—as with INGOs that are fully professionalized, disconnected from their mission, and heavily dependent on state funding—the authority of INGOs is seen to depend on maintaining that ideal-type reputation. INGOs will thus be well-served to explore this treatment of a difficult subject—authority differences among INGOs—while considering whether strategies that enhance their authority also advance their mission. Furthermore, none of our findings should be surprising to seasoned INGO staff, but the size of the gaps between INGOs—even household names—may be astonishing. It takes a *lot* to become a leading INGO. Many might approach the threshold, but few step through the door.

Finally, the frustrations of individual staffers in dealing with limits on their actions, and the insistence on vanilla victories that compromise on ideals but achieve buy-in across audiences, are confirmed in this book. Leading INGOs often cannot help *but* act the way they do, and change tends to occur only at the margins.

The Relationship between Status and Strategy

The influence or success of any actor emerges from an array of conscious choices and good fortune. We join with many other INGO scholars in focusing on the determinants of INGO strategies. The strategies employed by INGOs are plentiful: INGOs define missions, raise funds, form networks, design programs, deliver services, gather information, prioritize and frame issues, select advocacy tactics, represent constituents, measure outcomes, monitor compliance, advance new standards, and more (Keck and Sikkink 1998; Mitchell 2015; Green 2013; Carpenter 2014; Betsill and Corell 2008). Using an audience-oriented approach to authority, we argue that leading INGOs (and other INGOs) adopt different strategies because of their need to maintain deference from more (or fewer) audiences.

The Three C's: Collaboration, Competition, and Condemnation

There are three major strategic orientations that INGOs can adopt when dealing with various audiences: collaboration, competition, and condemnation. This simplification is a heuristic device for organizing the range of activities INGOs engage in (for a similar taxonomy, see Johnson 2016). An INGO's choice of frame, metric, or program will depend on the INGO's approach to the target it seeks to influence. First, in *collaboration,* INGOs agree with their audience about desirable goals and about the means to achieve them. In chapter 4, for example, we describe how the Canadian government and a coalition of small INGO activists worked together to advance the idea of an international treaty to monitor and slow the small arms trade. INGOs can also work in *competition* with their target, and will do so when they share a goal but disagree about the means to achieve it. In chapter 6, we show that all INGOs may agree on broad goals of human rights protection and poverty alleviation, but they might provide very different visions of how INGOs and others should advance these goals. Finally, INGOs can engage in *condemnation* when they disagree with both the means and ends of their target. In chapter 5, we explain how a few leading INGOs have condemned the United Nations Global Compact as providing political cover for corporations with poor environmental and human rights records. In practice, of course, these three approaches are sometimes adopted sequentially or simultaneously, but the tension among the orientations means one tends to predominate.

An INGO's authority shapes its choice of strategy. Weaker INGOs may regularly condemn states, corporations, and even other INGOs through protests, demands for boycotts, and colorful placards, but leading INGOs are more collaborative. Leading INGOs' authority gives them special access to states and corporations; when leading INGOs call, their targets are more likely to pick up the phone. For example, the Nature Conservancy has long worked with corporations in the protection of the environment through partnerships with Coca-Cola, Dow Chemical, and others. Collaboration works when the INGO partner—either state or corporation—defers to the INGO as a partner. Second, condemnation can be a riskier strategy for those INGOs that have developed robust relationships with state or corporate targets (Seabrooke and Wigan 2015). Those leading INGOs that do move from cooperation to condemnation do so delicately. These can be quite fraught decisions. CARE had to balance the concerns of its many audiences about its independence in deciding whether to accept money from the US government for relief and reconstruction in Iraq. At the last minute, CARE made the decision to reject this funding and later clarified that this rejection of funds from belligerents would last only during a conflict, not after (Stroup 2012, 202). Finally, leading INGOs are less likely to condemn their INGO peers, as doing so risks revealing petty fragmentation within the civil society sector they seek and are seen to represent.

Of course, not all leading INGOs are collaborative all the time, and condemnation can be a valuable strategic tool for shaming and awareness raising. Still, among the leading INGOs we identify, condemnation is rarely the sole strategy adopted. Greenpeace is perhaps the most combative of the leading INGOs. As we show in chapter 3, its authority is more limited to the media and the public. This gives valuable leverage. For example, when Greenpeace condemned corporations in 2006 for destroying the Amazon rainforest, McDonald's responded publicly to the allegations.[7] Interestingly, even Greenpeace has become more conciliatory toward businesses over time as it seeks to provide evidence of its efficacy in changing corporate behavior.[8]

Other Explanations for INGO Strategy

In developing this argument, we are aware of alternate explanations for INGO strategies. One is that INGOs craft their strategies in response to those on whom they depend for funds. Many express this argument in the formal language of principal-agent relations, where donors delegate INGOs some set of tasks (Cooley and Ron 2002; Bush 2015). Second, INGO strategies might emerge from the position they occupy in various networks (Carpenter 2014; Hadden 2015). Central nodes might set agendas while peripheral groups gather information (Lake and Wong 2009; Wong 2012). Third, strategies may emerge from the principled commitments or internal processes of an INGO (Brown, Ebrahim, and Batliwala 2012; Krause 2014), such as the claim that MSF's largely private fundraising is expressive of its principled commitment to independence from states (Redfield 2013). Fourth, a functionalist explanation holds that INGOs adopt the strategy best suited for the political opportunities or technical demands they face. Human rights INGOs might adopt evidence-based advocacy strategies as the most effective method of protecting rights (Clark 2001), whereas humanitarian groups focus more on service delivery.

Each of these explanations has substantial merit. To the extent that other factors condition the effectiveness of INGO strategies, they shape which INGOs rise to positions of authority. Yet we demonstrate that in the dynamic process of authority creation and maintenance, INGOs have substantial agency, and their responses to resource pressures and functional demands differ. Their choices result in more deference or less deference. The process of cultivating deference from multiple audiences involves speaking more than just the jargon of a single donor. Resource dependency thus might be a powerful explanation for INGOs like Catholic Relief Services that rely heavily on a single funder (Barnett 2011), but most leading INGOs have a diverse portfolio of funders with often very different preferences. Our logic thus suggests the reverse effect of the "multiple principals" problem (Hawkins et al. 2006), in which having multiple principals allows agents greater slack to pursue their own goals. That would be true for INGOs only if they did not care about maintaining their authority. But if INGOs *do* care about how audiences perceive them, then they will not neglect the relationship in which they enjoy authority, even if it means they have less freedom to pursue what they want. This effect is intensified if INGOs expect to have repeated interactions with the same audience(s) over time. By our reasoning, having multiple stakeholders *constrains* rather than frees INGOs.

Second, we agree that advocacy networks and project collaborations are a regular feature of INGO life, but the choices actors make within each issue network are shaped by outside relationships. This helps explain why leading INGOs regularly occupy central network positions across a range of issues and countries. Third, the principles INGOs adopt are still broad, and multiple strategies could be understood as supportive of values such as promoting freedom of expression or securing access to food. Thus a wide variety of strategic choices would be consistent with any moral stance, and stances could vary in terms of depth, scope, or reach. Finally, the functionalist explanation ignores the pervasive uncertainty that INGOs face. While INGOs may be rational actors that reject some strategies as ineffective, there is no clear, best strategy for achieving complex social change goals (Watkins, Swidler, and Hannan 2012).

An INGO's authority shapes the political constraints it faces and its access to resources. Of course, becoming a leading INGO is a consequence of successfully meeting political opportunities or building internal capacity. An INGO's political or social setting may select for particular strategies and repeatedly reward those organizations that fit its environment (Aldrich and Pfeffer 1976). That argument is not inconsistent with our account, but we reformulate environments as audiences and recognize that those audiences' preferences are not immutable. Political institutions, social norms, and salient topics are all social constructions that emerge from human relations. Organizations that more or less fit the expectations of some audience are more likely to receive deference from them. Having established their authority, INGOs are not solely at the mercy of these audiences.

They enjoy many forms of power, including the ability to constitute good prac-tice, frame emergent issues, and inform state interests. But the content of these efforts is likely to be incrementalism for those leading INGOs that pull their punches today to preserve their access for tomorrow.

Building Blocks of the Argument

In examining INGOs, we made several choices that shape the scope of this proj-ect. Our perspective is intentionally cross-sectoral, we focus on those INGOs that seek authority, and we approach INGOs as structured organizations rather than porous participants in transnational networks. We explain each choice below.

A Multisector Approach

Unlike most studies of INGOs, ours examines the authority of groups acting in a multitude of issue areas, including relief and development, environmental pro-tection, human rights, and beyond. We adopt this inclusive perspective for three reasons. First, while analysts may study these groups within a particular silo, the INGOs themselves do not stay in that box. Many have moved beyond a narrow definition of their work, such as when Oxfam began to work on climate change or when FoE incorporated indigenous peoples' rights. A cross-sectoral scope is necessary to understand how those issue area boundaries get constructed in the first place and to identify patterns among INGOs in general.

Second, INGO strategies are not simply determined by processes unique to human rights, relief, or environmental protection. In each sector, INGOs engage in service delivery and advocacy. In practice, human rights groups tend to favor advocacy, relief and development groups do more service delivery, and environ-mental groups engage in both political action and direct conservation, but the balance of these strategies within any one sector changes over time and reflects constructed categories of desirable action (for an example, see Nelson and Dorsey 2008). Furthermore, primary function does not determine whether or not an INGO is an "advocacy" INGO; most INGOs engage in some form of advocacy in the process of doing their work, whether through public education or their effectiveness in promoting their particular views on a topic. INGOs also all select decision-making and reporting structures (Lindenberg and Bryant 2001), and there is no clear pattern by issue area of how INGOs organize themselves. Oxfam and Amnesty have centralized advocacy offices with an increasingly global reach (Wong 2012). At Save the Children and FoE, new national chapters have been created in a more haphazard fashion (Stroup and Wong 2013; Wapner 1996).

CARE and HRW both have a strong central chapter that retains considerable informal and formal power (Stroup 2012).

A third reason for our cross-sectoral scope is that these causes compete with one another. Greenpeace and Amnesty are not only striving to outdo the Sierra Club and Human Rights First; they are also contending for the limited attention of policymakers and coverage by the media. In the short term, only so many newspaper articles can be written or charitable donations given. Granted, this competition across sectors may not hold all the time; an INGO trying to get aid supplies across an international border will address a wholly different set of audiences than one trying to promote the International Criminal Court. Still, our research demonstrates that competition and connection across sectoral boundaries is frequent and drives strategic selection.

In brief, closer dialogue among INGO scholars specializing in various issue areas yields new insights (Bell and Coicaud 2006; Gourevitch, Lake, and Stein 2012). Building upon excellent treatments of INGO authority and influence within specific sectors, we advance a more general understanding of INGO authority that differentiates these groups from other global actors while highlighting new questions. For example, why is service delivery in the human rights sector so rare? Leading INGOs such as Amnesty and HRW do relatively little to train lawyers or provide rehabilitation services for victims of torture, but these are as much human rights work as amicus briefs for the UN Human Rights Council.[9] Perhaps those strategies would endanger leading INGOs' status, or perhaps such strategies are second-best options for groups that lack the capacity and expertise for coordinated global advocacy. Our inclusive perspective raises new important questions about INGO strategies.

INGOs Seeking Authority

Not all INGOs seek to develop authority with some audience beyond their narrow donor pool or specific beneficiaries. Bicycles Crossing Borders is a Canadian NGO that runs a bicycle repair facility in eastern Cuba. Ecologia helps design environmental management standards for the International Organization on Standardization (ISO). Sea Shepherd employs controversial (and sometimes violent) methods to demand an end to whaling (Eilstrup-Sangiovanni and Bondaroff 2014). How do we distinguish among the happily obscure and the aspirants? We cannot offer a precise number but we expect that most INGOs seek some authority because they cannot afford not to. Few INGOs can become globally relevant through narrow appeals to small populations, and because INGOs often must justify their presence in the field, some form of advocacy is nearly always necessary. First, authority increases the potential efficacy of all INGO efforts. While advocacy clearly requires that some audience listen to an INGO's claims, so does service delivery. The transfer of goods and knowledge requires resources that must be raised externally, and deference from donors helps secure contracts and creates a regular flow of income (Gent et al. 2015). INGOs that successfully seek funding from the UN-REDD environmental program or the European humanitarian office ECHO have many more resources to channel to beneficiaries. INGOs hoping to provide services to disaffected areas also have to negotiate with governments or rebel leaders for access. In addition, there are many NGO registries, and these are, among other things, evidence that NGOs seek to be heard. At the United Nation's Department of Economic and Social Affairs, twenty-four thousand NGOs have registered in order to share their profiles with other global groups.[10] More than four thousand INGOs have received consultative status with the United Nations, and another six hundred applied in 2014.[11] While all INGOs may not be currently seeking coverage in the *Guardian* or participation in high-level meetings at the UN, that may reflect resource limitations rather than modest aspirations.[12]

We do not view INGOs as "power maximizers" (Mearsheimer 2001); such a view suggests that INGOs pursue their influence for influence's sake and little else. Instead, for INGOs that must preserve their well-being to advance their principled goals (Keck and Sikkink 1998), we see a number of reasons an INGO might seek greater authority. If its funding dries up, it must form new relationships. The group International Relief and Development (IRD) was accused of mismanagement and lost its US government contracts in 2015 but is now restructuring and changing its name.[13] If an INGO's programs are ineffective, it can look to others for help. After the Rwandan crisis, official and private aid agencies created a collective evaluation exercise to reflect on aid delivery and mobilize support for reform (Borton and Eriksson 2004). If an INGO's credibility is under attack, it can reframe its work and seek the approbation of new groups. After an internal revolt and external criticism from indigenous groups, FoE has shifted from a Northern-based environmental advocacy group to a Southern-based network committed to environmental justice (Doherty and Doyle 2013). An INGO might reconsider its work and conclude that the most effective path to change is on a national or global level (Stroup and Wong 2013; Arrington 2016). This is not an exhaustive list of the drivers of authority-seeking behavior, but it is support for our claim that most INGOs seek authority.

INGOs as Organizations

In this book, organizations are the primary unit of analysis. Many analysts see the boundaries of these organizations as porous, where individuals may sit in one office but work more closely with broader movements or networks (Carpenter 2014; DeMars and Dijkzeul 2015; Hillhorst 2003). We agree that those networks can be influential and sometimes transformative, but the networks are not actors in global politics. They are, like the authority we examine, an aspect of a social relationship. Throughout the book, we move back and forth between analyzing individual organizations and the audience(s) they seek to influence, as *which* INGO is accepted as an authority will vary depending on the audience. The study of social movements or networks within a particular area—as humanitarian groups or as human rights groups—involves a prior assumption that the International Committee of the Red Cross (ICRC) is more similar to the tiny group Feed My Lambs International (Polman 2010, 58–62) than it is to Amnesty. Our research reveals the problems with that issue-centric approach. The comparable global structures of the ICRC and Amnesty are a specific type of platform from which one could pursue social change. Given their global reach and cosmopolitan commitments, leading INGOs like these bring certain capacities and priorities to the networks in which they participate. Our study of the "nodes" of those networks thus complements a "network as structure" approach (Hafner-Burton, Kahler, and Montgomery 2009).

Our focus on individual organizations places these agents in their social settings but does not investigate large-scale changes in the global political context that INGOs face. Structural forces do shape the political opportunities INGOs confront, their ability to change market outcomes, and the larger frames and values available to them (Neumann and Sending 2010; Tallberg et al. 2013; Kapstein and Busby 2013). In the face of these structural processes, however, only some INGOs are able to take advantage of these opportunities or to construct value propositions that resonate with wide audiences. To take a concrete case, negotiations on international environmental agreements have become more open to INGOs, but only some organizations are invited to participate as either independent observers or participants in government delegations (Fisher and Green 2004). INGO efforts to demand greater access, without established authority, can often be counterproductive. Fisher (2010) describes how, at the 2009 Copenhagen summit on climate change, the protest tactics of outsider INGOs led to the revocation of access for many of the INGOs that had been able to work inside the Bella Center. The door at global governance institutions (and exclusive gatherings such as the WEF) may be more open to INGOs today than in the past, but only some are invited to enter.

The Book Ahead

It is hard to be an INGO. Even those INGOs that seem to have it all bemoan the challenges they face. As organizations seeking social change, INGOs have a hard row to plow and limited material resources with which to achieve their lofty ideals. Deference from multiple audiences is a boon. Without it, INGOs do not have the wide platform and loud megaphones with which to publicize their views. But with deference, INGOs find themselves at the mercy of the audience they have worked so hard to cultivate. To balance the tension between audience maintenance and getting the job done, leading INGOs often choose to pursue vanilla victories: incrementalist demands, mild strategies. This choice pushes against other INGOs' more abrasive demands for more ambitious proposals, thereby fragmenting the INGO community as a whole.

To make this argument, we employ a wide range of analytical tools, research methods, and data sources. The analytical work in the next chapter constructs a Weberian ideal type as a way of accentuating the distinct features of INGOs that form the basis of their authority (Jackson and Nexon 2009). The descriptive statistics in chapter 3 draw from new and existing data sets on media content, legislative proceedings, network ties among INGOs, and survey research. The case studies in chapters 4 through 6 were selected because the role of authority could be observed. Each of these case studies uses semistructured interviews with key informants, who were recruited through cold calling and snowball sampling. Interview data storage follows the protocol of individual and organizational anonymity with regard to specific responses, although we do identify participating organizations by type and name in the appendix. When requested, quotes were verified for accuracy with respondents prior to publication. We also made use of extensive secondary source material and print and online primary documents where available.

Chapters 4 through 6 each offer two cases with which we explore how status shapes strategy. Within the three chapters that cover three different audiences, we have selected cases that are similar but that include INGOs of different status to isolate the effects of status on strategy. The six cases presented in these chapters are all *collective* NGO efforts and *cross-sectoral*. A focus on collective efforts reduces the chance that we conflate the effects of status with the preferences of any one INGO. After we have identified a handful of leading INGOs, we can examine the logic behind the level and type of involvement (or not) in these collective efforts. The cases are also all cross-sectoral initiatives, which allows us to explore the role of status across a range of issue areas. If we looked at a case simply in the humanitarian sector, for example, where interactions among INGOs and their audiences are regularized, status differentials may be more taken for granted and thus less in need of defense. On issues that are less easily categorized—such as campaigns for financial justice or attempts at defining accountability—INGOs enter these arenas cautiously, conscious of the bases of their authority and the tenuousness of new ventures. One could argue that this makes our half-dozen cases "most likely cases." Perhaps, but the dynamic nature of global politics suggests that INGOs regularly face these sorts of challenges as new issues arise or old issues get re-examined. Leading INGOs play a key role in problem definition, even as they seek to frame new issues in ways that serve their cause or advance their authority. Thus, the 2010 earthquake in Haiti could be presented as a foreign aid issue, a humanitarian concern, evidence of sustained erosion and state mismanagement, or a chance to highlight international economic exploitation. As climate change became a dominant concern, Oxfam's adoption of the issue was shaped by supporters' interest in addressing systemic problems in global development (Crompton 2010; Cugelman and Otero 2010). INGOs across multiple sectors advance competing frames, but these frames are created with respect to the specific audiences whose deference they seek to maintain.

The remainder of this book explores variation in INGO authority and its consequences. We begin with two general questions: What is INGO authority, and how does it vary? Chapter 2 develops our conception of audience-based authority, discussing the contributions of this perspective and explaining how the authority trap works. Unlike states, INGOs are *an* authority, rather than *in* authority, and that authority is defined as deference. Because authority exists in the context of specific social relationships, we identify a range of relevant audiences INGOs seek to influence: namely states, corporations, and other INGOs. We argue that very few INGOs successfully secure deference from multiple audiences, and those that do we call leading INGOs. After they receive widespread deference, leading INGOs are constrained by the need to satisfy the varied values and preferences of their supporters, and they thus find themselves in the authority trap, incentivized to make moderate choices.

Once we develop our theory, the next challenge is to demonstrate the validity of our claims empirically. One key challenge scholars of authority face is how to measure authority consistently across contexts. We conceptualize INGO authority before multiple audiences that may have conflicting values and interests. We present our approach in chapter 3, leveraging multiple metrics to measure differences in how INGOs are seen by the aforementioned audiences. We also include metrics of deference by the general public, as public concern is often a leverage point for reaching INGO targets and can exert pressure on all three of our audiences of interest. We construct two samples: (1) a random sample of INGOs drawn from several registries, and (2) "most likely" leading INGOs, to demonstrate that most INGOs fail to achieve any deference at all from even one audience. We then identify a handful of leading INGOs, given our systematic differentiation of INGOs.

After establishing the variation of authority among INGOs, we move to address how leading INGOs' (and other INGOs') status shapes strategy. We trace dynamics in several audience-based chapters, each focused around two main case studies. These analyses help focus on dynamics unique to INGO interactions with each audience, and they also exhibit remarkable adherence to overlapping strategic choices. We show how leading INGOs and other INGOs face different incentives to use collaboration, competition, and condemnation.

We begin with states as an audience in chapter 4, as states have been a "natural" target for INGOs in many studies in the field of international relations. We examine two transnational INGO campaigns to change state practice to introduce a financial transactions tax (FTT) and create an Arms Trade Treaty (ATT). The two cases are similar in that both campaigns took off in the late 1990s, the issues in both cases target the practices of the United States and United Kingdom as relevant actors, and both engage issues that have traditionally been challenging for INGOs as "hard politics." The makeup of the INGO coalitions change over time in each case, allowing us to explore what the addition of a leading INGO does to the policy proposal and targets of the coalition. Leading INGOs are more collaborative with states than their more obscure peers are. In both cases, the entry of leading INGOs accompanied the reframing of the campaign's proposals to more reformist positions. This yielded a vanilla victory in the form of the ATT and even less for the FTT. We also show that status-specific concerns shaped the selection of state targets, with leading INGOs prioritizing the easy target states rather than the most important.

In chapter 5, we turn to the INGO-corporate relationship. The condemnation of corporate environmental and human rights records by many INGOs has created new political openings for collaboration, but only a few INGOs are invited to the table. We explore these dynamics through several examples of private, cross-sectoral regulations that emerged in the early 2000s. With the Sustainability Consortium (TSC) and the UN Global Compact (UNGC), early support from a few leading INGOs was critical to establishing the credibility of these initiatives. The limited substance of these efforts has discouraged many INGO supporters and yielded little more than vanilla victories. We then explore the alternatives to collaboration. Many INGOs still condemn corporate practices, but their efforts have not been sustained. Competition is possibly more fruitful for improving corporate practices, as the example of the Forest Stewardship Council (FSC) shows.

Our final empirical chapter takes up the politics of interaction among INGOs, an oft-neglected dynamic in most research. Chapter 6 highlights the pitfalls of assuming that all INGOs are alike. INGOs compete to offer specific visions of best practices for the entire INGO sector, and those visions depend on the INGO's authority. We explore two such initiatives, both formed in 2001, from opposite ends of the INGO authority spectrum. A small elite group of INGOs

TABLE 1.1 Summary of Comparative Case Study Findings

AUDIENCE	CASES	LEADING INGO STRATEGIES	OTHER INGO STRATEGIES	OTHER AUDIENCE-SPECIFIC OUTCOMES
States (chapter 4)	Campaign for Arms Trade Treaty (ATT)	Frequent collaboration (moderate demands)	Moderate collaboration	Vanilla victories achieved
			Frequent	Leading INGOs ally with middle-power states
	Campaign for financial transactions tax (FTT)	Moderate condemnation	condemnation (radical demands)	Two Goldilocks problems with number of leading INGOS and level of involvement
		Rare competition	Rare competition	
Corporations (chapter 5)	The Sustainability Consortium (TSC)	Frequent collaboration	Rare collaboration	Vanilla, but little victory
	United Nations Global Compact (UNGC)	Moderate condemnation	Frequent condemnation	Leading INGOs help launch private governance efforts, other INGOs in implementation
		Moderate competition	Rare competition	Competitive initiatives escape authority trap, but stymied by fragmentation
Other INGOs (chapter 6)	INGO Accountability Charter (AC)	Moderate collaboration	Frequent collaboration	NGOs compete to define good practice for the entire INGO sector
		Frequent competition	Moderate competition	
	World Social Forum (WSF)	Rare condemnation (ignorance instead)	Frequent condemnation	Real divisions among INGOs risk all INGOs' authority if made public

established the Accountability Charter (AC) to show that their organizational processes were transparent and egalitarian. A large group of other INGOs gathers almost annually at the World Social Forum (WSF), where INGOs see their role as pushing hard for alternatives to contemporary neoliberal globalization. Each initiative is a mix of collaboration and condemnation, and while the AC is decidedly vanilla, neither group has been particularly victorious.

Our conclusion revisits the main findings in this study, but since we are hopeful that our authority framework travels to other parts of IR, we discuss extensions of and exceptions to the authority trap. For this, we bring forth the example of the International Criminal Court, which, if anything, was not a vanilla victory. We also explore how the authority trap might work differently for non-INGOs, specifically nonstate groups that use violence, and for global governance generally. We show that while the authority trap may be difficult to escape, it is not ironclad.

There is no simple pattern of strategic choices that leading and other INGOs make across their relationships with varied audience. States, corporations, and INGOs have different preferences and bases of authority, which means that a leading INGO's propensity to collaborate with states does not automatically mean that collaboration is a generally preferred strategy. The rich case studies in each chapter, combined with other scholars' findings, allow us to identify distinct differences regarding each audience. Those findings are summarized in Table 1.1.

INGO sympathizers hope that the entrance of INGOs into global politics could create a more representative or more effective form of global governance. But there are a couple of problems. First, despite their best efforts, most INGOs remain in obscurity. Second, those INGOs that are well-known, including Amnesty, the ICRC, Greenpeace, and Oxfam, are no silver bullets. These organizations are visible targets for opponents, and their policy proposals can seem depressingly timid. These dynamics seem to hold regardless of whether the issue is environmental protection, international development, or human rights promotion. Our conception of authority accounts for the strategies that INGOs adopt, explaining why INGOs struggle to transform a system of global governance that is run by the very audiences on whom INGOs depend for their authority.

AUTHORITY AND AUDIENCES

In an era of porous borders and multistakeholder governance, the study of global politics has expanded well beyond the state. International nongovernmental organizations (INGOs) are one of the many actors on this crowded global stage, and their roles in this global order are shaped by their authority.

Authority is a necessary precondition for INGOs seeking to influence global politics. If authority is deference from other actors, then most INGOs do not have authority. Some INGOs, however, have authority from not just one actor or another, but from entire audiences (e.g. states, corporations, other INGOs) that influence global politics. The INGOs that have secured deference from multiple audiences are leading INGOs. Despite the reasonable expectation that leading INGOs would have the most latitude with regard to their strategic choices, authority constrains as well as enables. Paradoxically, more authority does not automatically yield more influence.

Leading INGOs have secured deference from multiple audiences around the world, but to maintain this status with diverse audiences, they must moderate their demands, resist radicalism, and find an idea they can sell to multiple interests. Leading INGOs *can* secure change, but these achievements are often "vanilla victories" rather than drastic shifts. Leading INGOs strive for incremental changes that avoid alienating the bases of their authority. Leading INGOs are thus trapped by their authority.

This book's argument is based on an audience-based understanding of authority, which we lay out in detail in this chapter. We structure the chapter in three parts. First, we explore the basic concept, explaining how INGOs can become *an* authority if they receive deference from some audience. The second section explores what it means to gain deference from an audience. We identify a number of audiences for which INGOs might be seen as an authority. We conceptualize authority as aggregating across audiences, which enables us to identify leading INGOs in chapter 3. Third, we explain the implications of the status differences between leading INGOs and other INGOs. We theorize in greater detail about the dynamics and constraints of the authority trap. We end the chapter with an extension to other actors in global politics.

The Nature of INGO Authority

Simply put, authority means having the right to act, not just the capacity to do so. While many understand political science as the study of power, international relations scholars have increasingly employed the idea of authority to study the complex world of state and nonstate actors to account for "soft" or noncoercive forms of influence. Hurd (1999, 400) characterizes authority as "perhaps the most interesting concept in social science," encompassing issues of legitimacy, control, and relations among private and public actors. In fact, if authority yields unquestioning submission, it may be more influential than coercive power; as Arendt (1961, 192) argues, "when force is used, authority itself has failed."

Authority is conferred by one actor onto another. It exists in social relationships and comes in various forms. To understand the different forms of authority that INGOs enjoy, we employ the useful distinction between being *in* authority and being *an* authority (Barnett and Finnemore 2004; Avant, Finnemore, and Sell 2010; Lake 2012; Flathman 1980). States and other actors *in* authority have been delegated that role by someone; for example, citizens delegate to the state, or states delegate to intergovernmental organizations (IGOs). Actors that are in authority have the right to issue commands, the ruled have an obligation to comply, and the ruler has the right to enforce its commands in cases of deviance (Lake 2012). By contrast, actors who are *an* authority have a right to speak because of their special knowledge, experience, or virtue (Friedman 1990, 80). They elicit deference not because they can ensure that their preferences are followed, but rather because their views are seen by some audience(s) as being correct and obligational; that is, they are seen as legitimate. Those that are an authority do not command, but they do have the right to be heard by audiences that defer to them.

Authority as Deference

For those who are accepted as an authority, some audience has surrendered its judgment (Raz 1986, 39–42). Authority requires deference. Authority, thus, is always relational rather than an attribute. This articulation is strikingly appropriate for thinking about INGOs. INGOs work without force, they speak with conviction and information, and an audience decides what they think about those actions and whether to defer. Sometimes that deference may be given based on instrumental rather than normative reasons. For example, a corporation may reject the authority of an INGO to report on its labor practices, either because of skepticism about the particular INGO's expertise or because the corporation does not share the INGO's values. Still, the corporation may defer to that INGO because a third audience—perhaps consumers or states—accepts the INGO as an authority and the corporation accepts the legitimacy of the market or state regulations. The key point is that deference is voluntary subordination to another. If an audience confers authority to an actor, it expresses clearly that this actor cannot be overlooked, even if its points are controversial or problematic. Some who defer to an INGO are celebrating its characteristics and choices, solidifying their shared norms. Others may only be deferring instrumentally, but they are still signaling the importance of that particular actor over others.

Authority must be earned, and the struggle to secure that deference is a political process. For example, aspiring experts interested in global governance constantly jockey for recognition and acceptance (Sending 2015). Intergovernmental organizations (IGOs) may be delegated certain tasks but then often work to increase their authority by expanding their expertise and promoting new normative standards (Chapman 2009; Hurd 2002). The very decision to place IGOs in authority can become politicized when others contest the legitimacy of that delegation (Zürn, Binder, and Ecker-Ehrhardt 2012).

Authority can become durable, but it is not permanent. Over time, an actor's status as an authority may become less contested and more taken-for-granted. Those who have authority can accrue the resources to protect it, and their continued visibility promotes unquestioned acceptance. Authority is always potentially subject to renegotiation, which may create anxiety. Still, sudden changes in authority are unlikely. For some, INGOs have authority because they are seen as credible purveyors of information, but not necessarily above reproach. Even so, authority has a tendency to be durable because it is based on a relationship rather than a one-shot interaction (Zürn 2017, 8–10). The lack of a clear chain of delegation, such as that which exists between the International Monetary Fund and its member states, might actually make principled or expert authority easier to preserve if it is not clear to whom an INGO should be accountable (Grant and Keohane 2005). Over time, even if in theory an INGO's authority is revocable, reliance on that INGO for information and arguments and the endorsement of that INGO by international institutions makes it more difficult for audiences to suddenly reverse course. Revoking deference to an INGO is costly for an audience, particularly if that INGO is already respected and well-known. This stickiness in authority should increase with the number of audiences from which an INGO secures deference.

Even if deference to a particular INGO becomes automatic, it is not unreasoned. For the audiences of INGOs, the two most common justifications are the INGO's recognized expertise or valued principled commitments (Stroup and Wong 2016). In terms of expertise, INGOs create knowledge by gathering information and advancing causal claims (Keck and Sikkink 1998; Haas 1990; Stoddard 2006). This information can be given additional credibility by the widespread assumption that NGOs are unbiased. The principled commitments of INGOs can add weight to their claims if the audience is sympathetic to the values promoted by the INGO. Those precise values travel the range of the political spectrum (Bob 2012), but, *in general*, the principled nature of INGOs gives them a particular form of authority. A third rationale for deference, delegation, is less common for INGOs. States and IGOs rarely delegate to private actors, and INGOs are much more likely to be entrepreneurs of their own rules (Green 2013). These various logics of deference do not always travel in lockstep. As Avant, Finnemore, and Sell (2010, 18–19) point out, the sources of authority may diverge, creating conflicting demands for the governor. For example, agents can be delegated tasks that trade off with their ability to maintain their level of expertise (Barnett and Finnemore 2004).

Our conception of authority departs from a couple of popular claims about INGOs. First, deferring to an INGO is different from being persuaded by an INGO. This is an important point, as many INGO analysts depict the modal path of INGO influence to be its ability to share new information and slowly shift the preferences of other actors (Finnemore and Sikkink 1998; Ahmed and Potter 2006; Nye 2004; Risse, Ropp, and Sikkink 1999; Khagram, Riker, and Sikkink 2002). But authority does not argue; it just is. If I am persuaded by evidence provided by Human Rights Watch (HRW), I accept the facts they provide from a position of equal capacity to evaluate that evidence, and I may dispute their claims. Their positions are subject to interrogation, and I need to be convinced by the quality of the evidence, the rhetorical strength of their leadership, and the sophistication of their materials. By contrast, if I defer to HRW as an authority, I accept that it occupies a superior position. Deference allows an audience to stop evaluating the merits of every single case and simply look to an authority to give the answer. The effects of persuasion are more ephemeral, though being repeatedly persuaded by an INGO may later result in deference to that group.

Second, although we agree in part with the popular framing of INGO authority as based on its pursuit of "the wider public interest" (Price 2003, 580), this can be a vague concept that actually occludes a set of audience-dependent evaluations. If all INGOs claim to work on behalf of others, the *specific* other varies by organization and confers different types of legitimacy. Broadly, INGOs can draw on one of two sets of widely accepted but divergent principles: representation and universality (Rubenstein 2014; Hopgood 2013). Both are general liberal principles, but they accord INGOs different moral positions. Those INGOs that claim to represent particular excluded groups draw upon a larger democratic norm that prescribes that those affected by policies should have a chance to have their views heard. Thus, the Madres de la Plaza del Mayo may have used a universal language of human rights, but they did so to defend their particular interests (Keck and Sikkink 1998). Other INGOs claim to represent universal principles, and an audience accepts the legitimacy of that claim insofar as they agree that the principles of human rights or environmental protection should be defended in policy discussions (Bob 2012; Barnett 2011). Thus, an actor's claim to be working on behalf of group A may be seen as legitimate by audience X, even if group A never consented to be represented by the actor. Because cosmopolitan values are (by definition) more likely to attract a wider range of audiences, INGOs that primarily advance universalist principles develop greater global authority.

Finally, our claims about authority in global politics are based on a precise focus on a single actor, INGOs. We embrace comparisons among different types of actors in global governance but emphasize that the ideal-type INGO enjoys status as *an authority* rather than occupying positions *in authority*. The two are not mutually exclusive. To illustrate, the United Nations has an office that is responsible for peacekeeping, but its authority can be enhanced by its principled commitment to neutrality (Barnett and Finnemore 2004). But the two forms of authority can also move in different directions. The United Nations maintains delegated responsibility for global peacekeeping operations (in authority), but the introduction of cholera to Haiti by UN forces in 2010 "undermin[ed] the world body's credibility and reputation"[1] (an authority). Still, IGOs are usually in authority and rarely simply an authority. This makes a direct comparison between INGOs and other actors like IGOs difficult. IGOs are created to govern a particular issue area and therefore nearly always have delegated authority to probe and expand even beyond original mandates (Johnson 2014). INGOs can also engage in private governance, but they must fight for these schemes to be seen as legitimate by growing numbers of stakeholders (Cashore, Auld, and Newsom 2004a; Sasser et al. 2006). This does not make INGOs weaker than IGOs, merely different. While other actors may be deeply involved in rule making (what some refer to as governance), rule making is just one tool in the INGO toolbox. INGOs gather information, demand attention to new issues, and shame states into adhering to their own regulations and promises (Bob 2005, Keck and Sikkink 1998, Hopgood 2006). Global actors enjoy authority for different reasons, and they subsequently do very different things with that status.

Attributes and Agency

One persistent question for scholars of power and authority is whether it comes from within, as some actor attribute, or is determined wholly externally. We land in the middle: authority exists in social relationships but does not emerge from thin air (see Finnemore and Sikkink 1998). The facts of INGOs' principled commitments and expertise emerge from the choices that INGOs make, and then some audience decides whether these are legitimate, desirable, or otherwise worthy of deference.

A number of scholars see structural conditions and external relationships as the primary determinants of INGO strategies and influence. Sending (2015) portrays different actors competing for recognition within distinct fields around issues like population governance. Alternately, research on global networks begins from the assumption that different groups come together within an established space (Carpenter 2014; Hadden 2015). Carpenter (2011, 74), for example, argues that "it is an organization's visibility in a particular network, not its resources per se, that enable certain organizations disproportionate influence over the network issue agenda." In this view, authority is not based on an actor's abilities, but comes about as actors compete with one another over the content and process of governance.

Whether conceived of as institutional fields, social networks, national environments (Stroup 2012), or other structures, these settings and the relationships within them shape INGOs' authority, strategies, and influence. Yet our approach differs from a purely structural one in several ways. First, each single network is not the only setting in which leading INGOs operate. Gatekeeper INGOs achieve their influence within a network because of their network position, but that network position is shaped by their authority outside the network (what Carpenter characterizes as their "betweenness"). Thus while some structures may appear powerful and immutable to INGOs that only operate in one field, they look quite different to leading INGOs, who work in many sectors before multiple audiences. Those that have achieved recognition and widespread deference participate in many networks and work in many fields, reducing the effects of any one set of deliberations on their strategies. When new issues emerge, leading INGOs are key players in the initial constitution of networks and the boundary making of fields; they are shaped by, but also shape, their environments.

Status as an Authority

Our claims about differences in authority of INGOs echo a large body of social science research on status. Status is the "collective beliefs about a given [actor]'s ranking on valued attributes" (Paul, Larson, and Wohlforth 2014). In this book, we evaluate the status of INGOs based on their authority before audiences. "High-status" INGOs are leading INGOs, and other INGOs have lower status. An actor's status is a social fact that can affect both its actions as well as how those actions are received. American golfing great Lee Trevino once quipped that "[w]hen I was a rookie, I told jokes, and no one laughed. After I began winning tournaments, I told the same jokes, and all of a sudden, people thought they were funny" (quoted in Podolny 2010, 10). Status has this same effect for INGOs and can create a virtuous cycle for authoritative groups. There can be an expansion of the social circles of an actor, or the "pattern of relations and affiliations in which the actor does and does not choose to engage" (Podolny 2010, 13). Those circles can more easily expand for leading INGOs.

High status thus comes with a number of advantages. For instance, higher-status individuals gain more recognition for their efforts than the same efforts made by lower-ranked individuals. Merton (1968) compared eminent scholars (Nobel laureates) and the way their research was rewarded vis-à-vis low-status scholars. With a stable of eager graduate students, postdoctoral fellows, and colleagues who want to coauthor, senior scholars multiply their already considerable advantages of having more experience and more years on the job.

Status may be especially important for INGOs compared to other actors, as INGOs exist in a particularly information-scarce and uncertain environment, which increases the importance of social status and reputation. With limited resources and operating across many regulatory settings, it is difficult to trace the spending, strategic choices, and accountability of INGOs (Burger and Owens 2010; Spar and Dail 2002). Status researchers argue that status and reputation become even more important in information-scarce environments (Kydd 2005; Fombrun and Shanley 1990). Status becomes the shortcut by which audiences evaluate the quality of a particular actor,[2] acting as a signal that can help audiences determine which INGOs serve their particular interests (Murdie 2014).

Differences in authority among INGOs create a status hierarchy. We label the ones that have deference from multiple audiences, and therefore the highest status, as leading INGOs. INGOs that have high status in some arenas may not enjoy the same in others. Tostan is respected for the innovative educational model it uses in a handful of African countries, but that does not translate into recognition when it comes to coordinating the global education cluster, a status enjoyed by Save the Children, a leading INGO (see chapter 3). Thus, for INGOs as for states, status involves privileging the claims of one actor over another, and only some voices are heard.

Before moving on to a discussion of INGO audiences, one more point about status and deference is critical. INGOs that are *an* authority must also be aware of, and concerned about, the possibility that their status could change. An audience can always withdraw its deference, and with no institutional position or delegated set of tasks, an INGO's access to that audience could quickly dissolve. For INGOs, and for other *an authorities*, being an authority and being recognized as an authority are the same thing; there is no authority status absent an audience. Throughout the book, we refer to INGOs' status shaping their strategies. More precisely, the omnipresent status-maintenance concerns of INGOs shape their strategic choices.

Who Defers? Authority and Audiences

The notion of audience is critical for understanding an actor's authority. While the legitimacy of individual INGOs varies in the eyes of the general public, policymakers, and corporations, *relative to other types of actors*, INGOs enjoy high levels of legitimacy. Cross-national survey research indicates that NGOs are more trusted than corporations, governments, and even churches (Boström and Hallström 2010; Pew Research Center 2003). Still, despite this broad favorability toward NGOs, each audience has its own values and preferences. In this book, we focus on states, corporations, and other INGOs as three important audiences.[3] These categories of audiences are still broad, of course: East Timor and the United States are both states, but East Timor arguably has much more in common with Palestine, with their shared recent histories of poverty, violence, and colonization. Our expectation is that while actual practice varies, the similar forms of authority that inhere in the United States and East Timor *as states* makes them more receptive to particular strategies.

Three Main Audiences

States, corporations, and other INGOs have different reasons to defer (or not) to INGOs, and these audiences have their own sources of authority that shape their engagement with other actors. INGOs then have choices about which audience to prioritize in their pursuit of political and social change, but careful attention to the particularities of each audience is more likely to yield deference.

The INGO-state relationship is at the center of INGO research. At least theoretically, state authority is high in level and broad in scope. States are in authority, providing order and rules and controlling the legitimate use of force. In practice, states often fail to meet these responsibilities or they pursue their self-interest in a way that harms or neglects others. INGOs can name and shame those states who fail to meet their commitments, and the authority of some INGOs as defenders of universalist principles can provide space to critique states' claims to care for their people in particular. In rights promotion and environmental protection, INGOs try to change state behavior via international law, pushing them to sign treaties or alter domestic practices (for a few recent examples, see Hathaway 2007; Betsill and Corell 2008; Conrad and Ritter 2013; Vollenweider 2013). The expertise of INGOs can be of particular value to states that lack information on conditions beyond their borders, which promotes collaboration. Sometimes, as in the boomerang model, states are an instrumental target for INGOs that seek to change the practices of some third party (Risse, Ropp, and Sikkink 1999; Deitelhoff 2009). INGOs can also change state behavior by establishing new norms that inform states' conceptions of their identities and interests (Humphreys 2004; Finnemore and Sikkink 1998).

Corporations have long been a key audience for environmental NGOs but are increasingly relevant for human rights and development INGOs as well. Multinational corporations have substantial material capacity and may be recognized as having the expertise and capacity to self-regulate. They often lack the credibility or authority that INGOs enjoy, however, and are seen as self-serving (Gourevitch, Lake, and Stein 2012; Vogel 2008). Thus corporations and INGOs are presumed to start from different value propositions. Sometimes, this makes corporations resistant to INGOs, and any deference to INGOs is likely to be instrumental rather than internalized. Elsewhere, these supposedly different values propositions may make INGO-corporate collaboration more likely. For example, Ruggie (2013, 74) found that in implementing internal human rights policies, Fortune Global 500 companies tended to favor NGOs as partners over business groups, governments, and the UN. Finally, some INGOs may in practice see little actual distance from corporations. The Environmental Defense Fund (EDF) has historically forged partnerships with McDonald's, FedEx, AT&T, and Smithfield Farms, in addition to the Sustainability Consortium discussed in chapter 5.[4] Nike, which in the 1990s and 2000s was the target of INGO campaigns regarding its labor practices (including the use of sweatshops to make its products), has started a campaign called "The Girl Effect" that partners with many well-known relief and development NGOs, including CARE, Mercy Corps, Plan, Oxfam, and Save the Children.[5]

The final important audience for INGOs is their peers: other INGOs. Among actors of the same type, the idea that INGOs are inherently authoritative—because of their stated commitment to principles or because they are presumed to be more effective—is contested rather than taken for granted. INGOs are best placed to evaluate their peers' practices and they are more deeply invested in discussions of moral principles. Deference by one INGO to another can emerge because of shared principled commitments or a recognition of the group's expertise, access, or capacity. Within coalitions, INGOs may delegate responsibility to other INGOs, which should then lead to deference from other coalition members. Meanwhile, otherwise obscure INGOs can secure deference from their peers, such as when they provide well-known INGOs with new information and ideas. For instance, Amnesty long worked in the field with local groups to report on human rights abuses and has learned about individuals in trouble not through its own work directly, but through partners (Wong 2012). Gatekeeper INGOs solicit ideas from "start-up" NGOs, hoping to find issues suitable for their campaign style and organizational expertise (Carpenter 2014).

IGOs are not included in this book as a separate audience. This was a difficult choice since our organizational focus makes us sympathetic to the debates over the authority of IGOs and their relationship to civil society actors (Fox and Brown 1998; Scholte 2011a; Reimann 2006; Boli and Thomas 1999). We expect that our conception of INGO authority should help explain INGOs' relationships with IGOs. Functional concerns can drive IGOs to open up to INGOs (Tallberg et al. 2013), but access still remains uneven, as radical INGOs that reject the basic value premises of IGOs or their member states are unlikely to be deferred to by states (Pallas and Uhlin 2014). This suggests that the IGO deference to INGOs is also concentrated in the hands of a few groups. The chapter on states discusses several cases where INGOs have pushed states to sign new treaties or change existing IGO policy, but this is an admittedly thin treatment. While we assume that the features that make INGOs authoritative with states may not be much different from those that encourage deference from IGOs, this deserves further exploration.

Aggregate Authority as a Determinant of Status

Our simple assumption is that the more audiences that confer authority to an INGO, the more authority the INGO has. We aggregate authority across audiences. To determine the status of a particular actor, we need to think about the multiple audiences before which it performs and the context in which these performances are accepted. The more audiences that confer authority to an INGO, the higher status it has. This does not mean that all INGOs try to be all things to all audiences. Some INGOs' causes might inherently appeal only to certain types of audiences, while others might make a strategic decision to focus on one audience and stand out from the competition.

Counting may seem pedestrian or too simplistic. After all, audiences are neither alike nor equally qualified to make judgments on the authority of INGOs. Some nonspecialists may be swayed by marketing techniques and lofty project descriptions, but we find it problematic to make judgments about whether certain audiences should have the power to judge and defer. Ultimately, qualified and unqualified audiences confer authority to all sorts of ideas and people in democratic countries, markets, and so forth. Citizens, governments, corporations, and other INGOs use a whole host of criteria to judge whether some organizations are better than others. These evaluations then allow those organizations to sit at the table, make rules, influence policymakers, and mobilize individuals to demonstrate in the streets.

Some additional concerns are how to weight different audiences or compare relative authority across audiences. For example, if INGO A has the support of Shell and BP but not fellow environmental INGOs, how do we assess its authority relative to INGO B, which has dozens of NGO partners but no corporate collaborators? Under the model introduced here, both INGOs would have the same amount of aggregate authority: one audience (multinational corporations for INGO A and other INGOs for INGO B). Aggregate authority errs on the side of breadth rather than depth.

This method sets aside both the rationale for deference as well as differences among audience members (the difference between Patagonia and Walmart, for instance). Still, in building a generalized measure of authority, such abstractions are necessary. We recognize that the proenvironmental commitments by corporations may vary in depth, shaping corporate-NGO relationships, but assessing this depth is itself challenging. After all, depending on who you ask, the decision to make Patagonia's business practices greener might not be impressive given that early on it adopted environmental sustainability as a primary informant of its decisions.[6] Meanwhile, Walmart's decision to consider the sustainability of its business model *is* quite revolutionary given its historic focus on cheap, high-volume sales. Ultimately, both instrumental and internalized deference boost an INGO's authority, and gaining more audiences, for whatever reason, boosts INGO status. Our conception of aggregate authority scopes out from these particular evaluations to assess which INGOs regularly have a seat at myriad decision-making tables and what they do once there.

The Authority Trap

As we show in the next chapter, our measure of aggregate authority yields an interesting outcome: there is considerable variation in levels of authority within the population of INGOs operating around the world. Some enjoy high status, others occupy niches, and most labor in low-status obscurity. Leading INGOs are often sought out as "the" INGO voice across a range of questions, but they are not a representative group.

A select group of leading INGOs has authority across the multiple audiences identified here. They are different from other INGOs. Their right to speak is unquestioned. They are simply perceived to be legitimate "by everybody" (for a discussion, see Collingwood and Logister 2006). They reach across social and political cleavages. Their messages resonate and therefore need to be addressed; they cannot be ignored.[7] For leading INGOs, audiences invoke their names, fund their work, invite them to comment, appropriate their logos, and seek out their guidance in uncertain situations. Consider the following example: In reporting on human rights abuses in Iraq in September 2014, both the *New York Times* and the *Guardian* relied on Amnesty's information.[8] Neither of these respected media outlets offered a description of Amnesty as an organization or gave a justification for using Amnesty's reports. The media's invocation of Amnesty legitimates their own reporting but also reifies Amnesty's status in global politics as a group that needs no defense when its words are invoked for consumption by multiple audiences. In that sense, Amnesty's status is durable and reproduced.

What Is the Authority Trap?

Leading INGOs seem to occupy a privileged status since they can command attention. Quite simply, they appear to have more influence. But does having deference from so many audiences actually help bring about more change? We might think that having more authority before more audiences yields more space to advance a cause, but leading INGOs are actually constrained in their choices. Leading INGOs moderate rather than agitate. Caught between communities, and aware of their need to maintain widespread appeal, leading INGOs must find solutions that resonate with multiple interests. Their dominant strategy is thus to find options to build bridges between their audiences rather than to gratify one audience in ways that might alienate another.

The authority trap ensures that INGOs that have the most authority in global politics rarely choose to leverage it for radical change. On the one hand, they have influence through the accrual of aggregate authority. On the other hand, they are hamstrung in the available strategies and the issues they can safely support by their desire to maintain their authority. This dynamic reflects "Gulliver in the chain gang," a fact Hoffmann wrote about with regards to US foreign policy in the 1960s (Hoffmann 1968). The authority trap constrains leading INGOs. Because of it, they work toward incremental change, and their issues and strategies are imperfectly representative of the many other interests in civil society. Yet because of their status, they are able to achieve policy changes while other INGOs are ignored. To flesh this out, we highlight several cognate claims from other areas of political science.

First, leading INGOs have little room in the short term to shift the ideational landscape in which they operate, and thus they hew to mainstream positions. To influence the activities of relevant stakeholders in global politics, leading INGOs must secure some position "in the middle" of a gamut of concerns and positions. In so doing, leading INGOs leave behind more critical perspectives in order to maintain their access. They ask for shifts in behavior and policy that various audiences can tolerate. As Busby found in his study of moral movements, one important factor was the cultural resonance of advocates' asks (Busby 2010, 11). While INGOs can creatively advance new ideas that rhetorically corner their opposition (Krebs and Jackson 2007), there are limits to their ability to create a coherent frame that meshes with existing claims and beliefs (Finnemore and Sikkink 1998). If the ask is simply too far from an actor's current perspective, it simply will not be comprehensible to the receiving audience.

Second, leading INGOs are brokers. They translate the demands of more radicalized components of global civil society into coherent, achievable asks that can travel to at least one more audience to alter the status quo. In the language of social network analysis, brokers link two otherwise disparate networks of actors, serving as the go-between for interaction between hostile or unknown parties (Hafner-Burton, Kahler, and Montgomery 2009; Goddard 2012). Brokers score highly on the network centrality measure of "betweenness" (Burt 2005; Padgett and Ansell 1993). By being "between" and thus able to connect with two networks that otherwise would not be connected, brokers display a remarkable ability to translate ideas. It speaks not only to the structural position of brokers, as network theory tends to emphasize, but also to the capacity that brokers have to relate to multiple audiences. Because brokers often bridge incommensurable or previously incomprehensible interests, they also must be moderate in their claims so as to maintain these ties. In a sense, brokers also fall into an authority trap because their menu of options for actions gets truncated once they bring different sides together. There are limits to the analogy, as leading INGOs go beyond brokership. Their authority does not come from the structural attributes of being a broker, but from their external relationships with each individual audience, which they then leverage to secure access and status. Brokering is simply a symptom of the multiple relationships of authority before different audiences. Thus, leading INGOs are not bound by network ties in the same way brokers are, but it is a useful analogy and suggests that the authority trap concept should inform the study of networks.

Third, even if leading INGOs try to keep their fingers on the pulse of more radical views within global civil society, they necessarily must temper these with opposing views. In this sense, leading INGOs' desire to appeal to multiple audiences creates a situation where they cannot fully represent the many views civil society groups might have. A parallel dynamic is highlighted in the median voter theorem, where in majoritarian systems, parties tend to move toward the middle of the ideological continuum in elections in order to gain more votes (Downs 1957). Extreme views are thus rarely represented in a normal distribution of voters. If most of the relevant stakeholders on a political decision are moderates, it makes sense to abandon the radicals in favor of appeasing the middle of the spectrum, where most of the votes are. We might expect leading INGOs to follow this logic, given that there will be many different sets of preferences articulated by audiences but converging toward the middle of any particular decision should be sufficiently satisfying to most of the audiences involved. Many leading INGOs are in fact careful to avoid making claims of representation themselves, but leading INGOs are still often asked by others to serve as "the" civil society voice, as if there is such a thing.

All of this is to say that leading INGOs have access to the stage of global politics, but they do not call the band's tune. Leading INGOs draw their status from holding the ears of many, but they compete for attention with other actors, truncating their options for action. Audience preferences can be envisioned as circles in a Venn diagram. Given the variation among audiences in global politics and their disparate interests, the area where those audiences' interests and values intersect is going to be quite small (see figure 2.1). The more audiences that defer to an INGO, the less room that INGO has for creative solutions. Put differently, the more audiences, the less "space" to find mutually agreeable solutions among multiple audiences.

Global Civil Societies

There are two "worlds" of INGOs. Global civil society is an imagined construct that is a convenient place for analysts and observers to dump unexplained outcomes and occasionally receive credit when something appears to push back against state or corporate interests. In reality, there are the "haves" (leading INGOs) and the "have nots" (other INGOs) when it comes to authority in global politics. Without authority, INGOs and other actors have very little hope of actually influencing political or social outcomes at the global level. The world of the leading INGOs follows separate logics of strategy and behavior from the other world, even if they are tied together by their organizational type (e.g. nonstate, nonprofit, and activist) and the issues they might tackle. Because of their status, leading INGOs are living quite different lives than most INGOs.

But if there truly is an authority trap, should not all the other INGOs just stop wasting their efforts? Doing so would prioritize short-term policy impact over the other processes in which INGOs are engaged. Among INGOs, there are

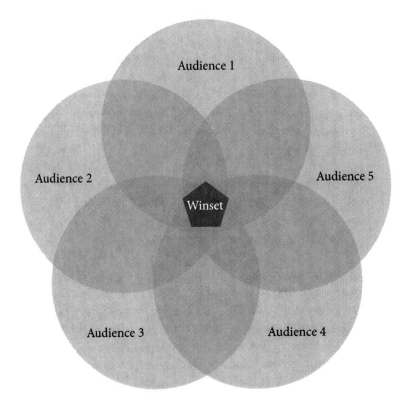

FIGURE 2.1 Audiences and leading INGOs

groups that better represent the interests of local groups and outperform lead-ing INGOs on executing local-, regional-, or domestic-level programs. Because of their proximity to pressing problems, other INGOs may be more innovative. Rare, a small conservation INGO that works with local communities, does exactly that, with the hopes of scaling up from individual projects to broader solutions.[9] Other INGOs often do the heavy labor of coming up with new problems that need attention, as we find in the financial transactions tax (FTT) case discussed in chapter 4. More concretely, other INGOs often take on important coordina-tive tasks in global coalitions, as in the Control Arms Coalition (also discussed in chapter 4).

It is not that other INGOs are not influential. Their problem is that their range is limited, and these effects are only felt at the local, regional, or national level. They are caught in the authority trap because their authority is nonexistent, or limited at best. To change global policies, an INGO must have the ability to com-mand attention from a variety of audiences, but this is something most INGOs are not positioned to demand. Other INGOs *need* leading INGOs to broadcast their work, spreading the insights from their work, getting bigger actors on board, and reframing the message in a more global way. The relationship between leading INGOs and other INGOs can sometimes be symbiotic. On the other hand, leading INGOs do have different special concerns because they seek deference from so many different audiences. Other INGOs do not have the same stresses, but they also do not have the same capabilities.

The great challenge for INGOs and other groups engaged in the business of social and political change is to generate outcomes that leave enough INGOs satisfied with the incremental progress that sometimes results and thus at least implicitly continuing to defer to leading INGOs. As some of the most visible members of global civil society, leading INGOs bear a heavy burden of articulating "what civil society wants" because they get access to the audiences that can change the way things are done. If leading INGOs have the most voice of INGOs in global politics, and if their tendency is toward vanilla victories rather than disruptive demands, other INGOs may conclude that they could do no better in similar circumstances.

For years, the state-centric default of international relations presumed that states start from a position of authority that they can lose, while private actors like INGOs start without authority and must construct it. More recently, theories of global power and authority have become much more nuanced, but one implicit assumption still prevails: more is more. More access leads to more authority, which leads to more latitude in decision making, which leads to more chances for actors to "get what they want." Our theory of authority challenges this equating of authority and influence by distinguishing between those in authority and those that are an authority. Lacking in authority status, INGOs need to reach many audiences, and they may adopt principles that will resonate with audiences and bring new information or technical expertise to demonstrate their added value. For actors in authority, more authority may create more opportunities for influence in various areas of regulation, or in defining new rules. Actors seeking to become *an* authority depend solely on deference from their own authority bases. As an INGO's authority increases, it may face more opportunities for influence but may also choose more constrained strategies as it worries about maintaining its status as an authority.

Becoming an authority is challenging; maintaining authority is difficult as well. Leading INGOs do not wield their authority without restriction. Unlike other INGOs, leading INGOs must work to maintain relationships with different audiences. They cannot just advocate anything they want or push their targets to the extreme. Leading INGOs, then, are trapped by their own authority, forced to maintain deference from multiple audiences. As a consequence, although leading

INGOs can bring in new ideas by other INGOs, create wide coalitions of other INGOs, and draw attention to deficiencies and solutions, they cannot actually push for radical changes from within the authority trap. Instead, leading INGOs opt for strategies that lead to vanilla victories, not too pushy, not too colorful, but widely acceptable change that appeals to a number of audiences.

Our focus on INGO authority as relational does not blind us to the different environmental and structural characteristics that shape the practices of INGOs. We build on structural theories by explaining the role of audience in the construction of actor authority as a feature of the *structure* of global politics. The environment in which INGOs find themselves shapes and interacts with organizational characteristics to determine INGO strategies. While there is considerable variation in INGOs' capacities and actions, only some INGOs get attention, and just a few strategies have widespread appeal. The relative authority of INGOs produces particular roles for these actors. Rather than revisit already excellent treatments of the importance of political opportunity structures and the existing normative landscape, we contribute to INGO scholarship by focusing on INGOs as actors navigating these environments.

There is no simple answer to the frequently asked question of whether INGOs have authority or not. Just like states and corporations, a few INGOs have a seat at the table while most do not. Getting that seat is no easy task. INGOs' individual capacities, expertise, and principled claims have to combine to both reach out to and resonate with myriad audiences. These theoretical claims raise two questions. The first is whether our supposition that leading INGO status is rare is empirically accurate. We take this up in the next chapter. The following question of how status shapes the strategies and ultimate influence of these groups guides the empirical cases in the three subsequent chapters.

THE EXCEPTIONAL NATURE
OF INGO AUTHORITY

Decades of extensive research have shown that INGOs can influence a wide range of global policies and practices. If INGOs in general have potential, however, only a few specific INGOs actually are high-status in the eyes of the audiences that they target. Groups like Amnesty, Oxfam, and Friends of the Earth (FoE) are familiar to analysts and the public because of their brand-name status. These INGOs are the rare exception rather than the rule.

In the previous chapter, we explained how authority emerges from the relationships that INGOs have with various audiences. In this chapter, we move from concept to evidence of audience-based authority. We offer a way to operationalize authority and identify which INGOs enjoy it. Recall that the authority trap has two parts: INGOs struggle to achieve status as leading INGOs so they can achieve their social change goals, but once they do, maintaining status becomes as or more important than advancing social change. This chapter focuses on the first half of the authority trap, demonstrating the extraordinary challenges of becoming a leading INGO. Only a few INGOs receive any demonstrable deference at all. Even more rarely, a handful of INGOs enjoy deference from multiple audiences, including the media, the public, states, other INGOs, and corporations. These are leading INGOs.

Although the complexity of a concept such as INGO authority presents significant measurement challenges, there are real and durable differences in the status of INGOs. We show this in two parts. First, we examine the life of the "average" INGO using a random sample. The evidence is clear: few INGOs enjoy authority before even a single audience, and most organizations struggle to get their voices heard. Second, we explore those groups likely to enjoy widespread authority with a sample of "most likely" leading INGOs. Even among these likely suspects, only a few INGOs enjoy deference from multiple audiences. Less than half of this group can claim more than two audiences' deference. A very few are leading INGOs. Interestingly, neither material capacity nor network connectedness appears to account for an INGO's authority. Authority involves more than just being rich or connected; it is about how those attributes are received in social relationships and then translated into deference.

Measuring Authority

INGOs seek audiences. They want to have the right to speak and to receive deference when they do. Yet few INGOs get attention, which seems particularly puzzling given the growing attention to NGOs since the early 1990s (Stroup and Wong 2016). More people are familiar with the idea of NGOs, and NGOs in general are viewed quite favorably. The Edelman Trust Barometer, which has been conducted since 2000, indicates high levels of public trust in NGOs in comparison to government and business.[1] If we move from NGOs in general to particular groups, some groups get singled out positively. Edelman surveys in several Western countries from 2001 to 2006 asked about a few "brand-name" INGOs—World Wildlife Fund (WWF), Sierra Club, Greenpeace, Oxfam, and Amnesty International—and found that they were received more favorably than corporate brands.[2] Many prominent studies of these groups have attempted to explain each INGO's path to power (Wapner 1996; Clark 2001; Hopgood 2006). In short, it might be reasonable to expect that NGOs have an easy time getting attention and being accepted as authorities. But, as we demonstrate below, the sort of deference from multiple audiences that Oxfam and WWF enjoy is the exception rather than the rule for INGOs.

We examine several audiences for INGOs in this chapter. States, corporations, and other INGOs are the key audiences that we consider in later chapters. To these, we add a fourth audience, the global public. Getting attention from these audiences, with their disparate preferences, is very much a challenge. Yet INGOs must rise to the challenge if they want to gain authority or become leading INGOs; these audiences constitute important stakeholders for INGOs, and they offer INGOs different paths to influence once they confer authority.

We face a number of challenges in measuring the distribution of INGO authority across these groups. First, even if the reach of INGOs might be global, they work to influence specific targets. To capture these specific relationships, we move beyond the total global population of INGOs to INGOs from the

English-speaking world, more specifically those registered at the United Nations or those headquartered in the United States, Britain, or Canada. We make no claim that these are representative of the global INGO community (Stroup 2012), but they are most likely to possess the resources and global reach to potentially reach many audiences (Tarrow 2005).[3] INGOs working at the global level with multiple country offices generally have a presence in one of these places. Second, the data on the reception of INGOs by corporations is largely focused on the environmental sector, a challenge for our cross-sectoral scope. The human rights and humanitarian relief sector have only recently turned to corporations as targets and partners. While today corporations are an important audience for INGOs across a range of sectors, the question of INGO-corporate relations has received the most attention in the environmental realm, and our analysis reflects that. Third, another audience, the general public, may serve as a leverage point for the three ultimate targets. We include media coverage and public attention in this chapter to capture the public presence that INGOs may seek in order to shape policymakers, corporations, and their peers. The public is admittedly fragmented across many different issues and settings, but broad indicators of public interest around the world can approximate public attention to particular INGOs.

Fourth, we face substantial challenges in gathering data on INGO authority. We are trying to capture deference, a social fact, and measure it for INGOs, organizations with limited transparency and whose characteristics are measured in haphazard ways. Deference is challenging to operationalize; it implies surrendering judgment (see chapter 2), but it is difficult to capture the rationale behind that move. In the measures below, we use attention as a proxy for deference. Audiences have to know *of* an actor before they evaluate that actor, making familiarity an important precondition for favorability.[4] Once known, audiences can respond in a variety of ways. They may grudgingly respond to or gladly embrace the claims of INGOs (recall the discussion of instrumental versus internalized deference from the previous chapter). There is no systematic way to capture the *intention* of audiences when they grant attention to an INGO, but we can at least tell which INGOs get attention and which do not.

Keeping these limitations in mind, we have mined new and existing data sources on INGOs to develop precise measures of INGO authority. While a number of scholars have explored differences in the status of INGOs, most work focuses on a single sector (e.g., human rights) or a single audience (e.g., states). We bring those different sectors and audiences together in this chapter to develop an aerial view of the global distribution of authority for INGOs. This multisector, multiaudience, multicountry perspective reflects the actual conditions INGOs face. They compete for attention to their cause, they choose among different audiences to target, and they must do so across multiple settings if they hope to influence global politics. We might liken the challenges faced by leading INGOs to an Olympic decathlon. Decathletes have to be elite athletes at ten different events, each requiring different skills. In general, decathletes will likely not be the best at any one sport, but they will be able to score exceedingly well across the board in ways that specialist athletes cannot. INGOs competing for audiences face a similar type of challenge. A handful of INGOs have enough authority to even compete on the Olympian stage of global politics, and just a few make the podium.

Elusive Authority for the Average INGO

If attention is a prerequisite for deference, it is difficult for INGOs to get noticed. To capture the frequency with which INGOs receive deference, we first focused on the experience of an average INGO. We created a random sample of 215 INGOs either registered at the United Nations or headquartered in the United States and United Kingdom (the sampling methodology and list of INGOs are discussed at length in the appendix). We then counted the number of times these organizations got attention from our audiences of interest: the public, policymakers, peers, and corporations. Whenever possible, we employed multiple ways of measuring the audience's attention. The evidence shows that most INGOs are ignored.

Public Attention

INGOs are most likely to be authoritative if they can command attention in multiple national settings, even if there is no such thing as a coherent global public that pressures policymakers (Grant and Keohane 2005). High levels of international media coverage and public awareness can thus be very useful for INGOs seeking political and social change. The public attention that results from media coverage can generate grassroots pressure on policymakers. INGOs can also use the media to bring new issues into the public arena, setting the agenda for policymakers (Wong 2012; Bob 2005; Carpenter 2007). In political systems that are hostile to direct confrontation, INGOs can use media coverage to create indirect pressure for policy change (Yang 2005). Advocacy via social media may allow INGOs to disseminate more information to a wider audience as a complement to their core political strategies (Kingston and Stam 2013). A visible public presence can help INGOs attract other INGOs as partners (Gourevitch, Lake, and Stein 2012). Finally, public awareness and media attention can result in new donors or new volunteers joining the organization. Thus public attention and media coverage can appear to be an end in itself for INGOs (Ron, Ramos, and Rodgers 2005).

While there thus are many incentives for INGOs to try to develop a visible profile, it is difficult for INGOs to get the attention of individuals, social groups, or reporters. Internet search data and media content offer different windows into public attention to individual INGOs. We start with data from Google Trends. Members of the general public may seek information about a particular NGO via Google if they are already aware of the existence of an organization. The Google Trends tool shows the popularity of a topic relative to all searches done on Google in a specific time period. It does not capture favorability, but it does indicate that members of the public are dedicating scarce resources to acquire information about a particular actor (Pelc 2013). The numbers reported by Google Trends range from 0 to 100. They are scaled, with 100 indicating the highest volume of search during a two-week time period. They are also normalized: the number indicates the volume of searches for the INGO relative to all searches on Google in that period (for more on interpreting this data, see the appendix).

We searched the random sample of 215 INGOs from January 2004 to December 2014 in Google Trends. Of those hundreds of INGOs, only Oxfam, FoE, and the World Economic Forum (WEF) were searched frequently enough to receive a score above zero.[5] The Google Trends data does demonstrate that public interest in NGOs in general has increased. Google searches for "NGO" were frequent, often even more so than for "United Nations."[6] But individual INGOs, at least according to the data on Google Trends, struggle to benefit from this growing interest. Most INGOs are not even registering on the Google Trends data; while they may be reaching out to the public, no one is reaching back.

Media coverage offers another avenue to public attention. Because the media informs the public about emerging topics, we might expect the media to report on a wider array of INGOs. Sadly for the average INGO, the media is a poor corrective for the problem of low information about the INGO sector. We searched the same randomly selected 215 INGOs in English-language world news publications from 2010 to 2012 in Lexis-Nexis, replicating a previous study of human rights INGOs (Thrall, Stecula, and Sweet 2014). Of the random sample, 54% had no mentions. Almost all the mentions of INGOs—96%—were of the top 10% of our sample. Four INGOs alone—Oxfam, FoE, WEF, and Rotary International—accounted for 50% of all mentions.[7] A look at a single media outlet over a longer period of time reveals a similar concentration of attention. The *New York Times* has historical coverage that allows a search of the full text from 1921 to 2012. We searched a truncated version of the random sample, excluding the UK-based INGOs which are less likely to reach the US-based *Times*. The term "nongovernmental organization" was mentioned an average 7 times a year, but the average number of mentions for the remaining 75 random sample INGOs was just 2.57 times per year since their founding.[8] As with the more recent media coverage, the top 10% of the sample received most of the mentions (84%) in the historical archives of the *New York Times*. NGOs in general have received more attention over time, but again, specific groups struggle for media attention.

In short, public attention clumps around a very small group of INGOs. Most INGOs get no attention, even though NGOs in general are increasingly prominent in the public eye. These two indicators, albeit imperfect, begin to help us measure what we mean by public attention.

Policymakers

Not all INGOs seek to make the front page of the global newspaper; many are expert specialists rather than household names. Thus it might be possible that INGOs fare better with legislators interested in the nuances of political agendas and foreign aid spending. Attention from governments directly constitutes authority when INGOs are called upon to provide information, give their opinion, and offer policy suggestions.

We gathered original data on INGO mentions in the full-text proceedings of the US Congress from 1970 to 2013. We searched a truncated version of our random sample, assuming that UK-based INGOs are unlikely to seek or receive attention from US policymakers. Overall, the term "non-governmental organization" appeared in the Congressional record about once every three days (5,346 times in forty-four years). Still, only a few specific INGOs get attention in Congress, whether they are based in the United States or working globally at the UN. Ten percent of the UN-registered INGOs accounted for 85% of the full-text mentions of that subsample, and the same share of the US-based INGOs accounted for 90% of all full-text mentions for that group.

Perhaps NGOs that lack public prominence still get attention from policymakers because of their technical expertise. Such attention should show up in the frequency with which specific NGOs have testified before Congress. Across the same time period as above, 97% of the witness appearances were made by 10% of the random sample of US-based INGOs.[9] Some of these INGOs are established specialists. For example, the International Campaign for Tibet, founded in 1988, had thirty witness appearances through 2012. But overall, congressional attention is focused on a small handful of INGOs.

For comparison, we ran similar searches of legislative proceedings in the United Kingdom and Canada, with random samples of INGOs headquartered in those countries as well as the UN-registered sample. Records in both countries are less complete, with limited full-text coverage or missing years. Still, for those dates available, we found a similar pattern for INGOs in each setting. In the UK, 10% of the random sample (both UN-registered and UK-based) enjoyed 90% of the mentions during the same time period.[10] Canada is slightly less skewed, with 10% (3 out of 29) of the UN-registered NGOs enjoying 74% of the mentions during the period from 1970 to 2013.[11] This is a marginal difference, however. The patterns among policymakers in the US, UK, and Canada follow those for the general public: most INGOs receive almost no attention.

Peers

INGOs are closely observed by their peers as potential collaborators and competitors. Deference from other INGOs may be harder to get and retain because INGOs are often competing with one another (see chapter 6). Despite these hurdles, peer INGOs are perhaps the most likely to be familiar with and connected to a wide range of INGOs. Surprisingly, however, INGOs defer to a small pool of other INGOs. We can see this in two realms: global network ties and surveys of US-based INGOs.

The fact that INGOs form networks is a truism. Importantly, members of a network must have at some point made a decision to listen to one another, based on their principles, capacity, expertise, or political access. We analyze data on global INGO networks provided in the Union of International Associations (UIA) yearbook compiled by Murdie and Davis (2012a). They generated a list of 4,378 INGOs across four issue areas from the 2001–2002 yearbook and then created a matrix of incoming and outgoing ties among those organizations. We can use these reported ties to assess and rank particular INGOs. Incoming ties signal that other INGOs are reporting that they partner with, and they also defer to, that INGO.

A few things stand out. First, the global INGO network is thin, which cuts against the assumption of widespread cooperation among INGOs. There are 17,170 ties in the Murdie and Davis (2012a) dataset, an average of only 3.9 reported network ties per year per organization. Second, within this network, there is a clear top tier. The top 10% of the sample had more than half (53%) of the incoming ties. Deference to multiple INGOs may be more frequent among INGO peers in comparison to the media and state officials, but attention is still concentrated on several hundred INGOs. Half the organizations in the sample (2,169) had zero or one incoming ties. Finally, globally active INGOs receive more deference from their peers. Consider the sample of UN-registered organizations. We chose from the category of groups that have the highest level of registration with the UN, and perhaps unsurprisingly, these 29 groups have a higher-than-average level of incoming ties.[12] Perhaps due to their extensive access to UN bodies, these groups enjoy greater authority in the eyes of their peers.

Beyond collaboration, another indicator of deference is favorability. An INGO's positive assessment of a peer may lead it to emulate strategies or partner with that INGO in advocacy and service delivery. We look at survey data on US-based INGOs working in numerous sectors.[13] From 2006 to 2008, researchers at the Transnational NGO (TNGO) Initiative at Syracuse University interviewed leaders of 152 INGOs.[14] In one question, subjects were asked to name five organizations within their field that they considered particularly effective. Only 30 INGOs, out of a total population of tens of thousands, were mentioned three or more times, and only 298 organizations in total were mentioned (Mitchell and Stroup 2016). Even though subjects were prompted to name five organizations, the average number of mentioned groups was 3.18. In short, INGOs have just a few organizations in mind when they think about which peers are effective.

The survey data may not perfectly capture an INGO's perceptions of its peers, as INGOs may feel pressured to promote themselves over others or default to recognizable INGOs rather than mentioning those they truly respect. While attention is less concentrated among INGOs as an audience, the fact that a limited number of INGOs are mentioned by their own peers as partners or objects of admiration suggests that very few INGOs have become household names even among their peers.

Corporations

Corporations are often a target of NGO efforts to improve environmental performance, protect human rights, and raise funds. Because of the sometimes adversarial nature of the corporate-NGO interaction, we might expect that deference to INGOs by corporations is often instrumental rather than internalized. Still, there is a growing interest in corporate social responsibility and the need that many corporations feel to signal their commitment to "good causes."[15] This can lead corporations to report relationships with NGOs. We expect that those INGOs are selected because corporations agree with their approach, value their expertise, or benefit from the stamp of approval provided by the INGO's principled commitments.

Though we lack data at the global level on transnational corporations and INGOs, data on the United States reveals that deference to INGOs by corporations is rare. Shumate and O'Connor (2010, 2014) searched the websites of 155 US Fortune 500 companies in 2005 for mentions of NGOs. As with other audiences, only a few INGOs were mentioned. The list of possible organizations is enormous, as the authors looked for any charity, domestic or international. Still, only 695 NGOs were mentioned. Of those, only 22 (3%) were mentioned four or more times (O'Connor and Shumate 2014, 116).[16] That 3% held 29% (232 out of 813 total ties) of the total number of ties between corporations and NGOs.[17] A third of the sample corporations (54 of 155) had no reported ties to NGOs, and another third (55) reported alliances with five or fewer NGOs. Multiple partnerships between US-based corporations and NGOs are infrequent. When those partnerships are reported, a few US-based NGOs get disproportionate attention from globally active corporations.

Discussion

As the data above make clear, claims about the authority of INGOs *in general* should be received with great skepticism. As discussed in the previous chapter, NGOs may in theory have access to authority because of their principled commitments or expertise, but few organizations are actually able to translate that into deference from an audience.

Across audiences, only a few INGOs get attention, creating a top tier and a dense bottom layer of what Carpenter (2014) refers to as "no-name" NGOs. This is clear for the public, global media, and policymakers. But even among the INGOs and corporations likely to do careful legwork on their potential partners (and thus perhaps more educated about the range of INGOs), attention is concentrated on a few groups. Just 10% of the globally active NGOs sampled by Murdie and Davis enjoyed more than half of the incoming ties from their peers. In the United States, 10% of the organizations in the TNGO Initiative survey enjoyed 37% of the mentions of effective peers (Mitchell and Stroup 2016). Less than 10% of O'Connor and Shumate's sample enjoyed more than half the incoming ties in the network of NGOs and US-based corporations. In short, the typical INGO in global politics is ignored.

That is the bleak first half of the story. Less depressing for INGO proponents, some INGOs do succeed in achieving deference from a single audience. More rarely, a few achieve that deference from multiple audiences. In the next section, we explore a group of INGOs that have become leading INGOs. To preface, it is exceedingly rare for an INGO to be seen as an authority beyond just one audience, let alone multiple audiences. While we may not be surprised by some of the names, we should be surprised by those that are missing.

Leading INGOs

Who matters in the INGO community? There are a number of popular lists that try to answer that question.[18] Among scholars, Clifford Bob and Charli Carpenter used the term "gatekeeper" INGOs to refer to the prominent, wealthy, and powerful INGOs that lead the human rights and human security sectors (Bob

2005; Carpenter 2014), while Michael Barnett and his colleagues (Barnett 2011; Barnett and Walker 2015) have referred to a "humanitarian club." A number of excellent case studies of prominent INGOs outline the specific strategies and influence of these organizations (on just Amnesty International, for example, see Clark 2001; Hopgood 2006). In short, INGO analysts (including ourselves) have followed the intuition that the INGO sector is dominated by a few groups. The research presented above offers evidentiary support for this hunch. The data above also advances our understanding of the breadth and depth of INGO authority by capturing the lack of deference by specific audiences to the average INGO. In this section, we push past this intuition to explore the differences among groups at the top, those most likely to become leading INGOs. Following the logic in chapter 2, we aggregate authority, assuming that the more audiences that defer to an INGO, the greater the INGO's authority. We also weight the audience scores the same, since each audience defers to INGOs for different reasons; it is problematic to conceptualize these as "outweighing" one another. We compare the reception of INGOs across a range of audiences and identify a short list of INGO leaders. Many of these are (unsurprisingly) household names, but others enjoy widespread deference despite a weak public brand.

Differentiation at the Top

An INGO's status as *an* authority exists in the context of specific relationships, and national and institutional context is critical.[19] In constructing a list of "most-likely" leading INGOs, we largely sampled from INGOs working in English or based in anglophone countries. Although we do not survey all possible INGO audiences, the most likely list includes groups with sizeable chapters in multiple countries who employ the international lingua franca to reach global media, global institutions, and globally powerful governments and corporations. Thus, while this list of leading INGOs is neither definitive nor exhaustive, it offers a systematic evaluation of those INGOs that might be considered gatekeepers.

To chart deference to INGOs at the top, we first constructed a list of most-likely leading INGOs and then searched mentions of these groups in the same way as for our random sample. We used existing explanations of INGO power to identify two possible factors that contribute to INGO authority: material capacity and network centrality. We identified a list of the largest environmental, human rights, and relief and development NGOs that are headquartered in wealthy countries and active in multiple national settings.[20] This list included thirty-six organizations (see the appendix for a discussion of comparing financial size across sectors). Second, we sorted through the list of INGOs with the highest number of incoming ties (using the data from Murdie and Davis 2012a) to include an additional nine groups. These forty-five organizations are listed in table A.1 in the appendix. The two right-hand columns of this table show each organization's founding year and 2014 expenditures. Half of the forty-five most-likely leading authorities (twenty-three) are from the relief and development sector. This is an undercounting of the number of relief and development INGOs in the population, but we assume that a disproportionate number of those INGOs are involved in primarily service delivery and may not always seek authority.[21]

Using the same databases and methodology as for the random sample, we searched for the number of times these forty-five INGOs were mentioned as a way to assess deference from the public, states, and INGOs. Recalling from above, we searched for frequency of Google searches using Google Trends, mentions in global media, mentions in US congressional and Canadian parliamentary proceedings, number of incoming network ties, and mentions as effective by INGO peers based in the United States. Unfortunately, we lack a database on the NGO-corporate relationship across sectors, though we discuss corporate relations with environmental NGOs below. As above, we searched each database across all available dates. While the uneven data range makes it difficult to make causal claims about the relationships among audiences, our widest possible net better captures the durability of authority for individual INGOs.

For each audience, we examined the same indicators as we used above for INGOs within this pool of most-likely leading INGOs. We start by discussing basic patterns in the distribution of authority. To begin, even among this top tier of INGOs, only a few organizations are established authorities in the eyes of single audiences. For example, consider media attention, assessed based on the number of times an INGO was mentioned in global news publications over a three-year period (2010–2012). We show these counts in figure 3.1.

These raw counts show that attention is concentrated on a few groups, despite the seeming advantages of wealth or connectedness that these groups enjoy (for the specific values used to construct these figures, see the appendix). Amnesty and Human Rights Watch (HRW) stand out as leaders, followed by a handful of other INGOs. Behind those few groups are a number of INGOs that get some attention. Many of these specialize in a narrower range of issues than the leading INGOs, including groups like the Carter Center (election monitoring), Rotary International (networking and community service), and International Planned Parenthood Federation (family planning).

Furthermore, some audiences defer to a wider range of INGOs than others. Public attention is concentrated, reflecting and reinforcing the status of "brand-name" INGOs like Greenpeace, Amnesty, and Oxfam. The same appears true for legislators in the United States and Canada, though some less prominent groups like the Environmental Defense Fund (EDF) and Catholic Relief Services have

FIGURE 3.1 Mentions of INGOs in global media, 2010–2012. Data drawn from LexisNexis news database.

successfully cultivated their authority before the US Congress.[22] By contrast, deference to INGOs is dispersed when it comes to INGO peers. There is no clear "industry leader" among INGOs, but rather a sizeable group of INGOs that have a substantial number of incoming ties or are described by their US-based peers as effective.[23] This dispersed authority makes sense, since INGOs likely know more of their peers *and* know more about them.

Finally, INGOs that appear to have many advantages, including wealth and location in a powerful country, often cannot transform those into authority. The random sample data presented in the section above reveals that the average INGO is ignored, and the story is not much better for wealthy or well-connected INGOs. A few organizations do succeed in achieving deference from a single audience, however, and a few are able to become leading INGOs. It is to that group that we now turn.

A List of Leading INGOs

The three audiences—states, other INGOs, and the public—defer to a limited group of INGOs. But how should we distinguish these leading INGOs from others? We start by ranking them. Table 3.1 lists the organizations from our most-likely sample that were the ten most frequently mentioned for each of our audiences across the six indicators. This is a simple view of the top; below, we consider an alternate and more fine-grained measure based on normalized scores. While the exact cutoff point is debatable, a list of the top groups captures their relative standing in comparison to other INGOs.

A number of groups are repeatedly listed in the top ten, including the usual suspects Amnesty and Oxfam, but also FoE, Salvation Army, and World Vision. A few do well before specific audiences. BRAC does well on Internet searches but does not make a dent with states or other INGOs. This prominence with the public should not be discounted. Deference from one audience is hard to achieve, two even more difficult, and three harder still. There are no economies of scale in building authority, since each audience has different preferences. Therefore, becoming a leading INGO is an unexpected outcome.

Figure 3.2 offers a visualization of those INGOs that have successfully gotten attention from multiple audiences by presenting the ranking data for all forty-five most-likely INGOs. Recalling that each of our three audiences is measured by two indicators, the maximum value on the Y-axis is 6. Out of our entire most-likely sample, only two INGOs, Amnesty and Oxfam, appear in the top ten list five or more times. Other INGOs receive deference on at least three indicators: World Vision, the International Committee of the Red Cross (ICRC), and CARE. Nine other INGOs have deference according to at least two indicators. In sum, using this measure, the fourteen INGOs on the left-hand side of figure 3.2 are leading INGOs.

TABLE 3.1 Ten most mentioned INGOs across six indicators

RANKING	PUBLIC AS AUDIENCE		STATES AS AUDIENCE		OTHER INGOS AS AUDIENCE	
	GOOGLE SEARCHES (WEEKLY) (2004–14)	MENTIONS IN GLOBAL MEDIA (2010–12)	MENTIONS AT US CONGRESS (1970–2013)	MENTIONS AT CANADIAN PARLIAMENT (1970–95, 2001–13)	INGO NETWORK TIES (2001/02)	MENTIONS AS EFFECTIVE BY US INGOS (2006–08)
1	Salvation Army	Amnesty International	Amnesty International	Amnesty International	Oxfam	World Vision
2	Greenpeace	Human Rights Watch	Human Rights Watch	Greenpeace	EarthAction	CARE
3	Habitat for Humanity	Oxfam	Salvation Army	Salvation Army	International Campaign to Ban Landmines	Oxfam
4	Amnesty International	Greenpeace	International Campaign to Ban Landmines	Red Cross	International Union for Conservation of Nature	Catholic Relief Services
5	Oxfam	Salvation Army	Environmental Defense Fund	Human Rights Watch	Amnesty International	Amnesty International
6	World Vision	Save the Children	Friends of the Earth	Oxfam	Save the Children	Save the Children
7	Human Rights Watch	Friends of the Earth	Habitat for Humanity	World Vision	Red Cross	International Rescue Committee
8	Save the Children	CARE	Freedom House	World Wide Fund for Nature	CIVICUS	Doctors without Borders
9	Bangladesh Rural Advancement Committee	Red Cross	World Wide Fund for Nature	Doctors without Borders	International Commission of Jurists	Mercy Corps
10	Red Cross	World Vision	Greenpeace	CARE	International Council of Voluntary Agencies	World Wide Fund for Nature

Sources: Data compiled from Murdie and Davis 2012a; Mitchell and Stroup 2016; and author calculations.

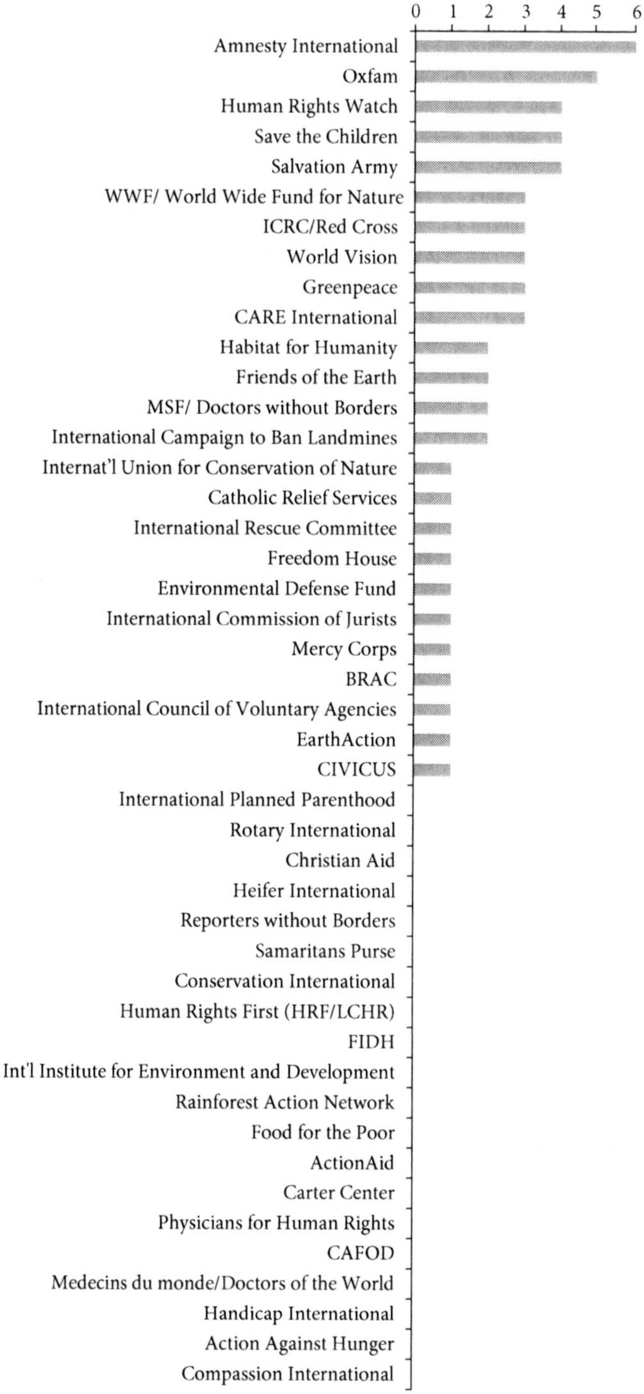

FIGURE 3.2 Appearances in top ten list for attention across six indicators

These groups are not uniform in their practices. Some, like Habitat for Humanity and Greenpeace, have a high public profile. Other groups, like Save the Children, have a lower advocacy profile (reflected in less standing before legislators) but still enjoy deference from peers and the public. All have actively sought to cultivate authority with multiple audiences and have done so fairly successfully. This project takes time; the youngest INGO here is the International Campaign to Ban Landmines (ICBL) (founded in 1992) and the average year of founding for leading INGOs is 1947 (compared to 1959 for the entire most-likely sample).

Another way to consider the distribution of authority is to look at the concentration of attention by each audience and see the gaps among different groups. To do this, we normalized the value of each indicator, setting the top score achieved by an INGO at 1 and expressing the other INGOs' scores as a percentage of this, ranging from 0 to 1. These normalized scores are reported in table 3.2. When we add these scores across the six indicators (the far right column in table 3.2), we can see the gaps among INGOs more clearly. The mean normalized score (reported at the bottom of table 3.2) is 0.86 and the median score is 0.46, indicating that the distribution of attention "scores" is skewed to the left. Table 3.2 shows a few high-scoring INGOs that account for much of the attention that INGOs receive, while most of the most-likely leading INGOs receive aggregate scores below 1 (out of a possible total of 6).

Table 3.2 also shows notable differences among the INGOs at the top. Amnesty scores 1.5 more points than its next competitor, the Salvation Army, and there is also a large gap between HRW and Save the Children. Like with the ranked scores, there is a clear cutoff in the normalized scores between the top eleven INGOs and the subsequent groups. The reordering of particular INGOs is a result of a scoring system that rewards INGOs that do very well with a single audience. Thus, Médecins Sans Frontières (MSF), WWF, and the ICBL fall in ranking while tiny EarthAction does well because of its high attention in INGO networks. While the ranking data better captures those INGOs that enjoy a breadth of authority, the normalized scores show the depth of authority that some INGOs enjoy with particular audiences.

Both breadth and depth of authority are important in the authoritative status of INGOs. We consider both in constructing a single list of leading INGOs, presented in table 3.3. We present the scores for each individual INGO in three different ways. First, we show the depth of deference. The first column represents the data from the far right column of table 3.2, the sum of the normalized scores across the six indicators. The next two columns capture the breadth of each INGO's authority. The middle column shows the counts (from figure 3.2) of the number of indicators along which the INGO appears among the highest

TABLE 3.2 Normalized scores for most-likely leading INGOs

NAME	AVERAGE STANDING IN WEEKLY GOOGLE SEARCHES	MENTIONS IN GLOBAL MEDIA	MENTIONS AT US CONGRESS	MENTIONS AT CANADIAN PARLIAMENT	INGO NETWORK TIES	MENTIONS AS EFFECTIVE BY US INGOS	TOTAL SCORE
Amnesty International	0.37	1.00	1.00	1.00	0.66	0.33	4.36
Salvation Army	1.00	0.62	0.69	0.29	0.13	0.13	2.86
Oxfam	0.33	0.70	0.12	0.17	1.00	0.50	2.81
Human Rights Watch (HRW)	0.16	0.96	0.98	0.18	0.31	0.21	2.80
Save the Children	0.16	0.57	0.15	0.06	0.66	0.33	1.95
Greenpeace	0.46	0.66	0.25	0.33	0.21	0.04	1.95
International Committee of Red Cross (ICRC)	0.09	0.25	0.65	0.20	0.45	0.21	1.84
World Vision	0.25	0.24	0.17	0.12		1.00	1.77
Friends of the Earth (FoE)	0.04	0.38	0.53	0.07	0.28	0.08	1.38
CARE International	0.03	0.33	0.05	0.08	0.20	0.67	1.36
Habitat for Humanity	0.41	0.13	0.45	0.05	0.19	0.13	1.35
EarthAction	0.00	0.00	0.00	0.00	0.95	0.00	0.95
International Union for Conservation of Nature	0.07	0.03	0.07	0.01	0.75	0.00	0.94
WWF/World Wide Fund for Nature	0.05	0.22	0.28	0.11		0.25	0.90
MSF/Doctors without Borders	0.08	0.17	0.10	0.09	0.19	0.25	0.88

(Continued)

TABLE 3.2 (Continued)

NAME	AVERAGE STANDING IN WEEKLY GOOGLE SEARCHES	MENTIONS IN GLOBAL MEDIA	MENTIONS AT US CONGRESS	MENTIONS AT CANADIAN PARLIAMENT	INGO NETWORK TIES	MENTIONS AS EFFECTIVE BY US INGOS	TOTAL SCORE
Catholic Relief Services (CRS)	0.01	0.03	0.20	0.00	0.17	0.42	**0.83**
International Campaign to Ban Landmines (ICBL)	0.00	0.00	0.01	0.00	0.76	0.00	**0.77**
Environmental Defense Fund	0.00	0.04	0.58	0.00	0.02	0.08	**0.74**
International Planned Parenthood	0.00	0.18	0.06	0.04	0.30	0.04	**0.61**
Freedom House	0.04	0.11	0.36	0.01	0.05	0.04	**0.61**
Christian Aid	0.05	0.12	0.00	0.00	0.32	0.04	**0.54**
International Commission of Jurists (ICJ)	0.00	0.05	0.04	0.02	0.36	0.00	**0.48**
Rotary International	0.05	0.06	0.03	0.05	0.14	0.13	**0.46**
International Rescue Committee	0.01	0.03	0.12	0.00		0.29	**0.45**
Human Rights First (HRF/LCHR)	0.00	0.03	0.19	0.00	0.12	0.08	**0.42**
CIVICUS	0.00	0.00	0.00	0.00	0.40	0.00	**0.40**
Mercy Corps	0.02	0.02	0.06	0.00	0.03	0.25	**0.37**
International Institute for Environment and Development (IIED)	0.00	0.02	0.01	0.00	0.34	0.00	**0.36**
FIDH	0.01	0.01	0.00	0.00	0.28	0.04	**0.35**

International Council of Voluntary Agencies (ICVA)	0.00	0.00	0.00	0.00	0.34	0.00	**0.35**
Reporters without Borders (RSF)	0.00	0.18	0.05	0.01	0.06	0.00	**0.31**
Conservation International	0.00	0.04	0.09	0.00	0.03	0.13	**0.28**
Heifer International	0.03	0.02	0.01	0.00		0.21	**0.27**
CAFOD	0.01	0.03	0.00	0.00	0.22	0.00	**0.27**
ActionAid	0.02	0.12	0.01	0.00		0.08	**0.23**
Physicians for Human Rights	0.00	0.03	0.08	0.00	0.05	0.04	**0.21**
Carter Center	0.02	0.08	0.11	0.00		0.00	**0.20**
Rainforest Action Network	0.00	0.00	0.01	0.00	0.06	0.13	**0.20**
Samaritans Purse	0.01	0.02	0.02	0.02		0.13	**0.19**
BRAC	0.13	0.04	0.00	0.00		0.00	**0.16**
Food for the Poor	0.00	0.01	0.01	0.00	0.00	0.13	**0.15**
Action Against Hunger	0.00	0.02	0.01	0.00	0.04	0.04	**0.11**
Médecins du monde (MDM)/ Doctors of the World	0.00	0.02	0.01	0.01	0.06	0.00	**0.10**
Compassion International	0.03	0.01	0.00	0.00		0.04	**0.08**
Handicap International	0.02	0.01	0.01	0.00		0.00	**0.05**
MEAN	*0.09*	*0.17*	*0.17*	*0.07*	*0.29*	*0.14*	**0.86**
STANDARD DEVIATION	*0.180*	*0.256*	*0.257*	*0.162*	*0.268*	*0.198*	**0.93**

Sources: Data compiled from Murdie and Davis 2012a; Mitchell and Stroup 2016; and author calculations.

ranks. The right column summarizes that same information in a different way. Recall that we selected two indicators each for three different audiences: states, corporations, and other INGOs. Because authority is more likely to be durable if it exists across many different audiences, we sorted the six indicators into their respective three audiences, and the far right column of table 3.3 shows whether those INGOs were highly ranked across multiple audiences (not just multiple indicators).

This group of leading INGOs has achieved widespread authority. Some INGOs have also gotten substantial attention from a single audience, and this could be a path to influence over some issues. There are a few surprises in this category. Groups like the Salvation Army and Habitat for Humanity are rarely discussed in the international relations literature but fall into the leading INGO category using both sets of measures. Habitat has successfully used its religious inspiration and narrow focus on housing to reach multiple audiences, well beyond its American roots. The presence of the Salvation Army on this list symbolizes the challenges of studying the INGO population. It works in 127 countries and is

TABLE 3.3 Leading INGOs

INGO NAME	ATTENTION SCORES FROM MULTIPLE AUDIENCES (NORMALIZED, TABLE 3.2)	NUMBER OF APPEARANCES IN TOP 10 RANKING (FIGURE 3.2)	DEFERENCE FROM AUDIENCES (0–3)
Amnesty International	4.36	6	3
Oxfam	2.81	5	3
Salvation Army	2.86	4	2
Human Rights Watch	2.80	4	2
Save the Children	1.95	4	2
Greenpeace	1.95	3	2
ICRC/Red Cross	1.84	3	2
World Vision	1.77	3	2
CARE	1.36	3	3
WWF/ World Wide Fund for Nature	0.90	3	2
FOE/Friends of the Earth	1.38	2	2
Habitat for Humanity	1.35	2	2
ICBL/Intl Campaign to Ban Landmines	0.77	2	2
MSF/Doctors without Borders	0.88	2	2

registered with the UIA, but its status as a religious institution prohibits US tax authorities from gathering information on its activities, and the heavy domestic component of its work complicates the question of whether it is a domestic charity or an INGO. By contrast, MSF gets a lot of attention from scholars, but its definitive public brand is not as powerful with other audiences. It does not do well before governments. Even though it is frequently thought of as a media darling (Redfield 2013), it is the definition of average with regard to this metric: its media mentions scores 0.17, the mean for our sample. Finally, the growth of BRAC has been hailed by some as evidence of the growing power of the Global South in development (Goetz and Gupta 1996), and the INGO is the largest in the world if the number of staff members is counted (Crack 2013). Still, BRAC has not translated this into widespread authority with global audiences, and this speaks to the fact that geography (i.e., location of offices) likely matters for getting one's issues before various audiences.

Our measures of leading INGOs do not capture standing with corporations, though this is an increasingly important audience for INGOs. We do know that corporate attention is also concentrated: "a very small number of NGOs play a central role in the NGO-corporate network" (O'Connor and Shumate 2014, 127). As discussed in the chapter introduction, this audience has been especially important for environmental groups but only recently so for humanitarian and human rights groups. We use data from Andrew Hoffman, who has explored the relationship between corporations and the sixty-nine largest American environmental NGOs (both domestic and international) (Hoffman 2009; Hoffman and Bertels 2010). WWF, Conservation International, and EDF are central to the corporate network, while FoE and Greenpeace are disconnected. Rainforest Action Network has many ties to businesses but it does not occupy a central position in the network, suggesting that it has lower authority in the eyes of corporations.[24] This differentiation among environmental NGOs in the ways they attempt to relate to corporations reflects a heated debate over NGO-corporate partnerships (Vogel 2008; Alcock 2008). Some environmental NGOs like FoE report that to partner with corporations can threaten their authority with other audiences, while others (like WWF) seem to have found a politically palatable and moderate path to widespread deference. We discuss this tension at greater length in chapter 5.

The evidence presented here may raise questions of how authority is constructed. While we largely focus on the consequences of the uneven distribution of authority, a few thoughts about its causes arise. Neither material capacity nor connectedness appear to be sufficient conditions for becoming leading INGOs, though both appear necessary. The INGOs considered to be leading INGOs are all wealthy *and* well-regarded by peers,[25] but so are some of the more obscure peers, such as Catholic Relief Services. This evidence suggests that claims like "wealth is power" or "network position is power" are oversimplifications. Wealth or connectedness alone is no guarantee that an INGO is on the path to high status. Founded in 1982, Food for the Poor reported more than $900 million in revenue in 2014, but it is virtually unknown except to a few of its peers. The International Institute for Environment and Development (IIED) is a UK-based INGO founded in 1971 that emphasizes partnership and cross-sectoral programming. Despite its many incoming ties, however, it remains invisible to most audiences. In the dynamic interplay of wealth, networks, and authority, the causal arrow runs both ways among all three factors. Wealth allows an expanded reach to more audiences and the chance to develop new expertise, while connectedness can yield new information or be leveraged into new relationships in and out of the INGO network. Reversing the causal claim, authority can attract more donors and more partners. Thus, rather than trying to unpack the causal chain, what we should acknowledge is that it can be a virtuous circle for INGOs that successfully balance their concerns.

Whatever the precise path, few INGOs have achieved deference from multiple audiences. Yet two important assumptions are implicit in that claim. First, we assume that deference emerges from intentional actions by an INGO to become an authority in the eyes of one or more audiences. Those INGOs listed as leaders did not become so by accident. But not all INGOs seek such status, and they are happy to work steadily in a limited sector with a particular group. Still, given limited sources and heavy competition, increasing one's status is one important factor that can help ensure basic financial security. Second, deference from multiple audiences is not equal to universal deference. Greenpeace may be highly regarded by the German government and the media but may be poorly received by American policymakers and INGO peers. While the concept of leading INGO can help differentiate among organizations in a variety of important contexts, the INGOs listed above may not be authoritative across all settings and time periods. Future explorations of the reach of these groups in other contexts would extend the research presented here.

These leading INGOs *are* authoritative in multiple settings, and that status can be quite durable. This durability has been noted by scholars of environmental groups (Bosso 2005), human rights INGOs (Welch 2001), and humanitarians (Barnett and Walker 2015), but the precise level and durability of an INGO's authority over time needs closer attention. Historical and longitudinal data from the *New York Times* (1970–2013), the US Congress (1970–2013), and Google Trends (2004–2014) indicates that those groups at the top stay at the top. Despite some annual variation, Amnesty was mentioned in congressional proceedings more than fifty times a year over a twenty-five-year period (1985 and 2010).

An organization with a much lower advocacy profile, World Vision, averaged twenty-two mentions a year during the same period, despite a budget that is perhaps ten times the size of Amnesty's. Nothing succeeds like success, and many INGOs that have achieved some measure of deference are able to translate that into new political access, new funds, and more salience.

Our comparison among INGOs across multiple audiences yields some important findings. First, we find definitive evidence of substantial differentiation among INGOs in their level of authority. Global civil society is not an egalitarian community of do-gooders. Rather, it is full of the sorts of inequalities and conflicts that exist in any political setting. In the global distribution of attention to INGOs, most INGOs are ignored and lack any authority in the global public sphere. Second, a few INGOs do achieve deference from multiple audiences. This is neither easy nor common. The ways these differences in status shape INGO strategies are the focus of the next three chapters. In unpacking how leading INGOs and other INGOs interact with their audiences, we can show how differences in authority shape the strategies of INGOs.

The previous two chapters have focused on the concept of and evidence for INGO authority. Before turning to the consequences of varied authority, we end with two points related to INGO authority in general. First, our understanding of authority, and the evidence we present, suggests the need to synthesize existing explanations of INGO capacity and legitimacy. The principled commitments that INGOs make are important in distinguishing them from other actors and may give them legitimacy as *an* authority, commitments that might fail without that principled basis. But principles alone offer no guarantee that anyone will listen to an INGO. Leading INGOs have the material capacity necessary to work in multiple settings, develop a deep well of expertise, monitor their own performance, and coordinate with other actors in the field. INGOs that develop these practices in isolation from their peers also fail to develop into leading INGOs. Peer networks may simply demonstrate good citizenship, spread an organization's name, or actually improve the practice of the members. Regardless, we return to the original insights implicit in Keck and Sikkink (1998). INGO networks are important, but so is the capacity of the individual members of the network and the principled aims they claim to advance. A focus on INGO authority can capture all three dimensions—the resonance of morality, the development of expertise and reach, and the ties among INGOs—while highlighting that authority varies substantially across the many relationships that INGOs seek to cultivate.

A second point, important for scholars of global governance, is that the concept of leading status is useful for a range of actors, not just INGOs. Authority is a difficult concept to capture and is often most evident in the breach of it, as in scandals involving INGOs. Attention is a necessary prerequisite for deference, and we have used that as a proxy for authority. Granted, that attention may come about because of questions about the actor's authority, what Zürn, Binder, and Ecker-Ehrhardt (2012) refer to as challenges to an actor's legitimacy. But it is worth noting that challenges to an INGO's authority constitute recognition of the authority of that INGO. An INGO with no authority does not need to be challenged. Alternately, attention to an INGO may be grudging rather than internalized. Still, "attention" captures an important dimension of an actor's authority and could prove useful for those that study the authority of corporations, states, and intergovernmental organizations. The global governance stage is a crowded one, and it can be difficult to separate character actors and bit parts from the main leads. The simple concept of leading authorities offers an organizing framework for distinguishing among the many actors, with their many capacities, active in global governance today.

TARGETING STATES

How do INGOs choose among different ways to relate to states? Considering the news from a single day in the summer of 2015, INGOs seem to use all three strategies—condemnation, collaboration, and competition—quite regularly. Amnesty International issued a report condemning the Indian government for failing to hold security forces in Jammu and Kashmir accountable for human rights violations. In Mozambique, World Vision signed a memorandum of understanding with the Ministry of Health to fight communicable diseases like AIDS, TB, and malaria. From the Netherlands, the Global Reporting Initiative announced new tools meant to encourage corporations to adopt sustainable practices, even when not required to do so by state regulations.[1]

In deciding among these broad approaches and more specific strategies, INGO authority matters. In this chapter, we examine two global campaigns—for an Arms Trade Treaty (ATT) and for a financial transactions tax (FTT)—to illustrate the effects of the authority trap on the strategic choices of leading INGOs and other INGOs. In general, we show that leading INGOs collaborate with states more frequently than do other INGOs. Leading INGOs command the sort of attention that makes states more likely to hear their claims. In addition, their substantial resources and global reach give them the expertise to make issues into salient policy proposals and the political standing to coordinate across many countries. This increased propensity for collaboration is no guarantee of goal attainment, however. The authority trap creates a number of challenging dynamics for leading INGOs in efforts to change state practice that shape their choices from among the three strategies.

First, their ability to speak to multiple audiences actually restricts them to moderate policy proposals. The influence they achieve can be thought of as a series of "vanilla victories," widely palatable accomplishments that can appear bland to more radical INGOs. This often requires that INGOs steer a path through the varied, established preferences of multiple audiences and find a midpoint satisfying to many groups. This also means that leading INGOs will tend not to use condemnation as a strategy because of the desire to attract, rather than repel, the audiences to whom they are speaking (in this case, states). INGOs are not simply reactive, however. They play a critical role in shaping the preferences of states on emerging issues, exercising what Barnett and Duvall (2005) refer to as "productive power." Yet while the productive power of leading INGOs as a whole may be substantial, the frames and proposals advanced by leading INGOs tend to be incremental rather than radical proposals that might alienate a key constituency. From the perspective of other activists, the asset of leading INGOs (their status) becomes a liability when it comes to designing policy demands.

Second, leading INGOs are focused not just on the question at hand but on their long-term authority and positioning within global politics. Leading INGOs need to emerge from a campaign claiming victory to keep their many audiences deferential and supportive. This shapes the selection of state targets, so that leading INGOs focus on already friendly states. States vary in their importance for a particular issue area and in their willingness to cooperate with INGOs on that issue (Betzold 2014). Thus, INGOs might shape target states' preferences, but some states are actively seeking out INGO partners or collaborating with INGOs. Across a number of INGO campaigns, middle-power states have been willing to work with INGO coalitions. Leading INGOs are particularly important in developing these alliances because they can build multistate coalitions. The responsiveness of midlevel states drives leading INGOs to collaborate with them so that they can demonstrate some policy change, even if those policies emanate from states that have little clout within the issue area.

Third, the status concerns of leading INGOs shape the cohesion (or lack thereof) within INGO coalitions and reveal the tensions among INGOs and other partners. Collective collaboration among INGOs might be a welcome choice, but INGO coalitions do not always work. Within and across our cases, the level and type of involvement by leading INGOs varies. These "gatekeepers" (Bob 2005; Carpenter 2014) or "advocacy superpowers" (Carpenter 2014) are critical for issue adoption, but more is not more. INGO coalitions face two types of Goldilocks problems that require careful balancing of interests. First, competition among leading INGOs can cripple rather than strengthen these coalitions. As the case of the ATT illustrates, a higher number of leading INGOs does not ensure more effective coalitions. Gatekeeping works best when there is only one gatekeeper. Second, particular campaigns can be more or less central to an INGO's overall advocacy profile. Leading INGOs that fully embrace a cause and put it at the center of their global agenda bring concerns over credit claiming and brand protection to the campaign. The case of the FTT suggests that leading INGOs like Oxfam are most valuable with a few committed staff members acting below the radar. In short, status concerns shape the evolution of collective INGO campaigns as well as the strategies of individual INGOs.

The authority trap works on both leading INGOs and other INGOs. If a few leading INGOs are trapped by their authority, other INGOs struggle because of their lack of widespread deference. They have no reputation—they are unknown—and struggle for attention. They may be narrow experts on a particular subject and struggle to reframe the issue. They need leading INGOs but often resent what happens when those big players enter the coalition (Chong 2009). Leading INGOs are not the only ones that adopt moderate policy positions or try to claim credit, but their authority makes it much more likely that they will choose these strategies *and* that these strategies will be taken up by INGO coalitions. Leading INGOs also tend to prefer any policy, however weak, to no policy. Bob (2012) calls these "zombie policies" and argues that they result from contests among competing networks. Weak treaties and policies are unsatisfying to many activists and can be counterproductive if they rob the issue of political attention or lower regulatory standards (Feinstein and De Waal 2015). From our view, zombie policies arise not just because the presence of opposing forces requires settling for second-best treaties, but because the demands of maintaining deference push leading INGOs to accept vanilla outcomes.

We structure the chapter to illustrate the implications of the authority trap. We begin with a brief description of the evolution of the ATT and FTT campaigns. The second section unpacks the moderating moves of leading INGOs within each coalition. Third, we show that alliances between middle-power states and leading INGOs may serve the self-interests of each type of actors but not necessarily the campaign's goals. The fourth section focuses on the challenge of getting the level of leading INGOs' involvement "just right." In the conclusion, we highlight several broader implications for understanding INGO strategies and authority.

Guns and Money: A Brief History of Two INGO Coalitions

Groups of INGOs have worked together on the regulation of small arms to attain the ATT and regulation of global financial flows via an FTT. The two cases share important similarities, and our comparison mitigates the confounding effects of external variables while offering insight into the role of status in shaping INGO strategies. Both the ATT and FTT operate in issue areas, security and finance, that are traditionally challenging for INGOs (Price 2003; Dryzek 2012). Leading INGOs might thus be particularly important for developing proposals for reform. Both issues are on the borders of the established sectors of human rights, environmental protection, and relief and development, which creates potential openings for a variety of leading INGOs to get involved. The primary state targets of each campaign are also similar; the US and UK are global hubs of both finance and arms production, followed by a group of middle-power states. Both campaigns coalesced in the late 1990s and are still active today. Finally, over two decades, both coalitions have changed substantially in terms of membership, strategies, and policy proposals.

Drawing on past scholarship and new research, we highlight the particular way INGO status shapes the strategic choices of INGOs. First we present a brief chronology of each case, focusing on the campaign's membership, strategy, policy demands, and outcomes.

The Arms Trade Treaty

Arms control and disarmament has been an issue of global concern for at least a century, but the modern campaign to restrict the flow of small arms dates to the late 1990s (Karp 2006; de Waal 2015). After the signing of the famous land mines ban treaty, the Canadian foreign minister expressed an interest in funding an NGO coalition around small arms. In response, researcher Edward Laurance brought together a group of INGOs, and the International Action Network on Small Arms (IANSA) was born (Bob 2012; Laurance 2013). IANSA's membership drew from both the North and South, and it considered an expansive number of issues rather than adopting a narrow policy position (Shawki 2010; Wong 2012). IANSA's initial efforts thus yielded some weak frameworks with little substantive content. The United Nations convened a conference on small arms in New York in 2001, but the outcome was a weak Program of Action with limited scope (Krause 2002). In frustration, one leading INGO, Human Rights Watch (HRW), closed its small arms program (Bob 2012, 140).

Following the disappointing UN conference, the NGO coalition reorganized, and in 2003 Amnesty, Oxfam, and IANSA launched the "Control Arms Campaign" (CAC) in seventy countries around the world (Green et al. 2013). Oxfam, Amnesty, and a few other INGOs led the coalition, while local NGOs participated in official state delegation, lobbied legislators, and publicized the humanitarian fallout within their own countries (Interviews 1003, 1006, 1011)[2] (Green and Macdonald 2014). The specific strategies of the CAC were to target public opinion and sympathetic middle-power states with a policy goal of achieving an Arms

Trade Treaty (ATT). The CAC launched a visually compelling "Million Faces" global petition in 2004, published a research report (*Shattered Lives*) making the case for tough regulation around arms, and showcased victims of the arms trade from more than fifty countries in "People's Consultations" in 2007 (Mack and Wood 2009).

At the time of the launch of the CAC, only three countries had publicly declared support for an ATT: Cambodia, Costa Rica, and Mali. By 2006, fifty states had come around to the idea, and seven of them formed a "core group" that introduced UN General Assembly Resolution 61/89 (Mack and Wood 2009).[3] Of the core group, the UK led the way, and its early declaration of support for the ATT in 2004 was the first from a major arms exporter. The UK's support paved the way for other states to join (Interview 1051). Other states, such as Canada, Norway, Sweden, Austria, Belgium, and Switzerland supported small arms regulation, and the US, France, and Germany, other major arms exporters, became supportive after the UK's initiative (Bolton and Nash 2010). In 2013, the UN welcomed signatures and ratifications for the ATT, and it came into force in December 2014. Today, almost all major arms exporters (France, Germany, Israel, Italy, Spain, UK, Ukraine, United States) have signed the treaty. The ATT covers all kinds of conventional arms in accordance with the UN Register of Conventional Arms, including small arms and light weapons. The ATT mandates that states establish a national arms transfer control system and assess whether a proposed arms trade has the risk to be used in terrorist activity, crimes against humanity, gender-based violence, or other ways that violate human rights (Green et al. 2013, 553).

The demands of the treaty are sizeable, and the ultimate effects of the ATT are still unclear. Some hail it as a major victory.[4] For example, Waltz writes that the ATT "breaks new normative ground" and that the CAC succeeded "against the odds" to connect the arms proliferation issue with human rights (Waltz 2014, 168). Others are skeptical that the ATT can be or will be enforced (Stohl 2015). Some INGOs are dismissive of the ATT, and arms companies do not envision the ATT affecting their operations (Feinstein and De Waal 2015).

The ATT is a visible achievement by a large coalition of INGOs, led by Amnesty and Oxfam. Not all coalitions achieve so much, of course. By contrast, the FTT has made its way to the global agenda but the outcomes of the campaign are much more modest.

The Financial Transactions Tax

Like the flow of guns, the unfettered flow of money around the world has been criticized by a number of analysts and activists. One well-known proposal for taxing global financial flows was advanced by Nobel laureate economist James

Tobin in 1971. He called for a tax to "throw sand in the wheels of commerce," reducing unproductive currency speculation while preserving the benefits of financial globalization. The "Tobin tax" began to get attention during the currency crises of the mid-1990s in Mexico, East Asia, Russia, and Brazil (Patomäki 2009). In 1995, the UN Development Program hosted a conference on the feasibility and effects of such a tax (Ul Haq, Kaul, and Grundberg 1996). Concurrently, a number of INGOs critical of neoliberal globalization began to call for a financial transactions tax (FTT) to be collected by an international institution. This group included War on Want in the United Kingdom, WEED (World Economy, Ecology, and Development) in Germany, the Tobin Tax Initiative in the United States, several chapters of Friends of the Earth (FoE), and the Halifax Initiative in Canada.[5] In France, a 1997 editorial in *Le Monde Diplomatique* led to the launch of ATTAC (Association pour la Taxation de Transactions financières à l'Aide des Citoyens et Citoyennes), an activist group constituted around the idea of an FTT. These different groups came together as a loose network. Many exchanged information and hosted conferences around the technical question of designing the global tax, recruiting financial services experts, and conducting feasibility studies (Wahl 2014).

The early work of these groups had little political impact in the late 1990s. A supportive resolution passed in March 1999 by the Canadian parliament was greeted with excitement, but the issue was still ignored by many finance ministries and the IMF.[6] In fact, American conservatives labeled the FTT a "United Nations tax" in the late 1990s and used it to justify withholding funds from the United Nations (Brassett 2010, 49–50). France was the important exception. The transactions tax proposal had support from almost all of France's political leaders (Landau 2004), and in 2001, 71% of French survey respondents expressed support for an FTT (Morena 2012, 278).

Two big global events were pivot points. By the early 2000s, the coalition had expanded into a diverse group including trade unions, church groups, and environmentalists, but the unveiling of that new coalition happened on the morning of September 11, 2001 (Interview 1031). Global attention shifted to terrorism, and the campaign lost momentum. The political winds swung back around a few years later. The 2008 financial crisis was a "game changer" for the FTT campaign, as Western governments and international institutions admitted that greater oversight and regulation of finance was needed (Wahl 2014). The IMF met with members of the Tobin tax coalition and for the first time seriously considered (though rejected) the proposal (Claessens, Keen, and Pazarbasioglu 2010). With continued opposition from the IMF, the FTT coalition shifted attention from global regulation to changes in national policies.

The more favorable political landscape attracted new members. The most notable entrant was Oxfam, a leading INGO. The campaign sought to capitalize on post-2008 public anger. British activists created a provocative YouTube video, "The Banker," in which actor Bill Nighy dryly conveyed the selfishness of financiers. The United Kingdom, the United States, France, and Germany were key targets, the first two leaders in global finance, the latter leaders in the European Union. Opposition in the United States and the United Kingdom remains strong. FTT legislation has been introduced various times in the US Congress, to no effect.[7] In 2009, British prime minister Gordon Brown suddenly announced his support for global adoption of an FTT, but the American treasury secretary said the United States had no interest in the idea.[8] The FTT achieved greater success in Europe. France and Germany proposed the FTT at a G20 meeting in 2010, but after meeting with lukewarm reception, they took the issue to the European Union. A special EU procedure allowed a subset of EU countries to move forward, and in 2013 eleven EU members began discussion of a proposal for a tax of 0.1% on stock and bond trades and 0.01% on derivatives.[9] These talks stalled, were revived in 2015, and stalled again.[10] The coalition has lost a member and the proposal has been pushed off the agenda, leading one media outlet to describe the EU FTT as "on life support."[11]

Observers vary in their assessment of the FTT campaign. Many coalition members are positive, citing "clear evidence" of changes in the policy process (Cambridge Policy Consultants 2012, iii) and highlighting the European campaign as a "showcase" for single-issue campaigns (Wahl 2014, iii). Yet no such tax has been instituted, and an EU-only tax may yet lead financiers to simply conduct trades elsewhere to circumvent the tax. Some long-standing proponents of the FTT see the current proposal as a small reform working within, rather than challenging, market mechanisms. From that perspective, the FTT campaign "hasn't achieved anything" (Interview 1038). Even if the FTT policy proposal were to pass, there has been no consensus on how the tax revenue would be used. Various proposals have been put forth, from spending the money to remediate global warming effects or creating a development fund to alleviate poverty. The growing FTT coalition has thus made the tax a salient issue, but as policy the financial transactions tax still seems a fairly distant possibility.

The ATT and FTT coalitions have shifted in membership and policy position over time, but they both meet a minimal definition of success as emergent issues rather than lost causes. Beyond that, however, there is no one perspective on the effectiveness of each campaign. Will the ATT impact the actual flow of illicit arms and reduce gun-related violence? Will an FTT be created, and if so, will it reduce dangerous currency speculation and raise meaningful sums for global public goods? Rather than offer a single evaluation of the success of these campaigns, we highlight the varied assessments of the two and focus on the particular strategies of coalition members. The increasingly moderate and narrow proposals of the two NGO coalitions can be traced back to the interests and strategies of the leading INGOs within them. The authority trap is inescapable; without those leading INGOs, the coalitions would have likely toiled without recognition from states, but with them, the proposals become less radical and more cautious.

In the next three sections, we compare these efforts—both across coalitions and over time—to reveal how the authority of some INGOs shapes three key strategic choices. Leading INGOs adopt moderate policy positions even when exercising "productive power" in actively shaping state preferences. They work with middle-power states that have the standing to create international law but little influence over important processes. Finally, their intense involvement in a campaign can hurt as much as help.

Multiple Audiences and Moderation

Leading INGOs tend to be more moderate in their demands and less confrontational in their approach. With their interactions vis-à-vis states, condemnation is not useful to leading INGOs, because they want to maintain access to multiple audiences. Rather, leading INGOs encourage reframing processes within an INGO campaign. In both the FTT and ATT, leading INGOs played a key role in reframing the policy ask, moving toward an issue that was more widely palatable and attractive to states. In so doing, they tempered their initial demands.

As a result of these concerns, leading INGOs determined the trajectory of the ATT and FTT campaigns, but they were not the initial policy entrepreneurs. This is a regular feature of INGO coalitions, where the initial interest in the issue usually arises from local or specialist INGOs (Keck and Sikkink 1998; Bob 2005; Cox 2011). A staff member at a leading INGO put the view from the top bluntly: "smaller NGOs tend to be innovative and then churn new ideas into the ideas marketplace, and most of those ideas die . . . unless the big guys come in because they can see an opportunity to scale it up" (Interview 1064). The smaller groups appeal to those INGOs with widespread authority to help spread their message, but that message gets altered according to the demands of the leading INGOs.

Framing the Small Arms Issue

On the small arms issue, the coalition began without a dominant frame. In the first few years of IANSA, leading up to the weak Program of Action in 2001, the coalition was a loose network for information exchange rather than a cohesive advocacy organization (Shawki 2010). IANSA adopted a laundry list of possible frames—sustainable peace and development, human security, and respect for human rights—reflecting the diverse concerns of coalition members about small arms (Grillot, Stapley, and Hanna 2006). The most successful framing at that point employed the language of humanitarianism to emphasize the indiscriminate harm caused by small arms and light weapons (Grillot, Stapley, and Hanna 2006). That framing depended heavily on the expertise and authority of HRW (Laurance 2013), a leading INGO. Drawing upon extensive legal expertise, HRW had effectively connected international humanitarian law with arms transfers in the anti-land-mines campaign, and it now brought that frame to the small arms movement (Waltz 2014). The disappointments of 2001, however, led HRW to substantially scale back its efforts on small arms (Bob 2012). HRW was also very wary of the political risks to its reputation. Domestic policy work on small arms would engage the staunch opposition of the National Rifle Association (NRA), and HRW was working closely with US government officials on the humanitarian impacts of the conflicts in Afghanistan and Iraq (Interview 1072). HRW stayed on as a member of IANSA and convened a disarmament summit on the twentieth anniversary of the founding of the International Campaign to Ban Landmines, but its arms control efforts focused on land mines and cluster munitions.

Amnesty and Oxfam, by contrast, expanded their work on small arms control, creating the CAC to push for a more expansive treaty and reorganizing what had been an egalitarian but leaderless IANSA. Oxfam had been working on arms control since the 1980s, and a narrow collaboration with Amnesty Europe on European arms exports in the late 1990s proved fruitful (Green and Macdonald 2014). The CAC was useful for Oxfam at a time when it was centralizing its global confederation, Oxfam International, to protect and promote its brand (Stroup and Wong 2013). In its first strategic plan, Oxfam International pledged to become a "global campaigning force," and the small arms campaign was one of a handful of campaigns launched through this new global structure (Scott and Brown 2004). Amnesty had been working on the human rights implications of small arms transfers since 1983, and the small arms campaign served the organization at a time when it was being challenged by its members and other human rights groups to expand into other issues besides political prisoners (Waltz 2014). As one observer describes, "as a leading human rights organization, Amnesty International certainly added value to the coalition's advocacy efforts, but the coalition work was also beneficial to AI" (Waltz 2014, 168). In response to challenges to its authority, Amnesty expanded its work on arms control, and CAC was its "first experience formalizing a campaigning partnership of this nature" (Waltz 2014, 158). Notably, that first formal partnership was with an INGO with similar approaches to advocacy but one that did not directly compete within the human rights sector (Stroup 2012). That partnership largely worked because of the collaborative approach of one key Amnesty staff member, Brian Wood (Interview 1072).

The reframing and restructuring was challenging, as Oxfam and Amnesty are both leading INGOs who are compelled to address multiple audiences. The CAC explicitly tied humanitarian and development concerns to the trade of conventional arms, shifting the discourse around weapons from one about state sovereignty to concerns over the safety, well-being, and rights of civilians in harms' way. Getting to this common frame was difficult, as Amnesty emphasized how the supply of guns violated rights, while Oxfam's development orientation suggested that the demand for guns was part of a vicious cycle of poverty and conflict (Waltz 2014, 160–64). Ultimately, the framework of the right to life and security spoke to growing concerns of key audiences for both Amnesty and Oxfam, and they met at a middle message. Their ability to then sell that message to other members of the small arms movement depended on the past failures of IANSA, whose structure may have been democratic but was also ineffective (Wong 2012). Some activists chose to participate in CAC despite complaints about its excessive centralization, while others critiqued the CAC and the resulting ATT as minimally reformist efforts that legitimized the commercial arms trade (Bolton, Sakamoto, and Griffiths 2012; Stavrianakis 2012).

Overall, the reframing made the ATT more politically palatable to states that championed human rights, but the CAC had a varied approach and was not uniformly conciliatory toward states. For example, the report that launched the campaign, *Shattered Lives*, condemned states for inaction and challenged them to regulate the global flow of arms. During the Bush administration, the United States was a harsh critic of arms control efforts, and the procontrol NGOs largely avoided costly advocacy with a hostile audience (Erickson 2007, 101–2).

Framing Global Finance

The framing of the FTT also changed with the entry of leading INGOs, according to their need to protect their authority. The initial Tobin tax coalition in the late 1990s was part of a critique of unfettered capitalism that called for greater regulation and taxation of currency flows at the global level (Stecher and Bailey 1999). German economist Paul Spahn's 1995 proposal for a two-tiered tax received substantial support from those interested in reducing the volatility of currency markets, while the UN Development Program's 1996 report emphasized the new revenue a tax would create (Weaver, Dodd, and Baker 2003). In the UK, War on Want and the spin-off organization it created, the Tobin Tax

Network, was primarily concerned with the tax's dampening effect on speculation (Interview 1040). The German NGO WEED adopted a similar frame in
a 1998 seminar on the Tobin tax (Interview 1041). These small radical groups
were foundational in creating a strong network of committed and informed
activists, but according to one campaigner, "in the first couple of years, we
seemed quite a lonely bunch" (Interview 1040). Leading INGOs like Greenpeace and Oxfam embraced the critical tone of the antiglobalization protests
in Seattle in 1999, for example, but they rejected the call by Seattle activists to
abolish the IMF and World Bank (Nelson 2002, 386). Because of fragmented
governance of global finance, hostility from the IMF, and the radical nature of
the frame, it was difficult to organize the campaign and move beyond public
awareness efforts (Nelson 2002).

These smaller activists then tried an alternate frame in the mid-2000s, one of
financing for development. After the announcement of the Millennium Development Goals in 2000, wealthy donor states met in Monterey in 2002 and committed to mobilizing new financial resources. In 2006, a leading group on innovative
financing for development was created, and a number of NGOs within the
group pushed for an FTT as a way to raise that money (Wahl 2014). As one
activist explained, this was a political move "in order to maintain momentum
and to stay in the game" (Interview 1041). The link between global finance and
global development remained tenuous, however, even among FTT supporters.
Members of the campaign were divided on whether to focus on the tax's effects
on financial markets or its potential as a source for development financing. At
first, campaigners tried to include both concerns, but that interfered with the
development of specific proposals, because "when the focus is on raising revenues to fund development the proposed tax rate is significantly lower than the
tax rate proposed when the focus is on stabilizing foreign exchange markets"
(Shawki 2010, 228).

While many FTT proponents remain committed to dampening currency
speculation, the global campaign definitively moved toward development
financing (except in the United States, as discussed below). After the 2008 financial crisis, policymakers and the public were more willing to entertain the idea
that one could make bankers pay for social harms. Oxfam then became critical
to the campaign's shifting demands and increasing attention. Oxfam had enter-
tained the FTT idea at various times over the previous fifteen years, but the 2008
financial crisis was a "perfect storm" of public anger, attention from politicians,
and declining aid levels (Interview 1032). In the UK, Oxfam had backed David
Hillman's rebranding of the Tobin Tax Network to the "Stamp Out Poverty Campaign" around 2005. The slogan invoked the well-known stamp tax and clearly
connected the proposal to global development. To avoid providing opponents

with ammunition, the new brand left behind the issue of financial market volatility, sidestepping the unresolved academic debate about the likely impact of
an FTT on markets (Interview 1038). After the financial crisis, the campaign
again rebranded, adopting the language of Robin Hood to capitalize on the public frustration with wealthy financiers. Today, FTT campaign networks in the UK,
France, and Germany have achieved substantial consensus: a tax to raise money
for public goods from the financial sector (Wahl 2014). What kinds of public
goods these funds might support, however, is still undecided.

With Oxfam's support, the FTT campaign became punchy and simple, and more
palatable to state officials. The reframing resulted in more attention from policymakers and the public. After the "Stamp Out Poverty" rebranding, the network
"went from having low-level meetings at the Treasury to having meetings with the
special advisor to Gordon Brown" (Interview 1024). Coalition members in a number of countries argued that "Oxfam had not necessarily added that much value
in terms of technical FTT knowledge" but had contributed substantial capacity
and expertise in public relations (Cambridge Policy Consultants 2012, 43). Oxfam
organized visible political stunts, reached out to legislators, and courted media.
The results of these efforts can be seen in counts of the number of mentions of the
campaign in English-language world news publications from 1993 to 2014 (Stroup
2016).[12] There are several small peaks in the mid-1990s, after the financial crises of
the late 1990s, and in 2001, but the Robin Hood and FTT language took off in 2009.
Oxfam's presentation of the FTT was more reformist than previous iterations
and more successful in galvanizing public attention.

The FTT coalition as a whole has had mixed success in changing state policies.
Germany and France have been sites of key victories, and Oxfam was involved in
both national coalitions, particularly in France. Unlike the CAC, which brought
in the global Oxfam confederation, the FTT campaign developed at the national
chapter level. Oxfam Great Britain has supported the national and international
campaign. Oxfam's publicity stunts have often used critical language to raise attention for the "Robin Hood tax" issue, but they have been more reticent to directly
critique Members of Parliament and bureaucrats (Cambridge Policy Consultants
2012). Across different countries, Oxfam mixed insider and outsider strategies with
condemnation and cooperation, consistent with its past practices (Stroup 2012).

The United States is an important but hostile target for the FTT campaign.
Rather than risk its authority, Oxfam America has played a very limited role in
the FTT coalition in the United States (Interview 1066; Interview 1035). Oxfam
America is a more conservative member of the international coalition, and the
campaign is a long shot. Oxfam America has chosen instead to maintain the
credibility with American policymakers it has fought hard to develop (Scott
and Brown 2004). The most prominent leading INGO active in the American

FTT coalition has been FoE, which has been "a great partner" to other coalition members and "critical" in mobilizing climate activists in the United States (Interview 1066). FoE has carved out a niche as a grassroots environmental NGO with a global reach and an expansive understanding of environmental protection (Doherty and Doyle 2013), which enables it to commit to campaigning on a cross-sectoral issue like the FTT. FoE has brought convening power to the FTT coalition and embraced the populist tenor of the US-based campaign, but its status has also created opportunities for collaboration with members of Congress.[13] A leading INGO like FoE could potentially bring more unity to the US campaign, but FoE has recently rebuilt its reputation around being a Southern-based, bottom-up organization, and it has not sought to centralize the US coalition. Thus, in contrast to the broader consensus elsewhere, the various US groups working on the FTT are fragmented, with some focused on tax reform while others emphasize global environmental protection (Interview 1066).

Vanilla Victories

The authority of leading INGOs like Oxfam, Amnesty, HRW, and FoE can be a major asset for issue entrepreneurs. Their expansive capacity and established reputation brings attention to an issue. These are victories, and that is an important point for those who would dismiss the influence of INGOs. Yet they are disappointing and bland for many of the local or specialist groups that have been working on these issues for decades, and hence they are vanilla victories. The concerns that a few prominent INGOs have about maintaining their standing with multiple audiences help explain the trend of increasing moderation in these campaigns and others.

An alternative explanation for the changing frame in each case might be changes in the external environment. One could argue that for small arms, the 2001 attacks on the United States dominated the discussion of security issues, pushing activists to find a different frame, while the 2008 financial crisis allowed for a bolder critique of financial markets. Of course, these structural concerns matter, but what matters more is how individual groups make choices about how to respond to these changing opportunities. Leading INGOs are particularly adept at reading these political winds, but they also may respond in a variety of ways, depending on how they view their bases of authority. As the US government ramped up the so-called war on terror, HRW walked away from the small arms issue to maintain its special access to US officials. Meanwhile, Amnesty and Oxfam constructed a shared development/human rights frame. In the FTT, Oxfam captured public anger at the rich but largely targeted sympathetic state officials to become part of the solution. FoE's embrace of the Robin Hood tax and global inequality issues supports its reputation as a Southern-focused INGO and offers a way to demonstrate its commitment to finding resources for climate change mitigation.

Choosing State Targets

In pushing for regulation of global flows of guns and money, INGOs face an array of possible state targets they can approach. Some states are more important in an issue area, and others are more willing to collaborate. In both campaigns, the United States and the United Kingdom were initially hostile but important. These states are frequent targets for many INGO campaigns because of their global influence (Drezner 2008; Betzold 2014). Many leading INGOs are headquartered in Western states (Smith and Wiest 2012), which gives them the domestic political standing to employ a range of strategies. Yet other states were more willing to listen to INGO activists. In both campaigns, leading INGOs collaborated with middle-power states to advance the global policy process. As in the case of the cluster munitions ban (Bolton and Nash 2010), middle-power states saw cooperation with NGO coalitions on the ATT and FTT as opportunities to advance their soft power in a particular issue area.

Allies in the ATT

Leading INGOs have the global reach and status to reach out to a range of states. Oxfam and Amnesty leveraged their considerable global reach by activating local affiliates or country programs to support the ATT (Green and MacDonald 2014, 4). Oxfam and the rest of the CAC also kept a running tally of different strategies to employ. For example, to prevent China from opposing the treaty, CAC activists pushed the ATT on African delegates important to the Chinese (Green and MacDonald 2014, 4). States have explicitly acknowledged the efforts of the CAC, Oxfam, and civil society (Stalker and Tibbett 2012, 5). Oxfam in particular has reported that its work was used by states in ATT negotiations, including the closing stages, and Liberia's president, Ellen Johnson Sirleaf, explicitly drew on Oxfam information (Green and MacDonald 2014, 6).

Despite the global ambitions of the CAC, a few middle-power states were particularly receptive to the CAC. A couple of small states were willing in 2003 to sign on to the idea of a comprehensive treaty covering all arms. Other states like Canada were supportive and had been critical in supporting the NGO coalition that would become IANSA (Krause 2002; Stavriankis 2012). Middle powers and INGO interests were aligned in many contexts. In a statement to the General

Assembly, Erkki Tuomioja, the minister of foreign affairs for Finland, stated that "we also owe a great debt to the representatives of civil society who played an active role throughout the ATT process helping and pushing us in finding solutions on various issues."[14] Australia signaled its intention to continue working with civil society in implementing the ATT (as cited in Bolton et al. 2014, 469). These state partners, in turn, led the charge among states to gather the support necessary to draft and ratify the ATT. Different elements of the CAC worked with different states, with Oxfam and Amnesty trying to leverage their existing strengths in their target states (Australia, Cambodia, Finland, France, the Netherlands, Kenya, Peru, Senegal, Spain, the UK, and the United States, among others), leaving other key countries such as Brazil and South Africa to other INGOs (Green and MacDonald 2014).

The ATT coalition was actually fairly successful in pressuring powerful states. In the late 1990s, the United States and United Kingdom were major arms exporters, powerful states, and hostile to arms control efforts. Yet in the ATT, in contrast to the middle-power plus INGO coalitions in land mines, cluster munitions, and the FTT, the UK came on board early and played a leadership role.[15] Two factors were important. First, domestic political concerns created an opening for ATT activists. A scandal on arms to Iraq had helped Labour get elected in 1997 and was part of their call for more transparency in government and a more ethical foreign policy (Erickson 2007). Second, in this political opening, a few INGOs were able to shape the British government's policy because of their authority and local roots. Amnesty and Oxfam are based in the UK, as is Saferworld, a specialist INGO that played a key role in the campaign. A key research coalition called Biting the Bullet gathered evidence on progress toward the 2001 UN Programme of Action. It was also headquartered in the UK and produced by Saferworld, International Alert (founded by former Amnesty secretary-general Martin Ennals), IANSA, and the University of Bradford.[16] These INGO coalitions leveraged their British members and presence in London to push key British policymakers (Interview 1072). These INGOs, working with state officials and industry groups, helped define a narrow procontrol arms policy for the UK (Stavrianakis 2012).[17]

By contrast, the United States opposed the formation of the ATT for years. In 2001, its singular objection nearly brought the entire arms control process to a halt. The resulting failure of the Program of Action led the CAC to shift to a new forum, the UN General Assembly (Interview 1063), a more sympathetic setting. After the election of Barack Obama in 2008, the US policy shifted, and in 2013 it signed the ATT. Still, strong domestic opposition, particularly from the NRA, makes Senate ratification of the treaty unlikely, even though most Americans favored regulation of the arms trade (Erickson 2007, 7–8). Several senators recently offered explicit criticism of the CAC as unrepresentative of the range of civil society views and restated their opposition to ATT ratification.[18]

A Few Willing Regulators in the FTT

Both the ATT and FTT campaigns started with the support of small states, but the latter campaign has seen little success in securing British and American support. French and German support has been critical for whatever victories the FTT campaign has achieved. Domestic politics played an important role in both cases, with both national INGOs and leading INGOs involved. France's sometimes role as a critic of neoliberalism created political space for the FTT. As Morena (2012, 289) writes, "up to late 2001, within French political circles and public opinion, the issue of globalization was high on the agenda and there was a general desire to reaffirm the state's position in the face of what was perceived as a menace to both France's culture and social model." France's support for the FTT—evident in legislation in 2001 and Chirac's commissioning of the Landau report in 2004 (Shawki 2010)—responded to this domestic policy pressure and offered an international expression of policy alternatives to unfettered globalization. By contrast, Germany's support for an FTT was unexpected by civil society activists. Chancellor Angela Merkel supported the FTT as a way to eliminate it as a wedge issue in the 2009 federal elections (Wahl 2014). Ultimately, the FTT was a national election issue in both countries, and public support for the FTT has been very high (Brassett 2012; Morena 2012).

Oxfam worked with a range of civil society groups in both countries. In Germany, Oxfam helped garner media attention and coordinate activists, but one German activist saw other civil society organizations as critical in building the foundational public support that allowed the FTT campaign to take advantage of political openings (Interview 1041). Oxfam's importance in the French campaign is more obvious (Wahl 2014, 11). French government officials credit the civil society campaign in France with sustaining political momentum for the FTT, and President Sarkozy used the specific Robin Hood tax language following a 2011 G20 meeting (Cambridge Policy Consultants 2012, 23, 28). Oxfam served as a resource for members of parliament seeking evidence, and Sarkozy's cabinet directly responded to an Oxfam ad in *Le Monde* (Cambridge Policy Consultants 2012, 23–24).

The United States and United Kingdom are centers of global finance but have resisted pressure to consider an FTT. In the UK, the campaign's rebranding in 2005 and subsequent adoption by Oxfam as the "Robin Hood tax" opened doors for meetings with the prime minister and Department for International Devel-opment (Brassett 2012, 267). A number of sympathetic British MPs reported that Oxfam could have more directly lobbied them rather than targeting the general public and a few high-level bureaucrats (Cambridge Policy Consultants 2012), but Oxfam may have avoided heavy spending on legislative lobbying because of intense opposition from Treasury officials and some MPs (Interview 1038, 1066). For example, George Osborne, an MP and chancellor of the exchequer, appealed to the European Court of Justice to block other EU member states from design-ing an FTT.[19] As a leading INGO, Oxfam faces difficult choices about which audience to mobilize. Simple and clever messaging may build public support, as in the case of Oxfam in many different national settings (Cambridge Policy Consultants 2012), but it also risks being seen as oversimplification in the eyes of other experts.

In the United States, Treasury officials have largely dismissed the purported expertise of INGOs and have argued that the proposed policy would disrupt beneficial financial flows or would be easily circumvented (Burman et al. 2015). A few small political openings have appeared. Treasury secretary Jack Lew seemed more open to the idea than his predecessor, Timothy Geithner.[20] FTT campaign-ers in the United States, however, have yet to develop a single message about its intended purpose (Interview 1066). Perhaps as a result, critics argue that transac-tion taxes are "answers in search of a question" (Cochrane 2013, 44).

Easy Targets

Leading INGOs are valuable to INGO coalitions because they sit at the nexus of several audiences, thereby drawing attention from state officials and setting global policy agendas. Quite simply, "people think that if Oxfam is conven-ing this, then it is serious so we ought to at least take a look" (Interview 1064). States differ, however, in their willingness to embrace INGO campaigns. Leading INGOs have regularly built alliances with like-minded, middle-power states to propose new treaties like the ATT or new financial regulations at the EU. The col-laboration may result because the state in question has internalized the norms of the INGO coalition or because the coalition's cause proves instrumentally useful for states seeking niche areas in which to exercise global leadership (Bolton and Nash 2010; Rutherford, Brem, and Matthew 2003; Brysk 2009). Either way, these are relatively easy targets for leading INGOs.

Support from these middle-power states is largely instrumental, however, as the ultimate goals in the FTT and ATT campaigns are to shape the flows of money and guns from powerful countries like the United Kingdom and the United States. We draw several lessons about the ultimate policy outcomes resulting from alliances between middle-power states and leading INGOs. First, the strategy *can* pay off, particularly if the INGO is headquartered in the powerful country, as with Oxfam and Amnesty in the UK on the arms trade. But both cases suggest that leading INGOs are generally cautious in hostile environments and are unwilling to risk their reputation in powerful states for a cause. In the ATT process, Amnesty, Oxfam, and HRW responded to specific political opportunities in their home countries. In the FTT process, Oxfam spent little in the UK on lobbying bureaucrats and MPs, avoiding potential risks to its reputation when asked about the intricacies of the tax proposal and instead focusing on public messaging. Oxfam America has avoided the issue altogether in the United States.

In considering which states are targeted by leading INGOs, we might ask whether lobbying easy state targets, who would agree without much effort, saps resources that could be leveraged to influence more reluctant but more important states. The authority trap requires that authorities demonstrate *some* output, and many leading INGOs plan their advocacy based on what they can achieve, rather than working backwards from the desired outcome. The interesting counterfactual is whether more campaigning in powerful states would yield a better or more comprehensive international agreement. After all, an alternative strategy focuses the vast organizational resources of these leading INGOs on important countries. By putting their eggs in one basket, these INGOs might alter the policies of the key states. They are unlikely to do so, however, as this would endanger their status.

When it comes to key state targets, leading INGOs are trapped. They are specially positioned to gain access to powerful states, but their organizational interests encourage them to protect their interests rather than stake their reputation on a single cause. The multi-issue work of transnational INGOs is thus in some ways political cover for incremental action in short spurts (Chong 2009). Leading INGOs recognize that the output they achieve is different from the impact they ultimately seek, but they argue that preserving their organization is necessary to ensure that someone is defending these universalistic causes over the long term. Thus they turn to middle-power states that can regulate domestically or push for agreements internationally.

When groups like Oxfam and Amnesty achieve formal agreements such as the ATT, they acknowledge the many problems that remain but argue that "some form of ATT is better than none" (Bolton, Sakamoto, and Griffiths 2012). This assessment is worth debating. Some issues become more intractable, not less, with the construction of formal international laws (Percy 2007). The vast literature on corporate codes of conduct suggests that weak regulation can deflect the sort of political attention that might generate stricter regulation (Vogel 2008). "Coalitions of the willing" between middle-power states and leading INGOs may advance their self-interests without actually achieving goals like reduced arms flow or stable currency markets.

Goldilocks Problems in Collective Campaigns

A close look at the ATT and FTT suggests that there are two Goldilocks problems INGO coalitions face in recruiting leading INGOs. First, a single INGO can adopt a campaign in a range of ways, as gatekeeping is not binary. The "just right" nature of Oxfam in the transnational FTT coalition is unusual, both for Oxfam and for INGO coalitions in general. Second, too many cooks spoil the broth. Considering the CAC in the context of other INGO coalitions, the close cooperation that was achieved between two leading INGOs is rare. Too many leading INGOs can introduce destructive competition into a coalition, while not enough attention from leading INGOs can keep an issue off the global agenda. Thus, collaboration can lead at times to competition between INGOs as they must balance their overall advocacy agenda with organizational-level interests.

The entry of a leading INGO can disrupt a campaign as well as promote its agenda, an outcome evident in both the FTT and ATT. In attracting support for their extensive but expensive policy work, leading INGOs increasingly seek to monitor their progress and demonstrate results, sometimes under compressed timelines (Coe and Majot 2013). Groups like Oxfam, Save the Children, and Greenpeace adopt campaigns in multiyear increments, and at the end they are challenged to claim victory (Interview 1023). This approach to advocacy has been widely critiqued, and several advocacy evaluations reveal that the need to demonstrate results can produce infighting over what policy positions to take and who gets to claim credit (Cox 2011; Coe and Majot 2013).

It is thus surprising that Oxfam came into a pre-existing network of FTT activists and contributed in both meaningful and seemingly collegial ways. From the perspective of Oxfam as an organization, the nature of its involvement appears to be the exception rather than the rule:

> When I compare this campaign with other campaigns, I think this campaign has been a brilliant model for coalition work. There are times when it should have been an Oxfam-only core, but we got [other groups] on because we just do *everything* with them. All the usual stuff around brand, and around data capture and all this stuff, it's just out the window. And I compare this to other coalition campaigns [such as X] . . . which just feels like such hard work, and the transaction costs

of that coalition, you could argue, outweigh the added benefit of working together. (Interview 1032)

According to a senior Oxfam staffer, the FTT campaign was "done largely below the radar in terms of Oxfam . . . and often, the really successful campaigns are the ones which initially don't have official buy-in, because they can be more flexible, they can do more alliances, they don't have so much sign-on hassle. But at some point you need the organization to get behind it, take it to scale, etc." (Interview 1064). Both interview subjects speculated that such flexibility may have emerged because Oxfam was the only big INGO on board and thus did not have to worry as much about branding and attribution (Interview 1032; Interview 1064).

Leading INGOs can participate in coalitions in a number of ways; successful coalitions seem to get it "just right." If leading INGOs bring all their resources (including reputation) to an advocacy coalition, then their authority with external audiences is on the line, which increases the chances that branding considerations and attribution will distract from an effective division of labor among coalition members. Of course, too little commitment is problematic too. FTT coalition members worry about whether Oxfam will continue its support for the FTT. The FTT is a long-standing INGO campaign issue, and "one of the many problems NGOs have is that they tend to work through three- or five-year plans . . . which is fine, but . . . that's not the way social change works . . . I mean, if it takes sixty years to get a Tobin tax, it's obviously a long time, but it's probably worth keeping going" (Interview 1040).

If coalitions struggle to get a single INGO's involvement just right, they must also be careful to involve the right number of leading INGOs. The second Goldilocks problem is that the involvement of too many leading INGOs is likely to create internal divisions within a campaign. The small arms coalition had a number of leading INGOs involved in the late 1990s, including sometime-competitors HRW and Amnesty. Once HRW left and IANSA restructured, the IANSA coalition became more effective. An IANSA secretariat was created to mitigate some of the conflicts that could happen between INGOs, but, nonetheless, mundane limitations have slowed down the process, as one participant explained about designing a petition in 2012:

> [E]ach organization has a certain language they like to use, or a language that they have to use. And then their own sign off processes are so complex and takes so long that it was actually little things like that that sound kind of small and insignificant but they could really hold things up for us as a coalition. . . . There were definitely differences like that in trying to just get things signed off where the language of what we were saying didn't resonate well with Amnesty, or Oxfam, so then we have to

find some kind of compromise and then they had to go back to their people, so stuff like that. (Interview 1054)

Leading INGOs bring resources and expertise in global campaigning, but they also brought the concerns of their members, donors, and many different national chapters. Thus the types of planning required for the CAC had to take into account "all sorts of really, really boring kind of practical considerations when you've got three organizations that all have ever so slightly different mandates ... procedures, policies, outlooks" (Interview 1063). These practical considerations often end up watering down demands as coalition partners seek common ground.

One might look at the list of FTT coalition members and see the same problem of too many leading INGOs. In fact, although a number of leading INGOs appear to be in the FTT coalition, they are generally contributing little besides their names. Consider leading environmental INGOs. FoE was a leading supporter in the 1990s, and in the United States it hosted meetings and wrote supportive briefs.[21] In Europe, FoE worked to overcome initial tensions with the new and critical ATTAC to create a big-tent alliance (Interview 1031). Today, however, FoE and Greenpeace are signatories to many campaign statements and participate in network meetings but "they say clearly they have no other resources and no other political will to play a leading role or active role" (Interview 1041). Greenpeace has been supportive but in a fairly passive way; the FTT is an issue where the INGO would "make the right noises and do what allies ask of us, but not an issue where we would take the lead" (Interview 1031). In short, behind the scenes, one leading INGO is present in each of the national campaigns, working with a number of less prominent INGOs and local civil society groups.

Implications for Other INGOs

INGO coalitions appear to be the rule in INGO advocacy, despite a few well-known examples of campaigns run by single leading INGOs (Clark 2001; Redfield 2013). The above discussion of strategic choices of a handful of INGOs should not sideline the importance of smaller or specialist groups in coalitions. One reason is that many local INGOs have better political standing to join government delegations, which gives them access to the sidebar state-level conversations that typical INGO activists cannot access (Interview 1011). Unknown INGOs contribute to various stages of policymaking, implementing international laws at home or monitoring international agreements (Betsill and Corell 2008).

Small or local INGOs still need larger coalitions for legitimacy, access, and resources. For local INGOs working with their home governments, the CAC brought a sense of independence from those state interests (Stalker and Tibbett 2012, 6). The CAC also brought visibility to smaller INGOs.

> I do think that there were a lot of benefits for smaller organizations in particular to be identified as a member of Control Arms, especially . . . in and around this time of negotiations. And some of it could be as simple as access to get to some of the meetings. Facilitating the passes, facilitating travel, all kinds of things. For a smaller group, if you were trying to go at it alone, you would come up against a lot of obstacles from the UN, member states and so forth. (Interview 1054)

Transportation and access to the UN meetings posed huge problems for smaller INGOs and NGOs, and CAC membership helped those groups.

For other INGOs, collaboration with states risks their independence, which is often the only credible signal of their legitimacy (Murdie 2014). This is particularly true for the more radical INGOs, whose transformative agenda may lead them to see collaboration as "selling out." Leading INGOs also need to be seen as independent, but the constraints are different. The durable status of their authority makes them less vulnerable to challenges to their principled commitments (Grant and Keohane 2005). In addition, working with states may yield policy changes for which leading INGOs can claim direct credit, reinforcing their elite status. This general tendency does not rule out radical actions by leading INGOs, as their credibility as pragmatic moderates can allow them to sometimes successfully push for more ambitious policy steps, especially in concert with sympathetic state officials. Moderation and technical expertise may yield little but might sap a campaign of energy, and leading INGOs may switch their tactics, as in the switch to a climate justice frame by groups like FoE at the Copenhagen COP-15 meeting in 2009 (Hadden 2015). Nonetheless, the differences in interests among coalition partners may also create tensions between leading INGOs and other INGOs, which might have contributed their share to a coalition but might not reap the same kinds of rewards as the more authoritative ones do. Competitive tendencies, which may not characterize INGO interactions in coalitions generally, may seep out as a result of working together.

Anecdotally, activists often struggle to attract a "gatekeeper" INGO to their cause. In a buyer's market, a number of potential issues simply get lost (Carpenter 2014). The cases above suggest that the challenge is actually even greater, as coalitions can suffer from too much support by these leading INGOs. Few INGO coalitions are able to effectively manage the Goldilocks problem, and as a result the coalition as a whole is trapped by the authority-maintenance concerns of a few members.

There are numerous case studies of INGO campaigns and coalitions, but few efforts attempt to unpack how status shapes the strategic choices of coalition members. In the cases of the FTT and ATT presented above, leading INGOs pursue vanilla victories in concert with middle-power states, and they sometimes endanger their own coalitions with their commitment. This is not to deny the influence of INGOs in global politics, but it suggests a rethinking of the type of outcomes that result. The hope of global civil society as a source of transformation is misplaced, as both weak and strong INGOs are caught in the authority trap. Most INGOs cannot influence states because they lack authority, and those INGOs that do have widespread authority are unwilling to sacrifice that durable status for today's cause. These dynamics then lead INGOs to make different choices about collaboration, condemnation, and competition with regards to states. As the cases make clear, the different authority levels of leading INGOs and others incentivize each type of actor to make strategic choices that may not translate into durable coalitions or meaningful policy changes.

We end this chapter with a few additional thoughts about INGO strategies. First, the research above speaks to the long-standing debate about whether INGOs are concerned about their principled aims and their organizational self-interest. Both are important for all INGOs. INGOs want to reach goals and claim credit for success, and thus they might go after easier targets. For example, Murdie and Urpelainen (2015) find that environmental NGOs generally tend to do relatively less shaming as a country's pollution emissions increase. But self-interest plays a greater role for leading INGOs, because the stakes appear higher. Having fought hard for attention from the public, policymakers, corporations, and their peers, leading INGOs equate their self-interest with service to the cause.

Second, our discussion of issue emergence and framing in the two cases above suggests that leading INGOs were critical in informing state preferences, not just reacting to them. Leading INGOs in the UK pressured British officials to translate vague political openings into specific policies. In France, ATTAC and Oxfam France made the FTT a national political issue. These examples point to the productive power of leading INGOs. It is possible that productive power is the typical form of INGO influence, and this will be magnified if we are examining leading INGOs. Drezner (2008) argues that INGOs are most likely to influence states when states do not know what they want. We could accept this proposition while disagreeing about the frequency with which state preferences are known. New research on constructivist political economy makes a compelling case that states are most often uncertain about the nature of the situations they face and the preferred strategies in each (Abdelal, Blyth, and Parsons 2010). The long process of issue emergence in each of the cases above reveals that leading INGOs are particularly adroit at recognizing those openings where states' preferences are unknown and at advancing new normative frameworks and policy proposals. Leading INGOs sit at the intersection of multiple audiences, which gives them insights into the different preferences of the various stakeholders. This intersection also gives them access. It is a strategically important and tactically useful position for policy change. In most circumstances, we might conclude that it is a position of great power because of the access and information an INGO might be able to gain.

If this seems to imply that openings for INGOs are frequent, however, the cases above also suggest that the productive power of INGOs may be largely reproductive of existing norms and structures. Sitting at the intersection of many audiences inherently makes leading INGOs moderate precisely because they want to keep this privileged spot, and what they produce may not necessarily be transformative. In short, leading INGOs might effectively target states, but their more collaborative choices may yield policy changes that fall far short of the original ambitions of the campaign. More is not more, especially when it comes to interacting with states. More authority brings more constraints concerning which states are targeted and which policy proposals are advanced.

INGOS AND CORPORATIONS

In a simple caricature, INGOs and transnational corporations are mirror images, one small and benevolent, the other large and self-interested. Are their relations with one another fraught or peaceful? Over the past several decades, there has been a general move among INGOs from largely contentious protests and shaming of corporate behavior to friendlier engagement with corporations (Spar and La Mure 2003; Sasser et al. 2006; Soule 2009; Snow and Soule 2010). There are a number of forms of collaboration. For example, Greenpeace has offered informal advice to Coca-Cola about its refrigerants, Oxfam has audited human rights conditions in Unilever's factories in Vietnam, and Save the Children and GlaxoSmithKline have partnered on drug development and distribution in poor countries.[1]

This chapter focuses on INGO engagement with two private regulatory efforts: the Sustainability Consortium (TSC) and the UN Global Compact (UNGC). In these private regulatory schemes, the authority trap once again catches INGOs. By the 1990s, INGOs as a group had been successful at condemning corporate practice that threatened consumer defection or state regulation. Yet when corporations open the door to collaboration with INGOs, the status of individual INGOs plays an important role in who gets invited to the table. Corporations are particularly open to initial collaboration with leading INGOs. Their high status increases the "halo effect," and leading INGOs possess the global scope and internal capacity to offer careful insight into ways to improve corporate performance.

This openness to leading INGOs is true for states as well, and leading INGOs generally embrace this cooperation with states when presented with the opportunity. The authority trap works in different ways when INGOs are targeting corporations, because the INGO community is deeply divided over the desirability of corporate self-regulation (versus state regulation). Many leading INGOs do choose to collaborate with corporations. When they do, the outcomes are also "vanilla victories," broadly palatable but offering only marginal, if any, change from the status quo. In TSC and the UNGC, many leading INGOs joined at the early stages, seeking access to big corporations in a single venue. But leading INGOs rejected sustained collaboration when it risked their reputation for independence with their key audiences. Both of those choices preserve INGO authority. As it became clear that both TSC and UNGC would demand minor or incremental change for company partners, many leading INGOs left or substantially scaled down their involvement, while a number of weaker INGOs came on board. The exit of leading INGOs further attenuated efforts to change corporate behavior.

Our claim that "status shapes strategy" may seem suspect if we argue that leading INGOs both embrace and reject collaboration with corporations. Ideology plays an important role as well, as there are very different worldviews that underlie each approach (Alcock 2008). But those who emphasize the differences between Friends of the Earth (FoE) and World Wide Fund for Nature (WWF), for example, neglect a comparison to other INGOs. Relative to that massive group, leading INGOs are more moderate and even conciliatory in their approach to corporations.

Of the fourteen INGOs we identified as leading INGOs in chapter 3, all but Greenpeace accept corporate donations. Some embrace a wide spectrum of corporations (CARE only rejects partnerships with producers of weapons and pornography), while others are more circumspect (such as FoE). Leading INGOs have a particular interest in corporate collaboration, as they can receive large amounts of money, scale up their already global operations, and claim credit for impacting corporate practice. Corporate financing or collaboration is a risky proposition for INGOs, whose foundation for authority rests on their commitment to serving the public's interests. As a result, even those INGOs with incredibly extensive corporate partnerships are careful to proclaim their independence.[2] Still, corporations seem to be an attractive partner for many leading INGOs. INGOs that boldly proclaim their independence from states—including Amnesty, Human Rights Watch (HRW), and Médecins sans Frontières (MSF)—are curiously quiet about the possibility of capture by corporate partners. Even Greenpeace, famously provocative for giving companies migraines (Larkin 2013), works with corporations (Yaziji and Doh 2009), sharing research on technical questions (Lyon 2010) and engaging in high-profile dialogues at the World Economic Forum (Mühle 2010). In short, while there are many different approaches toward corporations among leading

INGOs, they are as a group more willing than other INGOs to collaborate with corporations, particularly in the early stages of agenda setting and rule making.

As with INGO campaigns against states, the individual incentives facing INGOs of different status have important implications for the overall influence of INGOs on corporate behavior. It may be true that public shaming efforts to hold corporations accountable can work in concert with insider strategies to design corporate initiatives, a mix of purity and pragmatism (Conner and Epstein 2007). Yet there are two reasons to think that the diversity of INGO approaches is debilitating. First, these differences are not merely tactical; they reflect different worldviews, past practices, and ethical commitments that divide activists, making coordination among INGOs challenging (Chapin 2004; Hadden 2015). Second, while leading INGOs have the exact sorts of global campaigning structures that might create more cohesion and yield more influence (Wong 2012), individual INGOs that try to simultaneously collaborate and condemn corporations will appear to be untrustworthy partners.

The chapter begins with an overview of corporate self-regulation and a brief history of TSC and the UNGC. Second, we explore the strategic choices of both leading INGOs and other INGOs in choosing whether to engage or condemn these two initiatives. The engagement of leading INGOs offers a veneer of credibility to new corporate initiatives with little change in actual practices, leading to results that are decidedly vanilla, and perhaps not even victories. In the third section, we explore how the authority trap catches even those INGOs who chose condemnation or competition. The need of leading INGOs to protect their authority before multiple audiences leads them to moderate the demands of critical campaigns and ignore the poor social and environmental records of many corporations. Finally, we explore the implications of the continued differences among INGOs on whether to collaborate with corporations. While an effective division of labor might be desirable, fragmentation among INGOs is more common, leaving corporations free to define the parameters of reform for themselves.

Private Regulations for Many Stakeholders: The TSC and UNGC

Private authority plays a critical role in global governance. Although the idea that nonstate actors play a role in global politics has been around since the 1970s (Keohane and Nye 1977), recent work has begun to consider the kinds of authority that such actors wield as *distinct* from and not dependent upon the authority of states. Despite some superficial convergence, NGOs and corporations ultimately enjoy very different forms of authority (Risse 2010), with correspondingly contrasting interests in specific forms of governance.

A number of studies suggest that INGOs can influence corporations by promoting voluntary, market-based, and private regulatory instruments (Cashore 2002; Cashore et al. 2004; Bernstein and Cashore 2007; Auld, Renckens, and Cashore 2015). The historical record shows that this entrepreneurial rule making is the most common form of private authority (Green 2013). Around the globe, corporations and many states and citizens embrace the legitimacy of market liberalization and market-based action, enhancing the power of these private governance systems (Bernstein 2001). Proponents argue that market exchanges can result in binding norms for participants (Cashore 2002; Bernstein and Cashore 2007). One such system celebrated by many INGOs is the Global Reporting Initiative (GRI). Originating from civil society collaboration with the United Nations, it is a multistakeholder organization that provides businesses with ways to report their progress on sustainability that include environmental, social, and governance concerns (Abbott and Snidal 2010; Abbott 2012).

Corporations have a number of reasons to adopt private regulatory schemes. Private regulations can enhance the reputations of participants if they are seen as difficult but valuable commitments (Cutler, Haufler, and Porter 1999; Potoski and Prakash 2005; Vogel 2005; Prakash and Potoski 2012). They may also stave off more onerous public regulations (Vogel 2008).[3] In order to achieve these ends, the arrangement must be seen as legitimate by the public and state regulators, and the inclusion of INGOs as independent or impartial voices can enhance the legitimacy of these efforts. Yet an INGO's endorsement is costly. First, there are substantial risks involved. NGOs and businesses struggle to hear the other's demands and struggles (Interview 1055), and they appreciate one another as entities with divergent interests (Huxham and Vangen 2000). In addition, INGOs will often insist on much higher standards than a firm might prefer (Yaziji and Doh 2009, 134). Private regulatory schemes that have support from INGOs may thus be costly for corporations to establish but still preferable to state governance.

Holding these potential costs constant, global corporations prefer to work with leading INGOs in creating new standards and codes. When corporations seek to demonstrate their commitment to sustainability or interest in human rights protection, they borrow legitimacy from NGOs, and the more authoritative the INGO, the greater the boost to the corporation's reputation. This "halo effect" is not the only potential benefit, however. Yaziji and Doh (2009) offer a useful list of benefits to corporations from partnering with NGOs: legitimacy, social awareness, new networks, and technical expertise. We would add an important caveat: the size of these benefits depends on the extent of the partner INGO's authority. While all INGOs bring their principled commitments, for example, only some are well-known, and those prominent organizations are more likely to have extensive civil society networks into which the corporation can tap.[4] They are also better able to access global policymaker networks, can better mobilize the public, and have contact with the media. In short, leading INGOs bring a bigger halo and more resources and therefore face a wider set of opportunities for engaging corporations.

This early preference for partnership with leading INGOs may change once these private regulations move to design and implementation. Specialist INGOs can bring technical and analytical expertise and a commitment to discretion and problem solving (Interview 1071). Local INGOs can help corporations achieve political support, understand resident conditions, and anticipate problems. Consider the example of the Kimberley Process, an effort to eliminate the "blood diamond" trade. A then-unknown human rights organization, Global Witness, launched the campaign against the diamond industry, proposed a certification scheme, and served as official NGO observer (Haufler 2009). Leading INGOs like Amnesty, Oxfam, World Vision, and ActionAid were heavily involved in awareness raising, but they left soon after the certification scheme was created (Bieri 2010).[5] Meanwhile, a few local and specialist INGOs continue to work to improve the inspection and certification procedures of the Kimberley Process.[6] In the Kimberley Process and elsewhere, however, there is no guarantee that other INGOs will avoid "tragic choices" (Avant 2004).

In short, leading INGOs face different opportunities and incentives, relative to other INGOs, to cooperate with corporations in designing private regulatory standards. Before analyzing the choices of specific INGOs, we provide a brief history of two cross-sectoral initiatives in which INGOs have played an important role, TSC and UNGC.

Sustainable Retailing: Walmart and the TSC

The Sustainability Consortium (TSC) draws largely from North America but is global in its effect, as it includes global production and retail networks across thousands of products. The TSC story begins with Walmart, one of the most controversial private actors in the world. Walmart employs more than two million people in stores in twenty-seven countries and generates more than $1 billion in sales daily (Gereffi and Christian 2009). Its retail success and logistical capacity are often depicted as, for better or worse, emblems of American societal values and economic structures (Dicker 2005; Bianco 2006; Fishman 2006; Moreton 2009; Quinn 2012; Massengill 2013; Klein 2014).

Walmart's visible brand and extensive global reach has made it a prominent target for environmental and labor rights activists. In the late 1990s, Walmart came under investigation for using child labor in Bangladesh and Central America and for paying low wages in the United States (Gereffi and Christian 2009).

Meanwhile, Walmart's stated commitment to environmental sustainability seemed superficial, and consumers were reportedly avoiding the store because of its labor and environmental practices (Plambeck and Denend 2008). Thus, in 2005, CEO Lee Scott announced new initiatives around renewable energy, waste reduction, and the sale of sustainable products. The last required the development of a sustainability metric, to be constructed by a new multistakeholder group. In 2009, Walmart unveiled TSC, composed of fellow retailers, suppliers, civil society groups, and several universities, including Arizona State University and the University of Arkansas.[7]

The initial goal of TSC was to define and assess the sustainability of the products Walmart sells in its stores (typically between 120,000 to 150,000 products), and to eventually communicate these assessments into information for consumers.[8] Today, TSC seeks to develop new methodologies for measuring the environmental and social impact of the production of specific goods. TSC is expansive in its scope and includes nearly the entire universe of consumer goods. It does not provide information based on individual products (e.g., T-shirts) but on entire product categories (e.g., clothing and textiles). There are currently 110 product categories that have sustainability profiles on the life cycle of individual products. These profiles help TSC members identify "hotspots" in each category where improvement is needed. In these hotspots, a set of questions gets addressed through Key Performance Indicators (KPIs). Member businesses can use these KPIs to design their own policies on sustainability or to demand that their suppliers make changes.

TSC operates in an increasingly crowded field of initiatives meant to assess the environmental impacts of corporate practice (Hoekstra et al. 2014). TSC seeks to improve environmental sustainability throughout the entire supply chain, and the membership of TSC includes both retailers, such as Walmart, and producers, such as Cargill and Dow Chemical. Yet this expansive scope introduces a wide range of diverse concerns. The construction of KPIs can be quite contested as different interests must come to a single set of hotspots. The TSC's measurements also attempt to balance scientific rigor and bottom-line usefulness. The science of these "life-cycle assessments" (LCAs) is extremely complicated, as analysts use imprecise data to model future impacts upstream and downstream in the production process (O'Rourke 2014). The impetus behind such assessments is to assess possible environmental tradeoffs while figuring out more efficient ways to obtain raw materials or streamline manufacturing processes to make them more sustainable (see EPA 2006). In the face of this uncertainty, TSC prioritizes workable measures that serve corporate members' needs. The TSC's assessments depend on "the cooperation of companies with vested commercial interests— long term if not immediate—in the results" (Freidberg 2015, 176). Ten working groups oversee the development of KPIs, giving feedback and debating what should be included. The working groups are composed of corporate and INGO members and membership is by invitation only (Interview 1045).

Many of the challenges that TSC faces are shared by other sustainability efforts, but TSC has been singled out for both praise and criticism. While Walmart's move to "go green" was at least in part a defensive maneuver to stave off criticism, more sustainable practices may be desirable, profitable, and serve as a model for other corporations (Meeks and Chen 2011). Yet some see Walmart's sustainability commitments like TSC as little more than slick marketing (Mitchell 2013). Even if Walmart and TSC have helped by minimizing members' environmental impact without altering the bottom line, more overreaching environmental or wage protection is difficult for corporations that are still required to show a profit.[9] The particular impact assessments of TSC are largely done in isolation, which contributes to overlap and confusing duplication across a range of product life-cycle assessments (Subramanian et al. 2012).

The UN Global Compact

Critiques of corporate practice went well beyond Walmart in the 1990s. After campaigns against Nestle, Nike, and Shell, corporations became sensitive to claims of social irresponsibility. The United Nations (UN) offered a potential venue to both discuss global regulation of corporations and engage corporations in the fight against global poverty (Post 2012). In 1999, UN secretary-general Kofi Annan launched the UN Global Compact (UNGC) at a speech to business leaders at the World Economic Forum. He described it as a "strategic policy initiative for businesses that are committed to aligning their operations and strategies with ten universally accepted principles in the areas of human rights, labor, environment and anti-corruption."[10] The UNGC is an ambitious umbrella initiative that encourages both environmentally and socially sustainable business practices, taking into account human rights, labor rights, and transparency, in addition to environmental standards.

The UNGC aims to facilitate dialogue and mutual learning among businesses, and it offers members access to UN agencies, trade and labor unions, the public sector, academics, and INGOs (Ruggie 2001; Kell and Levin 2003; Rasche 2009; Williams 2014). Today, the UNGC claims more than eight thousand business participants from 145 countries.[11] Through two primary mechanisms, an annual Communication on Progress (COP) and participation in regional and national networks of learning, businesses work with the UN to "weave a web of joint values" (Rasche 2009, 514). The UNGC networks focus on developing best practices, external impact, and public-private partnerships (Ruggie 2004). Ultimately, the

UNGC is not designed to enforce standards but to facilitate voluntary compliance with growing norms of doing business (Post 2012; Ruggie 2013; Williams 2014).

The UNGC has its champions and detractors. It claims to be the world's largest corporate social responsibility initiative, and its membership has grown substantially. Proponents argue that the UNGC is central to a new social contract being negotiated among government, business, and society (Post 2012). Critics see a number of problems. Some argue that the UNGC does not actually result in improved corporate performance in line with the UNGC's ten principles (Sethi and Schepers 2014). Antiglobalization activists decry that the UNGC lends legitimacy to extractive and self-interested actors, "bluewashing" member businesses (Berliner and Prakash 2015) by covering questionable practices with a veneer of UN legitimacy. Analysts of international institutions argue that the UNGC is undemocratic and lacks transparency (Thérien and Pouliot 2006). All of these critiques reflect the centrality of businesses in decision making in the UNGC.

Both TSC and the UNGC are ambitious cross-sectoral initiatives meant to improve the environmental and social performance of members. Both initiatives have sought NGO partners to certify their credibility and promote dialogue among key stakeholders. The response of NGOs to these overtures has been quite varied. In the following sections, we discuss how leading INGOs and other NGOs have engaged with TSC and the UNGC, and how the status of individual INGOs played a critical role in shaping the level of collaboration or condemnation they adopted in each case.

Vanilla Victories

A number of leading INGOs have sought engagement with corporations at the UNGC, TSC, and elsewhere. For some leading INGOs, collaboration with the brand-name corporations of TSC and the global policymakers of the United Nations can offer opportunities to claim credit for advancing corporate social responsibility. As with states, the outcomes of those collaborations have been "vanilla victories," small movements that are broadly palatable to a wide swath of audiences. In comparison to their dealings with states, the outcomes may be even smaller victories, as the self-regulating nature of these private arrangements requires that INGOs moderate their demands even more to avoid alienating the corporations upon whom they depend for enforcement.

WWF, CARE, and TSC

The presence of Walmart, the world's leading retailer, in TSC has encouraged other large corporations to come aboard (Interview 1007). This has made TSC an attractive place for INGOs to meet up with powerful corporations (Interview 1058). In addition, the fact that so many powerful corporations meet in a single place makes TSC a more efficient mechanism for the comparatively smaller staff of INGOs to reach business leaders (Interview 1059).

TSC has twenty-six NGO partners, including two leading INGOs, WWF and CARE.[12] To demonstrate its commitment to incorporating civil society perspectives, TSC explicitly sought two leading INGOs from different sectors that were willing to engage with corporations, and CARE and WWF were invited to join the board of directors in 2011 (Interview 1059). In announcing the appointment, TSC highlighted the expertise and global reach of these two NGOs.[13] WWF has been a leader in working with brand-name corporations to design specific accreditation standards, first in partnership with Unilever to create the Marine Stewardship Council (Yaziji and Doh 2009, 133), and now at TSC. CARE is one of the few nonenvironmental INGOs in TSC. CARE has long worked with a number of corporations to support its relief and development programs (Stroup 2012). Its involvement in TSC reinforces other partnerships with corporate TSC members General Mills, Walmart, Proctor & Gamble, Coca-Cola, Johnson & Johnson, and Kellogg's.[14] CARE's role in TSC is recognized by its NGO peers, but CARE did not attend a 2011 working group of civil society organizations interested in TSC.[15] One limit to CARE's deeper engagement in TSC is the challenge of quantifying the *social* impact of production for the life-cycle assessments generated by TSC. This would be a difficult task for any organization but particularly for an organization like CARE, whose technical expertise is in particular projects and programs (Interview 1059). CARE remains a TSC member, though it no longer serves on the board.

Other INGOs with more limited authority have also worked in close collaboration with TSC and its members. The Environmental Defense Fund (EDF) has planted its flag in the ground (literally) in Bentonville, Arkansas, Walmart's headquarters, signaling its long-term commitment to work with Walmart. It remains the only one with such concrete commitments, and it works in tandem on both EDF priorities (e.g., hazardous chemicals) and Walmart priorities (e.g., zero waste) (Interview 1001). Other INGOs have had a history of engaging with Walmart in and out of TSC, such as Conservation International (Crawford and Smith 2012), the Nature Conservancy, World Resources Institute, and the Natural Resources Defense Council. In 2016, EDF and the Nature Conservancy occupied spots on the board of directors. For other INGOs, collaboration with TSC offers the possibility of becoming more authoritative in the eyes of corporations. One interview subject suggested that INGO participation can help corporate members such as Walmart identify future partners for work beyond TSC (Interview 1053). In other words, TSC may yield new resources for corporate-friendly INGOs.

TSC provides a forum for corporations and some NGOs to develop closer ties, and it seeks practical approaches to improving the social performance of businesses. A decade after Walmart's stated commitment to responsible sourcing, however, there is no guarantee that the research generated by TSC will change member practices. From the outset, there were different levels of knowledge among working group participants about the basic concepts of sustainability (Interview 1060, 1061). In addition, there is no certification for TSC members, so one company might take the research on household goods and do nothing, while another might pursue change with suppliers, informed by TSC tools. Walmart is the only retailer to date that has made significant use of TSC findings. It has used annual questionnaires, based on the KPIs, to generate scorecards that then reward certain producers with sustainability "badges" displayed on its website.[16] Even if TSC metrics offer the promise of affecting global corporations along different points in the supply chain all at once (Interview 1044), such change comes slowly:

> We all realized we were only going to be able to take it so far. That distance was incremental at best. It might raise the floor, but . . . whether or not it raises the floor is a very, very big question that is still far from answered. It certainly does not look like it's going to raise the ceiling. (Interview 1048)

The process of decision making at the TSC can often be frustrating, as deliberation within working groups and participation more generally are both time-consuming (Interview 1012, 1059).

Even more troubling, the input of some NGOs and more progressive corporations has been sidelined. For example, WWF was excluded from a TSC working group in May 2011 because of its stated support of rigorous certification by the Forest Stewardship Council.[17] The Forest Stewardship Council itself participated in some early working groups of TSC but has since walked, as have more progressive corporations such as Seventh Generation. WWF has given up its board seat and is less involved in TSC today (Interview 1048). The structure of TSC privileges the staff at the supporting academic institutions and the corporate members driving TSC. According to one NGO member, the reliance on corporate members for support can create unequal dynamics (Interview 1060). Given the dues structure of TSC, corporations foot the bill of operations, and there is a tension in managing disagreements over methodologies and evaluative mechanisms on which INGOs and corporate views may diverge. INGOs that continue to participate recognize this problem:

> There [are] a lot more corporate voices and industry voices than there are NGO voices. So most of the time . . . [NGOs ensure that the discussion] still gets on the right hot spot and we're sending the right signals

and it doesn't get watered down to the lowest common denominator of what's acceptable by the industry. (Interview 1057)

The lack of transparency at TSC makes it difficult to evaluate whether member INGOs have been at all successful in that regard. In a parallel from the UNGC, Berliner and Prakash (2015) find that members of the UNGC make improvements in superficial ways, while actually faring worse than nonmembers on labor rights protection and environmental performance. In this context, leading INGOs have scaled back their involvement in TSC, seeing little space for their expertise and potential risk for their brand. Thus the output of TSC is decidedly vanilla, and perhaps not much of a victory, for those seeking to improve global supply chains.

UNGC: Ambitious but Elusive Global Partnership

Since its inception, the UNGC has argued that INGO and civil society participation is critical because it provides credibility for the UNGC and the capacity to monitor corporate practice. In a survey of top international companies, the most favored external partner was INGOs (Ruggie 2013, 74). For corporations at the UNGC, INGOs are generally seen as the "watchdogs" of the agreement (Hurd 2003; Williams 2004). In fact, UNGC proponents claim that it does not need to have any formal compliance mechanisms because INGOs are expected to fill that role. INGOs also lend legitimacy to the project and allow the UN to credibly claim that it is an honest broker between businesses and INGOs (Hurd 2003, 108). A key author of UNGC principles posits that "international NGOs serve as a bridge between the global and local levels" (Ruggie 2013, xli).

Leading INGOs were particularly important in early attempts to establish the credibility of this initiative. The successful launching of a major UN initiative to encourage corporate responsibility required well-known INGOs from the environmental and human rights sectors. Amnesty, HRW, WWF, and Transparency International joined the more than forty global corporations at the launch of the UNGC in New York in the summer of 2000.[18] Transparency International was critical for the inclusion of anticorruption as a UNGC principle in 2004.[19] According to one early count of UNGC supporters, seven of the fifty-seven signatories were civil society organizations, and all seven are fairly authoritative by our metrics (Bruno and Karliner 2000).[20]

Yet INGOs have little influence at the UNGC, and many leading INGOs have withdrawn their early support. The value of the UNGC to INGOs was unclear from the outset, and some leading INGOs that signed the early compact were tentative in their commitment. For example, in announcing its support, Amnesty argued that an effective and credible UNGC required independent monitoring and enforcement.[21] The evolution of the UNGC has driven Amnesty, HRW, and other leading INGOs away. Just a few other leading INGOs are today in the pool of 565 global NGO members.[22] Leading INGOs like the International Committee of the Red Cross have occasionally engaged in various working groups convened by the UNGC.[23] Oxfam was an early member that criticized the weak accountability mechanisms of the UNGC, but it has since worked with the compact to promote the use of its poverty impact assessment tool and to advance human rights principles with UNGC business members.[24]

One problem for many INGOs is the exclusive structure of the UNGC. In terms of governance, INGOs have four of thirty-three total board seats.[25] Of the remaining seats, twenty-one represent business interests, and the vice chair is Sir Mark Moody-Stuart, the former chairman of Royal Dutch Shell. No leading INGO has been represented on the UNGC Board of Directors, however, and Transparency International, a long-standing board member, has not offered public input on the UNGC since 2009.[26]

Meanwhile, a large group of leading INGOs have either condemned or ignored the UNGC. Greenpeace and FoE joined a long list of mostly Southern INGOs that voiced their opposition to Kofi Annan's proposal in 2000. Amnesty and HRW have since joined ActionAid, FoE, and Greenpeace in issuing pointed criticisms of the UNGC (Berliner and Prakash 2012, 6).[27] Other INGOs have described the UNGC as providing cover for companies with poor records in environment, labor, and human rights (Bruno and Karliner 2000). MSF has largely avoided the UNGC except to argue that the humanitarian sector in which it operates should not become a new market for private corporations.[28] Finally, many corporate members mention their donations to groups such as Habitat for Humanity and the Salvation Army in their annual Communication on Progress submitted to the UNGC, but service-oriented groups like these are largely silent on the merits of the UNGC.

Meanwhile, hundreds of other INGOs, as well as almost two thousand local NGOs, have joined the UNGC.[29] These include some corporate-friendly INGOs such as Conservation International, International Union for the Conservation of Nature, International Institute for Environment and Development, World Resources Institute, and CERES. Plan International and Planned Parenthood have also joined in the past five years. The specific networks that have emerged from the UNGC have engaged civil society on narrow issues (Mwangi, Rieth, and Schmitz 2011), though this does not hold across all countries. A number of corporate-INGO partnerships have also emerged from the UNGC. Berliner and Prakash (2012) find that corporations from countries with higher numbers of INGOs are less likely to join the compact. They interpret this as a preference for weak regulation, based on the assumption that all INGOs reject the UNGC. Yet an alternate interpretation is that corporations in countries with high number of INGOs have plenty of chances to either find NGO partners or hear NGO criticisms, especially since countries with numerous INGOs are the home countries of leading INGOs (Stroup 2012). Corporations from countries with few INGO members may thus join the UNGC to access those local or specialist INGOs that are interested in partnership.

All Vanilla, Not Much Victory

The seeming willingness of many corporations to engage in conversations about their environmental and social responsibilities has not yielded much at two expansive initiatives, TSC and the UNGC. The former generates research that focuses more on user-friendliness (for managers and consumers) than on scientific rigor, while the latter involves a range of networking events whose outputs are limited.

This will not surprise many who are skeptical of the substance behind corporate social responsibility and NGO-corporate collaboration (for an example, see Dauvergne and LeBaron 2014). Both TSC and the UNGC were initiated by corporations in concert with other actors (academics for TSC and the UN for the UNGC), with a circumscribed role for INGOs. The limited prospects of these arrangements raise the question of why leading INGOs would even risk their reputations and spend their limited resources on such initiatives. There are at least three reasons for leading INGOs to join the early stages of these initiatives. First, they can claim they are authorities by virtue of the fact that corporations seek their involvement. Second, corporate partnerships can benefit the programmatic work of INGOs that need technical, logistical, or financial assistance, and the ability to demonstrate efficacy in their programming is critical for INGO claims to their audiences. Finally, the appearance of principled pragmatism is necessary for leading INGOs. The comments from Greenpeace's director, Gerd Leipold, to the 2007 World Economic Forum are telling:

> [H]ow can I justify my participation on behalf of Greenpeace in the World Economic Forum? Simply because it is important that the agenda setting is not left to the powerful. It is because those relatively few delegates affect the lives of billions of people who are neither present nor represented at the WEF. It is because someone needs to mention that good intentions for the future do not replace the responsibility for the past. It is because those corporations which make genuine steps forward deserve acknowledgement and support—and those who only want to do greenwashing, must hear on the spot that they will not get away with it any longer.[30]

Faced with businesses at least willing to discussion corporate responsibility, a group such as Greenpeace believes that it risks looking rigid and dogmatic to multiple audiences if it does not meet these overtures.

Leading INGOs are particularly well-placed to change corporate practices. Their high status makes them attractive to corporate partners, and they have, by definition, the ability to reach many different audiences. Yet these groups are caught in the authority trap. Their long-term interest in maintaining their status shapes their short-term reactions, whether collaborative or critical. Those that engage must still demonstrate their independence and efficacy, which makes them intolerant of initiatives that show little progress. Even if they walk, however, their initial support for the endeavor helped launch the initiative as a credible one. Those leading INGOs that criticize corporate practices remain fairly moderate in their tone, as when HRW, which has published numerous reports on Walmart, explicitly argued in a 2012 investigation of Thai shrimp farmers that a boycott would be counterproductive, arguing instead for Walmart to take responsibility.[31] Leading INGOs must balance between demonstrating their independence from corporations and proving their credibility as effective partners, which privileges a middle-of-the-road strategy that neither stays the course of building private regulation nor pushes painfully on brand-name corporations.

Beyond Private Regulations: INGO Status and Corporate Relations

Private regulatory initiatives such as TSC and the UNGC are only one form of INGO-corporate interactions. Those more optimistic about the possibility of leading INGOs influencing corporate behavior might point to the wide range of corporate condemnations that have been issued by groups like Oxfam, FoE, Amnesty, and MSF. Perhaps the authority trap does constrain a small handful of INGOs that tried to collaborate on unenforceable, corporate-led initiatives, one could argue, but it is less powerful when leading INGOs bring the full force of their global reach to condemn or compete with corporations.

In this section, we build upon the cases above, as well as on a vast literature on NGO-corporate relations, to illustrate that the authority trap has an expansive reach. We argue that leading INGOs use condemnation more selectively, and less harshly, than other INGOs, but we do see more possibilities for competition to yield changes in corporate practices. When condemning corporations, those INGOs that are the best placed to push back against corporations are also the least likely to do so. Competitive initiatives offer some possibility of allowing leading INGOs to protect their reputations while pushing for more demanding regulations, but the proliferation of initiatives threatens to fragment and confuse the task of social and environmental auditing.

Condemnation

The two cases of INGO-corporate collaboration above reverse the pattern seen in the chapter on state targeting; the early days of the two initiatives were dominated by leading INGOs, with less powerful INGOs joining later on (and perhaps replacing their authoritative peers). In these situations, a group of elite INGOs and elite corporations agree that something must be done, and they all benefit from their initial affiliation. When it comes to condemnation in anticorporate campaigns by INGOs, we return to the well-noted pattern of issue entrepreneurship by smaller INGOs, with the later entry (for better or worse) of leading INGOs (Keck and Sikkink 1998; Bob 2005; Carpenter 2014). One illustrative example is Oxfam's 2001 campaign to "cut the cost" of AIDS drugs, an issue adopted by Oxfam after it had been promoted by a range of other activists (Sell 2002). As they do when condemning states, leading INGOs repackage and promote causes launched by other INGOs. In doing so, leading INGOs reorient their condemnation toward the easiest targets and repackage the campaign into a more moderate set of demands for the corporation.

INGOs tend to go after the low-hanging fruit of corporations that have already committed to corporate responsibility. Research on corporate campaigns suggests that all INGOs are drawn to a particular set of targets. Bartley and Child (2014) find that large corporations that have invested in developing visible brands and reputations for social responsibility are more likely to be targets of antisweatshop protests. Brand-name corporations offer tempting targets for INGOs seeking to draw attention to a cause. According to SIGWatch, the ten biggest global corporations combined were the target of the majority of the campaign actions of over 7,500 NGOs in 2015.[32]

If large, prominent corporations that have tried to develop reputations as being socially responsible are likely targets for INGO activists, the key question is whether INGOs differ in their approach to these brands depending on the INGOs' status. Both logic and evidence suggest that the answer is regularly yes. Consider the distinction between leading INGOs that hold corporations accountable to existing standards and other INGOs that use campaigns against corporations as a proxy for a critique of larger processes and institutions (Yaziji and Doh 2009) in lieu of formal participation. Other INGOs have more freedom in going after corporations because of their narrow but committed support base, while leading INGOs are fettered by their need to please many audiences. In a simple contrast of corporations and INGOs, Yaziji and Doh (2009, 85) write that "the greater institutional complexity of firms relative to that of NGOs underlies the need for multivocality and thereby limits options for both responding to conflicting institutional pressures as well as the possibility of being institutionally entrepreneurial." This same logic holds for comparisons *among* INGOs as well. Leading INGOs have less room to advance new causes and fewer options for pleasing their many stakeholders.

In addition to these concerns created by the need to please multiple audiences, leading NGOs also dilute their criticisms because of direct ties with their target. Corporations are increasingly key funders or partners of leading INGOs, which gives them even less room to be critical. HRW faced one particularly confounding situation in the mid-1990s. One of its long-standing board members, Bruce Klatsky, was the CEO of Phillips-Van Heusen (PVH), an apparel company being criticized for intimidating worker unions at a plant in Guatemala. A group of US-based activists threatened to picket the HRW annual fundraiser.[33] In response, Klatsky facilitated an HRW investigation, and the INGO published a report titled *Corporations and Human Rights* in March 1997.[34] The report highlighted strengths and problems in the treatment of workers, and Klatsky pledged to recognize the union and "deal with" personnel responsible for antiunion discrimination.[35] Still, the problem of worker rights continued for PVH and the apparel industry in general, and in 1999 PVH was accused of closing a plant in Guatemala to discourage unionization.[36] This example illustrates the trap for leading INGOs. HRW had to respond to allegations against PVH in order to maintain its reputation for independence, but its critiques could not be so harsh as to alienate a key supporter. The report HRW generated was a discrete output that helped change conditions in a small factory for a few years. For other antisweatshop activists, Klatsky's position at HRW created a political opening for holding PVH accountable for its treatment of workers (DeWinter-Schmitt 2007). Klatsky's stated commitment to human rights made PVH a more viable target for all activists.

Leading INGOs go after the easiest targets, those already ostensibly committed to corporate responsibility, and offer incremental changes as a way to placate critics. A more recent example is Oxfam International's Behind the Brands campaign, which targets the social and environmental practices of the top ten global food and beverage companies and rates their performance.[37] The ratings system is meant to shame some but also encourage better practice, a mix of condemnation and collaboration. Meanwhile, the heaviest polluters and worst rights abusers are left alone. Lenox and Eesley (2009) find that corporations with the worst environmental performance are the least likely to acquiesce to activists' demands and may not have even been targeted in the first place. As with states, leading INGOs target those corporations likely to change their practices, not necessarily those corporations whose practices are the most consequential in labor abuses and environmental degradation.

Competition

While most studies categorize NGO-corporate relations along a two-dimensional spectrum ranging from hostile to friendly, there is an additional approach that many NGOs have adopted. NGOs can compete with corporate-led regulations, broadly agreeing with seemingly shared goals of environmental and social protection while disagreeing about the best means to design standards and monitor performance. Here leading INGOs may be able to better leverage their authority into effective pressure on corporations.

For an illustration, we examine the issue of forest certification, which has not only received substantial scholarly analysis but also inspired a number of other certification efforts (Auld, Gulbrandsen, and McDermott 2008, 188). Today, roughly 10% of the world's forests fall under a global certification scheme.[38] There are perhaps sixty different certification systems around the globe today, with a handful of dominant initiatives, including the Forest Stewardship Council (FSC), the Sustainable Forestry Initiative (SFI), and the Pan European Forest Certification Schemes (PEFC) (Anderson and Hansen 2003).

The key point of competition has been between the FSC, supported by some leading INGOs, and the SFI, driven by US-based corporations. The FSC began as an effort to create a labeling system for tropical timber after a failed attempt in the early 1990s to create a global convention on forestry. WWF, FoE, Greenpeace, and the Rainforest Action Network sought input from a variety of stakeholders, including local groups, environmental NGOs, governments, and industry (Synnott 2005; Dingwerth 2008) and expanded to include a range of forest products. FSC adherents must commit to general principles, evaluated according to whether members meet specific criteria. FSC also has chain of custody requirements that tracks products from forest to marketplace (Auld and Cashore 2012, 137–38). FSC itself does not issue the certification but instead accredits others to inspect and issue FSC labels.

The competitor SFI has courted US-based industrial forest companies (Cashore, Auld, and Newsom 2003b), as the United States is the largest market in the world and largely depends on domestic sources for forestry products. SFI was started by an industry group, the American Forest and Paper Association, as a response to the FSC (Cashore, Auld, and Newsom 2003a, 232). Unsurprisingly, the SFI has heavily favored business interests in the United States (Cashore 2002, 508). SFI data are compiled by member organizations and submitted to an expert panel for review without public reporting (Cashore, Auld, and Newsom 2003b).

SFI initially did not allow third-party certification, instead relying on first-party reporting (self-auditing) or second-party verification by an industry group, the American Forestry and Paper Association.

The FSC is not perfect, but it has much more support from leading INGOs than does the SFI. Some claim that the FSC performs better than other leading competitors on sustainability and ecological health measures (Clark and Kozar 2011). The FSC requires more costly changes in corporate practice, though this can vary by country (Espach 2006). Other accounts of the FSC have been less enthusiastic, showing differential effects of FSC certification, depending on the audience (Overdevest and Rickenbach 2006; Rickenbach and Overdevest 2006). There is mixed evidence on whether the FSC has affected deforestation practices (Marx and Cuypers 2010). Still, despite the many problems facing the FSC, it is accepted as legitimate by many more actors than is the corporate-dominated SFI (Schepers 2010). Leading INGOs have played a key role in promoting the FSC and contributing to its reputation for independence and stringency. The WWF has remained consistent in its support. FoE and Greenpeace were founding members, and many of their national offices are still FSC members though both organizations have publicly critiqued FSC (Auld 2014). Recently, a 2014 Greenpeace report argued that uneven requirements in the FSC certification process threaten its credibility, but this criticism is a call to strengthen, not abandon, the FSC.[39] Meanwhile, Oxfam/Novib (Oxfam's large office in the Netherlands) has also been an FSC member, though it and the larger Oxfam confederation have raised questions about FSC audits.[40] Other INGOs with very different approaches to corporate collaboration are also FSC members, including the Nature Conservancy and the Natural Resources Defense Council, as well as Dogwood Alliance and Rainforest Action Network. By contrast, there are no leading INGOs that support the SFI.[41]

The competition between the two forestry standards can be confusing for consumers, loggers, retailers, and auditors themselves. Still, a collaboration with a competitive standard led by NGOs is arguably a superior outcome to collaboration with a corporate-dominated certification initiative. Faced with the FSC's greater legitimacy and potentially more rigorous standards, the SFI has evolved to more closely resemble the FSC (Cashore, Auld, and Newsom 2004; Overdevest 2010). The FSC's support from NGOs does come with its own challenges, as it has had to protect its own credibility in the face of NGO criticism while attracting corporate members. On the latter, it has increased the representation of business in its governance structures (Cashore, Auld, and Newsom 2003a). But it has also recently announced further efforts to synchronize its various standards and auditing mechanisms, potentially increasing its rigor (Fernholz et al. 2015).

In short, private certification schemes in which INGOs play a central role are no panacea, but they appear less problematic than TSC and the UNGC, where leading INGOs helped launch new initiatives with little to show in terms of changed corporate behavior. The forestry case suggests that competition can provide positive external pressure on corporations while still maintaining the reputation of leading INGOs. Still, the long-term success of these competitor initiatives may still hinge on whether they serve the status concerns of leading INGOs. FoE, WWF, and Greenpeace all have slightly different bases of authority. FoE has become increasingly committed to serving its local chapters as a sort of global group of grassroots coalitions of environmentalists and indigenous groups (Doherty and Doyle 2013). FoE has been a vocal internal critic, raising its member organizations' concerns, but it ultimately supports FSC as the most desirable, if imperfect, timber certification scheme (Auld 2014). Greenpeace depends on its visible public profile, and its recent report of problematic FSC cases suggests that it will exit FSC rather than see its reputation suffer. Finally, WWF's authority derives as much from its close relationships with policymakers and corporations as it does from its public support, and the FSC still offers WWF the chance to claim credit for achieving a workable private partnership. FoE and Greenpeace are more likely to be troubled by problems in the auditing chain, while WWF is more likely to feel threatened by reduced corporate membership. Ultimately, an FSC with a weaker reputation for NGO backing will make it less competitive than other forestry schemes.

Division of Labor or Fragmentation?

Academics and practitioners have generated a deep literature on NGO-corporate interactions, describing their many forms and theorizing about their importance. The frequency with which INGOs and corporations interact varies by sector and over time. For example, despite divestment calls from antiapartheid activists and global efforts at the United Nations to establish a code of conduct for transnational corporations, corporate activity has stayed off the agenda of many leading INGOs. Though environmental INGOs regularly targeted corporations in the 1970s, INGOs in the human rights and development sectors did not embrace corporations as a key target until the 1990s (Lindenberg and Bryant 2001; Chandler 2009). Regardless, across issues as diverse as diamond mining, labor rights, carbon emissions, and disaster response, INGOs and corporations regularly work alongside one another.

Regardless of sector, INGOs face choices about the strategies to employ when engaging with corporations. Research on anticorporate campaigns repeatedly suggests that collaboration and condemnation, working in tandem, complement one another. Radical tactics can be effective at raising awareness and shaming corporations, even if they are not easy to translate into workable policy propositions (Yaziji and Doh 2009). Meanwhile, collaboration with corporations can yield specific commitments or new guidelines, but without public attention the firm can water down these commitments or walk away. Thus, at least in theory, equal adoption of these positions could yield an effective division of labor. According to a staff member of one leading INGO, "we invite [companies] to the table, but if they aren't motivated, then sometimes it's up to the other [environmental] NGOs to soften them up a bit . . . when they're a little bruised, they'll come back to us to help make the pain go away" (Bertels, Hoffman, and DeJordy 2014, 29).

These kinds of opposing strategies can pose problems for INGOs working with companies, however. To begin, it is not easy for a single organization to adopt both strategies simultaneously. Oppositional tactics are likely to alienate corporate audiences, while collaboration can make activists look like sellouts. The sorts of coordinating structures necessary to manage complex campaigns are more prevalent at leading INGOs (Wong 2012), but it is not clear that a good cop/bad cop approach by a single actor will be well-received by corporate partners (though see Greenpeace's collaboration with Unilever in Africa and condemnation of Unilever on Malaysian rainforests (Larkin 2013)). Some groups like FoE have recently created a more decentralized structure that allows these contrasting strategies to exist within the same organization, but the mixed signals sent by different chapters of the same "brand" may impede those groups' future as a campaigning organization (Doherty and Doyle 2013).

To complicate matters, leading INGOs might approach such questions differently from other INGOs because of their need to appeal to multiple audiences. The consequence of this is that leading INGOs occupy a middle ground strategically. They do not universally condemn corporations, as radical tactics might alienate not only corporations but other audiences like private donors or state officials who generally embrace the authority of the market (Bernstein 2001). On the other hand, they have to be careful to maintain some distance from corporations, as compromised independence reduces INGO authority with other audiences as well. Within that middle ground, leading INGOs lean toward either collaboration or condemnation. Each strategy offers leading INGOs the chance to demonstrate their efficacy; radical protest events can yield substantial media attention, while collaboration can be cited as evidence that the INGO has a foot in the door. Such credit claiming is necessary for leading INGOs to maintain their status and support their vast organizations. Ultimately, competition among INGOs for legitimacy and supporters prevents public recognition of the importance of both approaches and spills over into very public divisions over the future of any one movement.

By way of conclusion, we raise issues that suggest the increasing salience of INGO-corporate interactions. The Syrian refugee crisis, at time of writing, has captured the imagination of much of the world, and with thousands of refugees pouring across European borders each day, the cracks in the global humanitarian system have been showing. Enter a new slate of problem solvers: a company called Alarm Phone, with an online mapping platform that fields distress calls from boats in the Mediterranean and contacts relevant authorities to help the situation. Refugees Welcome provides an Airbnb-like interface to link refugees with people with rooms to let. Even the UN Refugee Agency has jumped on board the "new" economy by crowdfunding to support refugees alongside local crowdfunding efforts.[42] These for-profit efforts are supposed to remedy the slower responses formulated by the bureaucratic global humanitarian community largely composed of leading INGOs and a handful of state and IGO funders (Barnett and Walker 2015). Nonprofit and for-profit agencies compete to offer solutions to the refugee crisis.

The popular narrative about evil companies and virtuous INGOs is suddenly not so simple. The Syrian refugee example highlights the challenge for leading INGOs, who watch with concern as these supposedly small, agile companies face off against large, plodding bureaucracies. In actual practice, then, the lines between the two actors seem to blur, with INGOs adopting the jargon and structures of their for-profit counterparts while corporations talk about social responsibility and social entrepreneurship. NGO-corporate collaborations can reduce the costs for leading INGOs to take on new infrastructure and approaches while preserving both their authoritative status and their abilities to do their work. Unfortunately, the authority trap prevents the output of corporate-INGO collaborations from yielding substantive changes in troubling corporate practices.

DEFERENCE FROM INGOs

For INGOs, there is a popular assumption that birds of a feather flock together. In truth, INGOs enjoy a diverse array of relationships with other INGOs. They collaborate in networks, condemn their peers' strategies and priorities, and compete to define best practices for the INGO community (Murdie and Davis 2012a; Carpenter 2014; Hadden 2015). In fact, the scholarly literature on INGOs suggests that peers might be their most important audience, insofar as collective action within civil society may be a necessary precondition for influence over other actors. Peers may also be the most challenging audience for INGOs. This is the one audience where an INGO's principles are just one of many points of discussion, alongside strategies, resources, and partnerships. INGO peers are most informed about INGO decisions and simultaneously compete with one another for deference from states, corporations, and the public. Put bluntly, INGOs know each other's struggles but are the least likely to let each other off the hook. Even if INGOs in general might benefit when some become authorities in global politics, they do not all see their preferences realized.

In this chapter, we evaluate how INGO authority shapes strategic approaches to peers in two cases, the INGO Accountability Charter (AC) and the World Social Forum (WSF). The AC, an exclusive project started by leading INGOs, is a modest victory in terms of defining the accountability and transparency of INGOs. The AC has developed a set of strict reporting and assessment guidelines aimed at securing the approval of state donors and target corporations. In spite of its best efforts, it has gotten little attention, making it a "vanilla victory" even for its members. The WSF is an inclusive annual gathering of an enormous number of other INGOs who reject collaboration with economic and political elites. The claims of WSF participants are not vanilla, but they are also not victories, as the WSF remains obscure. Drawing from opposite ends of the INGO authority spectrum, the two initiatives are limited collaborations among a subset of INGOs that offer competing conceptions of good practice for INGOs.

As with other audiences, both leading INGOs and other INGOs are caught in an authority trap that shapes their strategic choices. Other INGOs often collaborate to survive, and they condemn leading INGOs that seem timid defenders of principled causes. Leading INGOs frequently compete with other INGOs, occasionally collaborate, and rarely condemn other INGOs. This last point is particularly interesting. Leading INGOs condemn their peers not through loud "naming and shaming" as with states, but through silence and apathy. Condemnation takes this silent form because leading INGOs cannot publicly denounce their peers, as such seemingly petty infighting or divisiveness might undermine their authority with other audiences. As discussed in the introductory chapter, this is akin to the *Fight Club* rule: the first rule of being a leading INGO is that you do not talk about your authority. Instead, leading INGOs largely ignore the weak, except when their status with other audiences is threatened.

We begin with a brief history of the AC and WSF. Second, we explore how each initiative offers a mix of collaboration and competition. At each initiative, the status concerns of individual members shape the group's output. The third section describes the limited level of influence that each initiative has achieved, with the AC decidedly vanilla and neither particularly victorious. Fourth, we explore why condemnation, a strategy frequently employed to target other actors, is a risky strategy for targeting INGOs.

Two Cases: The Accountability Charter and World Social Forum

The AC and WSF are useful cases for evaluating how status affects strategy with regards to an audience of other INGOs. First, both are cross-sectoral initiatives that bring together INGOs from a variety of issue areas. In addition, both initiatives bring together INGOs of varied status, which allows an examination of status concerns within each group. The AC is mostly made of up leading INGOs, while the WSF is dominated by small and local groups. Finally, both are places where INGOs have collectively gathered to answer the question of "what do you stand for?," a question involving both substantive content and normative legitimacy. The AC emerged because governments and corporations asked leading INGOs to defend the legitimacy of their privileged positions by showing how they themselves were accountable to those people whose interests they claim to defend. By contrast, the WSF arose out of the "alter-globalization" movement, whose critics have responded with "we know what you're against, but what are you for?" (Smith 2004). In the simplest terms, WSF participants have credibility as representatives of excluded voices on the global stage, but have been searching for capacity and coherence as a path to influence, while AC members have internal coherence and access to decision makers, but seek to guard their authority as legitimate defenders of neglected principles and peoples. We briefly describe the evolution of the two groups below, focusing on leadership, goals, and structure.

The INGO Accountability Charter

Accountability has become a key buzzword and major challenge for INGOs. INGOs have long faced questions from both friends and foes about what gives them the right to push for social and political change (Edwards and Hulme 1996). INGOs' claims to serve or speak for unrepresented groups or principles have been increasingly contested as INGOs have been given more access to state agencies and intergovernmental organizations (Zürn et al. 2012; Tallberg et al. 2013). Corporations and governments—frequent targets of INGO campaigns—have accused INGOs of promoting Northern rather than universal values, of failing to accurately represent the interests of their intended beneficiaries, and of being ineffective or incompetent (Collingwood and Logister 2006, 179–80; Lyon 2010).

A number of these pointed challenges to the legitimacy of INGOs emerged in the early 2000s. As the US-Iraq conflict unfolded, right-leaning groups in the United States posed questions about the power and independence of INGOs.[1] In response, several small groups of leading INGOs began to meet informally (Lindenberg and Bryant 2001). A 2003 meeting convened by the Hauser Center for Non-profit Organizations and the INGO CIVICUS brought twenty INGO leaders together, which led to the inaugural meeting of the International Advocacy NGO network at the headquarters of Transparency International in Berlin (Brown 2008, 98–100). The network quickly focused on crafting a defense of their accountability (Interview 1014). A subcommittee of leaders from leading INGOs—including Save the Children, Oxfam, Greenpeace, and Amnesty—drafted an "Accountability Charter" (AC), which was endorsed publicly in June 2006 by eleven INGOs (Brown 2008, 112). Within a year and a half, another fifty organizations had signed on.[2] The initial AC states that "our right to act is based upon universally-recognized freedoms of speech, assembly and association, on our contribution to democratic processes, and on the values we seek to promote."[3] Those values are explicitly cosmopolitan principles and include human rights, sustainable development, environmental protection, and humanitarian response.

Soon after its formation, the AC and its members moved from a general sign-on statement to creating specific reporting standards for members. As one participant described the evolution, "We got these beautiful words, but what do you do—where does the rubber hit the road? Is there any rubber involved anyway?" (Interview 1039). The AC secretariat expanded and was moved from CIVICUS to the International Civil Society Center (ICSC) in Berlin. The ICSC is collectively owned and financed by eleven INGOs (most of them leading INGOs) and serves as a kind of think tank for identifying long-term trends.[4]

Among the at least 350 self-regulatory initiatives that have been created by INGOs (Deloffre 2010; Lloyd, Calvo, and Laybourn 2010; Crack 2013), the AC is perhaps the only one that seeks to create standards for INGOs regardless of sector. It has created a set of specific reporting requirements for members and an independent review board to assess member practices. The AC has also worked to expand its membership to other INGOs. In doing so, it faces a difficult trade-off: a demanding set of standards is more likely to placate external critics, but more onerous requirements push away other INGOs that may be interested in accountability but unwilling or unable to meet the specific standards. In short, the AC is not designed for all INGOs. It emphasizes professionalization, process, and accountability. In its own words, "[it has been] signed by most of the most *global NGOs.*"[5]

History of the WSF

In sharp contrast to the AC, the World Social Forum (WSF) is an inclusive group of largely unknown INGOs. The vision for the WSF emerged from conversations among antiglobalization activists from France and Brazil who were frustrated by the exclusive and narrow base of the global economy. Bernard Cassen was director-general of *Le Monde Diplomatique*, a leftist French monthly, and founder of ATTAC, an antiglobalization network. Cassen met in early 2000 in Paris with two Brazilian activists, Oded Grajew, a former businessman committed to social responsibility who had just returned from the World Economic Forum (WEF), and Chico Whitaker, a Brazilian architect and activist then visiting Paris.[6] While these activists may not have come from leading INGOs, they are well-known in their home countries and well-regarded by other INGOs. Imagining an alternative to the WEF and building upon the energy evident in protests like the 1999 "Battle in Seattle" against the World Trade Organization, the three decided to launch a "World Social Forum" in Porto Alegre the following year.[7]

There are two notable features about the tactical choices made by the founders of the WSF. First, even among this small group, there were conflicting understandings of the purpose of the WSF meetings, and this tension continues today.

For Whitaker, the WSF would provide an agora, a discursive space in which deliberation itself would strengthen civil society. For Cassen, by contrast, such gatherings could and should develop clear policy proposals that could be injected into global politics (Hoskyns 2014). Second, the WSF was explicitly designed to bring together activists across a range of issue areas. Just as the AC emerged from an interest in transcending sectoral boundaries among advocacy INGOs, the WSF was a new moment for global justice movements in that it brought together activists who had previously met just around single issues such as human rights, women's empowerment, and environmental protection (Rucht 2012).

In contrast to the highly structured processes of the AC and its members, the WSF has a loose and ever-changing governance structure. An International Council (IC) was created in 2001 as a fairly fluid steering committee, and today includes 155 members. The WSF has not become a highly formalized organization, contrary to what most social movement scholars have predicted (Pleyers 2012). The IC has undergone several reforms,[8] pushing back against the way formalization privileges "only those with the financial resources and time to attend the meetings" (Della Porta 2006). Larger INGO members of the council include ActionAid, ATTAC, Greenpeace, Oxfam, and Via Campesina, but smaller or national NGOs play important roles (Steger and Wilson 2012). This generally informal structure has given radical actors relatively greater opportunity to influence the form and content of the WSF (Smith and Wiest 2012). This is both a strength and a liability. Some argue that the WSF "has been hijacked by its 'parents' and 'mothers', a closed group of organizations (and increasingly, individuals) that has no political capital or representative function beyond their role in organizing the Forum" (Scerri 2013).

The WSF has met almost annually in a variety of places, and sometimes many places at once as a "polycentric" meeting. Because each meeting does not result in a final statement or cohesive position, it is difficult to assess the changing "output" or "effectiveness" of the WSF over the past fifteen years. It has served as a networking platform for civil society groups working on particular issues, including resistance to war and imperialism (Reitan 2009) and climate justice (Goodman 2009). Each year, tens of thousands or hundreds of thousands of people gather at these multiday events. As more place than organization, it is not the WSF, but the actors that meet there, that seek to influence others.

Collaboration and Competition

The AC and WSF are collective INGO efforts and thus necessarily involve some level of collaboration. A wide range of INGO analysts and practitioners claim that working together is essential for INGOs to achieve social change. The critical questions, however, are collaboration *with whom* and *for what*. The AC and WSF embody both collaboration and competition; they offer specific but very different conceptions of what good practice looks like among INGOs. The process of developing goals and standards are driven by the status of members. The AC creates close collaboration among a small number of leading INGOs to create transparency around their organizational processes. The WSF, by contrast, creates new ties among a wide range of other INGOs to build resistance to hegemonic globalization. The AC competes to define specific mainstream practices as legitimate, while the WSF competes to demonstrate the importance of more radical goals. In this section, we explore collaboration and competition at the AC and WSF and in the process reveal how authority affects how INGOs approach their peers.

Standards for Whom? Accountability at the AC

Members of the AC have developed specific reporting requirements and created greater transparency about organizational practices. It is a daunting task to create a global standard for INGOs across multiple sectors. Initially, the AC sought to be the "gold standard" for all INGOs.[9] The logic was that a single high bar would create convergence in organizational practice and reward truly accountable INGOs. The AC soon realized, however, that member INGOs "have very different structures and areas of work and objects and purpose" (Interview 1017). Thus the AC fell back to creating a sort of umbrella standard that identifies commonalities across existing reporting requirements. In the words of former Oxfam International director and AC board chair Jeremy Hobbs, "we are not proposing a single scheme, which is likely to divide proponents of different codes, but we are proposing a framework for inter-operability between various regional and national level codes."[10] In 2014, eight national INGO coalitions formed a partnership with the AC to identify core standards.[11]

In a crowded field of private INGO regulations, the AC can encourage healthy competition if it helps INGOs improve their performance.[12] Members report that the AC offers a place for a "more open and honest conversation" with peers (Interview 1018). Those conversations can help members assess the costs and benefits of new strategies, such as how to expand advocacy activities (Interviews 1014, 1037). The AC has worked to become more than a rubber stamp, developing an extensive oversight mechanism and dense internal network. AC members attend annual meetings, submit annual reports, receive feedback from an independent review panel, and participate in peer advice networks and workshops.

Still, the AC has faced problems in improving INGO practices. First, the functional requirements of anticorruption work, humanitarian relief, environmental protection, human rights advocacy, and civil society support vary substantially, so certain AC requirements are of limited utility across all members (Interview 1017). Even the CEOs of the national offices of AC member organizations have little familiarity with the AC's reporting requirements and review.[13] Second, achieving greater transparency inside leading INGOs may not actually be desirable, as transparency provides information to enemies as well as allies.[14] Third, the AC has been unable to develop reporting uniformity within single INGOs, a challenge that reflects the variety of organizational forms they can adopt. Some AC members (like Transparency International and World YWCA) are loose federations of affiliated chapters, while others (like Amnesty and Greenpeace) are highly centralized. AC membership does not require reporting by all affiliates of the same INGO "family." Sometimes an entire federation signs on, while in other situations just a single national chapter or international secretariat could join. For example, only the Transparency International secretariat, and not individual national chapters, reports to the AC (Interview 1017). Finally, annual reporting is costly, and even wealthy INGOs have had trouble investing in monitoring and evaluation. AC members like Amnesty, Oxfam, and World Vision may have "an army of people" working on monitoring and evaluation, but Plan and Greenpeace—still sizeable INGOs—each have only one person working part-time on the same tasks (Interviews 1037, 1039). Some leading INGOs have declined to join, feeling they have sufficient methods for demonstrating their credibility and accountability; Human Rights Watch (HRW) is a notable nonmember.[15]

In short, the AC's independent review panel and standardized annual reporting requirements do offer a more wide-ranging form of oversight and greater transparency than other initiatives. Yet even wealthy INGOs struggle to find the resources to meet these reporting requirements, and membership remains small. AC members must pay annual dues that range from €1,000 to €25,000. This sliding scale subsidizes smaller organizations but is still a substantial fee. A British NGO with income under €1 million would pay less than €350 to join BOND, a robust network that supports and advocates for British development NGOs.[16] Thus, even with intentional efforts to attract small INGOs, most of the AC members are large INGOs; in 2012, only six of the twenty-four members had annual incomes of less than $10 million.[17] Rather than reshaping the INGO sector, the AC has reinforced pre-existing ties among powerful INGOs like Transparency International, Amnesty, Greenpeace, and Oxfam (Interviews 1017, 1028, 1069), maintaining a small club of leading INGOs. It is likely to continue in this vein; the AC's "prospect list" of potential recruits prioritizes large and prominent INGOs like World Wildlife Fund (WWF), Médecins sans Frontières, HRW, and Christian Aid (Interview 1017).

The AC standards reward formalized and moderate organizations rather than informal movement groups engaged in radical tactics. This standard may be attractive to large donors or might provide sufficient pushback to corporate critics, but it is *not* palatable for many INGOs, for whom conforming to the demands of a state or corporate audience would be tantamount to defeat. Critics argue that leading INGOs ignore everyday realities (Naidoo and Tandon 1999, 199). Appeasing non-INGO audiences thus plays to the "vanilla" status quo and creates schisms within civil society. For example, to meet the commitment of "environmental responsibility," AC members must (1) implement a written "environmental management system," (2) specify how it will minimize environmental impact, and (3) monitor and report on its environmental performance. Environmental responsibility does not include activism, such as protest in front of the White House to protest the Keystone pipeline.[18] As one observer explained, civil society organizations are "much more diverse than the purposes captured by the organizations that traditionally make up our large international NGOs" (Interview 1022). The AC's narrow vision of good practices thus rewards only certain INGOs and reinforces gaps between INGOs.

Fighting for a Cause at the WSF

In contrast to the process-oriented focus of the AC, the WSF is built on the proposition that the appropriate role for INGOs in global politics is opposition "to neo-liberalism and to domination of the world by capital and any form of imperialism."[19] The WSF is a popular forum for collaboration among many less well-known INGOs. For participants, the WSF meetings are *the* primary space where people come together to envision themselves as part of a global community, effectively displacing those meetings that used to be convened by the United Nations (Smith and Wiest 2012). Others argue that the WSF is the "intellectual and organizational epicenter" of the global justice movement and that the debates at the WSF meetings have produced a fairly cohesive "alter-globalization" ideology (Steger and Wilson 2012). Regular participants argue that the WSF provides a networking opportunity that would not otherwise exist (Interviews 1074, 1075). Proponents of the WSF praise the meetings as "one of the most dynamic and important political events in the world" (Becker 2007), where the global public can overcome poor organization or limited global consciousness to achieve influence.

WSF meetings may foster new ideas or relationships that cut across issue areas. One example is environmental protection. Environmental frames at the WSF extend across meetings, and environmental organizations regularly participate in events addressing indigenous concerns, public services, and neoliberalism (Kaneshiro, Lawrence, and Chase-Dunn 2012). For a major environmental NGO like Friends of the Earth (FoE), the WSF has regularly exposed its campaign staff to activists within other networks (Doherty and Doyle 2013), which may bring about shifts in "conventional" activist thinking. In their study of leftist environmental networks, Reitan and Gibson (2012) trace how the 2008 WSF helped a newly formed climate network, Climate Justice Action, connect with indigenous activists. By being inclusive, the WSF can create unexpected coalitions that adopt new frames.

Still, the WSF's ability to promote a coherent antiglobalization agenda, either within or beyond its meetings, is limited. While the key challenge for the AC has been to develop specific reporting requirements, WSF participants have grappled with defining a clear alternative to the status quo. Both proponents and critics of the WSF agree that while a number of specific proposals have been debated, its participants have not collectively identified a viable alternative to neoliberal globalization (Fisher and Ponniah 2003; Pinsky 2010; Rucht 2012).[20] The WSF has not established a recognized brand that competes with the internationally known WEF meetings in Davos.[21]

In addition, the WSF has not substantially altered the strategies of leading INGOs, many of whom attend the WSF. First, the leading INGOs that have supported the WSF are already committed to supporting Southern activists. Oxfam and other prominent development INGOs such as Christian Aid and CCFD (a French Catholic relief group) spend much of their money through partner organizations in the field rather than operating programs themselves (Stroup 2012). Their support for Southern partners at the WSF is thus a manifestation of pre-existing relationships. Second, the WSF may have given smaller groups a chance to organize sessions, but this does not negate the influence of leading INGOs. Ranking the twenty most central organizations at the 2003 and 2005 WSFs, Byrd and Jasny (2010) find that Christian Aid, CAFOD, and FoE were in the top four, while in 2005 ActionAid, Oxfam, InterAction (an American NGO umbrella group), and CIVICUS were also central to WSF events. Their analysis of ActionAid's approach to the 2005 WSF suggests that information runs top-down, not bottom-up, since the INGO took the opportunity for different parts of the organization to meet and build skills, including training of organizers and plan for larger campaigns and projects (Byrd and Jasny 2010, 367). This was also evident at the 2016 WSF meeting in Montreal, where Oxfam Quebec planned its WSF sessions around its existing work on global inequality and tax havens (Interview 1073). With their extensive organizational capacity and established organizational priorities, leading INGOs may attend the WSF as much to teach as to learn.

Finally, while the WSF may be *the* place for the alter-globalization movement, it is only *a* place for leading INGOs. The rejectionist position that is the foundation of the WSF is itself rejected by many leading INGOs, as evidenced by their continued participation in the WEF in Davos. From 2013 to 2015, the heads of leading INGOs made multiple appearances there: three visits by HRW and two appearances each for Amnesty, Oxfam, Save the Children, the ICRC, and the International Food Policy Research Institute. Greenpeace, CARE, World Vision, CIVICUS, the Environmental Defense Fund, WWF, Islamic Relief, Plan International, and Habitat for Humanity have also had spots as featured speakers.[22] At the same time that World Vision advocacy and country staff members were hosting a number of events at the 2004 Mumbai WSF, they sent their leaders to Davos.[23] Leading INGOs may bemoan this choice, at least publicly. Writing as then head of CIVICUS in 2007, Kumi Naidoo (2009, 217) highlighted the group's regular participation at the WEF but said that "for me personally this is sometimes unfortunate, as my heart is usually not in Davos, but with the concurrent World Social Forum." Leading INGOs highlight their civil society roots, but their status depends on continued relationships with state and corporate elite.

Status and Strategy

The AC and WSF are collaborative INGO initiatives that draw from opposite ends of the authority spectrum. At each, INGO status determines the content of each group's efforts to define good practice. For the leading INGOs that dominate the AC, INGOs should develop and meet uniform standards while offering high levels of transparency. If implemented, this standard would reward formally organized and professional INGOs, which would allow them greater access to resources and perhaps higher levels of public trust. By contrast, the largely unknown INGOs that drive the WSF agenda argue that the heterogeneity of the INGO sphere is a strength, rather than a weakness, for groups whose responsibility should be the representation of excluded voices and resistance to those structures that create that exclusion in the first place. If successful, this competitive initiative would reveal how elite actors—including some INGOs— neglect human rights, poverty, and environmental degradation, and it would provide an alternate political vision that allows for more equal participation by numerous groups, particularly from the Global South.

Fifteen years on, neither of these contrasting visions has been particularly successful. In the next section, we explore the AC's efforts to silence external critics and the WSF's efforts to increase the influence of the powerless.

Some Vanilla, Even Less Victory

The AC and WSF are based on opposing but equally plausible political logics. The few AC members hoped that their club of leading INGOs would pressure other INGOs to adopt their benchmarks for good organizational practice and silence states and firms who question the accountability of INGOs. The AC is a standard that pleases a few external audiences and creates a "vanilla" outcome. The WSF founders hoped to challenge the lead actors in neoliberal capitalism through the collective resistance of a massive number of INGOs and activists. Both efforts fall far short of these goals. Neither the vanilla proposition from elite INGOs nor the ambitious attempts to empower the powerless have had much influence.

Silencing Critics and Defending Privilege

The AC seeks to achieve a "high standard of transparency, accountability, and effectiveness."[24] The particular standards of the AC are designed help leading INGOs demonstrate that they have a place at decision-making tables, in response to state and corporate critics. This is a defensive, competitive maneuver to validate the practices of member INGOs in the eyes of states and corporations rather than peers and beneficiaries.

Both as a gold standard and an umbrella standard, the AC developed particular reporting requirements for its members. Before doing so, the AC had to consider which audiences would be examining these reports, as certain indicators may be more or less important to each. For example, the formal complaints mechanism of an INGO might be of interest to government donors that want to encourage participatory development programs, but a private donor interested in sustainability might care more about an INGO's total greenhouse gas emissions by weight.[25]

The AC has formed partnerships with two initiatives that are familiar to corporations and state agencies. The first is the Global Reporting Initiative (GRI), a project primarily designed to enable reporting by corporations on environmental practices (Levy, Brown, and De Jong 2010). Because the GRI was an established framework with which corporations were familiar, INGOs (particularly environmental ones) that use the GRI have an easy answer when pressed by corporations to defend their own accountability (Interview 1039). In practice, INGOs find the GRI standards difficult to adapt for their own reporting. Many INGOs find even the reports on corporate procedures and reporting of little use, and INGO participation in the GRI process has declined markedly (Levy, Brown, and De Jong 2010, 103). The GRI emphasizes transparency over performance measures. As one subject described, an actor that reports its plans to blow up the world tomorrow would get high marks from GRI because it is being transparent (Interview 1036). By January 2014, the AC board of directors decided to move beyond some of the GRI requirements, and additional qualitative indicators of performance have been developed.[26]

The AC also works with the International Aid Transparency Initiative (IATI). Created in 2008 and largely financed by official donor agencies, IATI aims to increase the availability of data on foreign aid from public and private sources. The AC secretariat has been in discussion with IATI since 2011 and formally joined in 2014.[27] For AC members, IATI membership accomplishes two goals. First, it is a public demonstration of the members' commitment to transparency, protecting them from charges of hypocrisy as they push states to "publish what they fund."[28] Second, it also helps members meet the requirements of key donor agencies, many of whom are IATI signatories. The UK's Department for International Development (DFID), for instance, requires IATI reporting for the NGOs that receive funding, and a third of AC members have special funding agreements with DFID.[29] For the AC, a partnership with IATI helps members meet existing or future requirements, and the familiarity of IATI to donor agencies shortcuts the discussion of INGO transparency. Yet many INGOs, particularly smaller ones, have expressed concern about the high costs involved in IATI reporting, and only 125 INGOs reported data to IATI as of October 2013.[30]

Other possible stakeholders get less attention. For example, all INGOs pay tribute to the idea that "beneficiaries" are their most important stakeholders (Hammad and Morton 2011), and the AC claims to place primacy on "peoples (including future generations) whose rights we seek to protect and advance."[31] Yet critics argue that beneficiaries are "relatively powerless stakeholders" in the AC and do not receive the same attention as governments and donors.[32] The AC is also not designed for INGO staff and the general public. As one staffer reflected, "the audience we are writing this for, does that really exist? . . . None of the beneficiaries . . . are going to read it. Why the hell would they?" (Interview 1037). Charter members recognize that the AC "is not in any way in the public mind—or even within the sector, I think there are a lot of people that are not aware of it" (Interview 1028).

These efforts to satisfy external critics have had limited success, as the AC has low visibility and little brand recognition.[33] Yet members report that while governments and firms may not initially be aware of the AC brand, they are impressed by its requirements and its review mechanism (Interview 1028). If the AC does achieve greater prominence, this could actively disadvantage other INGOs, who fear the costs to them if official donors start to require AC membership (Hammad and Morton 2011, 16). This possible future for the AC shows that even vanilla victories come at some cost. An initiative that is widely palatable to external audiences may punish powerless INGOs that are either unable or unwilling to meet the bar defined by AC members.

Trying to Build a Platform for the Powerless

For the WSF to move beyond an agora and become a platform, the relationships and policy proposals developed there must have some staying power. The independent influence of the WSF has been limited to date.

First, the challenges of convening the annual events are substantial. From its inception, it has been an intentionally Southern-based network. Brazil has been a locus for WSF events and for the WSF's coordinating structures. By convening in Southern locales, the WSF attempts to overcome resource constraints or visa problems for participants (a goal evident in lengthy debates over whether the 2016 WSF should be in Montréal).[34] Yet limits on participation remain. The 2007 WSF in Nairobi, on a big continent with poor roads, saw only a few Africans, with most of the African participants dependent on major partners from the North to cover their travel expenses (Siméant 2013). In Caracas in 2006, the highway from the airport to the inland capital was closed, which turned a thirty-minute trip into one lasting a half-day or more (Hammond 2006). Montréal in 2016 faced fewer infrastructure-related challenges, but participation from the Global South was quite low.[35] In short, the WSF's locations have expressive and practical value, but WSF participants still face the mundane limitations of bringing together activists that lack resources.

Furthermore, the WSF seeks to include a diverse array of participants. Though civil society has a tendency to organize into formal organizations, the WSF seeks to be a forum of people rather than of big names (de Sousa Santos 2006). Yet big names and local elites are inevitably most capable of participating. For each event, the largest number of participants comes from the host country, and the bulk of participants are members of formal groups: trade unions, farmer's groups, indigenous associations, and NGOs (Rucht 2012). Poorer activists rely on Northern sponsors to fund their WSF participation. This almost automatically selects for individuals with French- or English-language skills, university degrees, and international experience (Siméant 2013), in short, the elite of the Global South. These elites are also better placed to exploit the opportunities of the WSF. In Dakar in 2011, for example, last-minute venue changes and water shortages had little impact on middle-class NGO professionals, but poor African women with no cellphones faced great challenges in regrouping (Scerri 2013).

Finally, it is difficult to discern whether attending WSF meetings has an independent effect on global networks. For instance, Siméant (2013) suggests that the WSF can be a key moment for African activists in a career of international work, but she finds that most WSF participants are already relatively privileged and internationally aware. The great majority of WSF participants in 2005 self-identified as "white" (Álvarez et al. 2008). Of those 2007 WSF participants surveyed by Kaneshiro, Lawrence, and Chase-Dunn (2012), more than 70% of those from the Global South were affiliated with an NGO with international scope. In short, they were already known to INGOs, which is likely how they learned about WSF to begin with. The greatest effect perhaps then is on the local activists in the host country for whom the WSF offers a chance to consider the international dimensions of their local concerns. Local participation in global justice events does not necessarily ensure continued movement activism, however, as Hadden and Tarrow (2007) show for the 1999 protests against the World Trade Organization.

Stiff Competition

INGOs differ in many ways, including their level of authority. This shapes what they each offer as visions for what INGOs "should" do. These are not deliberations among a community of equals (Risse 2000). Hierarchy exists both within the entire INGO community as well as within each collaboration. The AC mirrors and reinforces the existing distribution of authority, concentrated in the hands of a few. The WSF's decision-making structures privilege the weak in an attempt to equalize the gaps in authority between NGOs. Like challengers elsewhere, members of the WSF do not actually have the capacity to challenge the system, but they do articulate an alternate vision for their field (Fligstein and McAdam 2011).

These are contests among rival networks. Unlike conservative and liberal groups that compete over policy goals (Bob 2012), the members of the AC and WSF ostensibly share the same side of the political spectrum. They adopt varied strategic choices, however. Leading INGOs in the AC frequently collaborate with states and corporations, while WSF members challenge the very legitimacy of state and corporate power. These INGOs "remain unimpressed" by one another (Bob 2012, 30). INGOs may thus face their most challenging audience when engaging their peers, as this is the one audience where an INGO's principled commitments offer no special claim to authority. In addition to competing for funding and attention (Cooley and Ron 2002; Prakash and Gugerty 2010), INGOs compete to define the standards by which they should be evaluated.

INGOs adopt competitive strategies when facing one another, but the content of the initiative varies based on status. Leading INGOs selectively collaborate with less-powerful INGOs, and they do so on their own terms, asking smaller groups to meet the particular AC standards or paying for less fortunate groups to attend the WSF. Some collaboration with other INGOs may be necessary for leading INGOs, insofar as it helps them demonstrate their "roots" in civil society and gives them special access to information that then reinforces their gatekeeper status. By contrast, other INGOs engage in higher levels of inter-INGO collaboration. This is largely out of necessity, but such collaboration may end when the moderate policy position of leading INGO partners threatens their own principled commitments. Some INGOs active in the AC and WSF have chosen a middle path between the powerful and powerless. One such INGO is CIVICUS, which views itself as a conduit between INGOs of different capacities that will strengthen civil society more generally.[36] Such an INGO, positioned as a "broker" (Goddard 2012), acts as a bridge between leading and other INGOs, but such inclusivity limits its ability to expand its authority with external audiences.

The vanilla victories leading INGOs achieve with other audiences are perhaps most subject to criticism from INGO peers. The hierarchy that exists within the INGO community is not legitimate for those at the bottom. Unfortunately, their attempts at competition are limited by their low status, where they have little access to resources and no audience for their claims.

The Tricky Business of Condemnation

In the introductory chapter, we characterized competition as a strategy where actors largely share the same goals but differ on tactics. This is not always the case, as INGOs can differ on the goals themselves. Yet our examination of the cases above suggests that condemnation of other INGOs is rarely employed by leading INGOs.

The idea that INGOs offer harsh proclamations of states' and corporations' behavior is not news; their "naming and shaming" and protest activities are familiar (Bandy and Smith 2005; Sasser et al. 2006; Hafner-Burton 2008; Soule 2009; Krain 2012; Murdie and Davis 2012b). Condemnation is antagonistic and can involve colorful displays of people, slogans, and a variety of stunts to make a point, as when Sea Shepherd chases down illegal whaling vessels in the Antarctic, or when Amnesty International places two hundred body bags on the beach to highlight the plight of migrants across the Mediterranean.[37] A popular stereotype of INGOs expects them to express dissatisfaction with the world by making noise to express their opposition.

Such condemnation strategies are dangerous when deployed against INGOs ostensibly working for the same cause. Airing the dirty laundry of the INGO community risks undermining the reputation of INGOs as defenders of the public good and is a challenge to their authority. Evidence of divisions among INGOs can restrict the political access of all INGOs, as happened in climate change governance when faced with competing INGO networks (Hadden 2015). Moreover, assaulting another INGO's inconsistencies or funding problems leaves one's own record open for condemnation.

For other INGOs relying on the political or financial support of their more powerful peers, condemnation risks alienation. Still, challengers with little authority may have less to lose. At the WSF, leading INGOs are targeted by the WSF even while they make the WSF possible. In the first five years of the WSF, critical financial resources were provided by large Western INGOs, including Oxfam, Action Aid, CAFOD (a British Catholic development NGO), CCFD, Christian Aid, and MISEREOR and EED (two German church-based relief groups) (de Sousa Santos 2006). During this period, support from these INGOs totaled 4.6 billion USD and accounted for 30% of the WSF's average total income.[38] Yet the large presence of these prominent INGOs in Mumbai in 2004 and Nairobi in 2007 sparked criticism of the "NGO-ization" of the WSF and led to a renewed emphasis on privileging grassroots groups (Gautney 2012; Pleyers 2012).

In addition, the recognizable brands of leading INGOs are natural targets for other activists seeking to change broader agendas. When then Oxfam ambassador Scarlett Johansson endorsed the SodaStream drink dispenser in January 2014, pro-Palestinian activists decried Johansson's support of a company operating in the West Bank. A group tried to deliver a ten-thousand-signature petition to Oxfam America's offices in Washington DC and Boston.[39] Such public condemnation used the celebrity status of both the actress and the NGO to draw attention to the Israel-Palestine issue. This was not the first time Oxfam had been publicly criticized by its partners: Southern activist Walden Bello publicly criticized the reformist orientation of Oxfam's Make Trade Fair campaign (Mertes and Bello 2004; Reitan 2007).[40] Leading INGOs are often castigated, as in articles titled "how Glo-Bono-Phonies and Trojan Horse NGOs sabotage the struggle against neoliberalism" (see also Wallace 2009).[41] Of course, such attacks on brand-name INGOs need not only come from the left. Over the past decade, Canadian Patrick Moore has used his story as a "Greenpeace dropout" to offer a broad critique from the right of climate science and activism.[42] For sympathizers and skeptics, the high status of certain INGOs makes them more likely targets for condemnation.

Leading INGOs are well-positioned to call out their ideological opponents. When they publicly call out their like-minded peers, however, they risk looking petty and defensive. For these groups, it is easier to ignore their critics than to engage them. The literature on leading INGOs as gatekeepers supports the idea that apathy is an easier response. This is not always the case, as evident in the heated back-and-forth between Kenneth Roth and Neera Chandhoke over the tactics of Human Rights Watch (Bell and Coicaud 2006). Overall, however, at both the AC and WSF, there is not substantial public condemnation of specific INGOs. Our interpretation of this finding is that while condemnation can serve as a form of leverage politics in influencing other actors, it is a dangerous strategy when directed at INGO peers. For leading INGOs in particular, the public condemnation of a sympathetic INGO endangers their claim of working for the public benefit rather than organizational self-interest. Leading INGOs may be self-critical behind closed doors; as one AC board member quipped, while member INGOs may have global operations, "round the board table . . . we are often still too 'pale, male, and stale.'"[43] Such statements are an acknowledgment of the concerns of external critics, but they are also sentiments rarely aired in public.

When interacting with other audiences, INGOs benefit from the presumption that they have principled commitments. That presumption led many early INGO analysts to celebrate the potentially transformative role of these groups and to gloss over disagreements among INGOs. Since then, practitioners and scholars have shown that collaboration is difficult in the face of substantial differences. We bring to that conversation the important role of status in shaping inter-INGO politics.

Like all other actors, INGOs collaborate and compete with one another (with occasional condemnations). Multi-issue, leading INGOs have a large megaphone with which to promote their strategies, but they can be outflanked by more radical groups (Warleigh 2000) dedicated to very different ideals. INGOs create competing visions of what is good practice for all INGOs. The AC and WSF are two examples of INGO collaborations that do just that. Leading INGOs adopt different strategies from other INGOs because they have political access and media attention. Perhaps even less than for corporations, however, these different strategies are unlikely to yield a division of labor. The basic political purpose of INGOs and the methodologies they should employ are long-standing questions within global civil society, and there is no consensus.

In choosing strategies, both leading and other INGOs are caught in the authority trap. Leading INGOs' status-maintenance activities may look like cooptation to other INGOs, but those peers lack an audience to hear their claims. For leading INGOs, the authority trap works differently when the target is other INGOs. Unlike other audiences, INGO peers have similar principles and claims to expertise, so leading INGOs must *earn* deference from other INGOs. Securing authority before other INGOs is important to bolster their standing before other audiences. Meanwhile, other INGOs may be well-regarded by their peers, but they still face the mundane problems of scarce resources and disparate concerns. Ultimately, the limited success of the AC and the WSF speaks to the fragmentation of INGOs that make up global civil society.

AUDIENCE-BASED AUTHORITY IN POLITICS

More access does not always yield more influence. As we argue in this book, authority can create both opportunities and problems for INGOs. Most INGOs do not enjoy deference from the actors that determine global policy or shape social practices. A few groups secure deference from multiple audiences to become leading INGOs, but they then face a new set of challenges in balancing the competing views of those audiences. Pleasing these audiences requires reconciling disparate values and priorities. The authority trap discourages those that have the biggest megaphone from choosing more radical visions and incentivizes them to moderate their claims.

These dynamics lead to "vanilla victories," or changes that yield only incremental improvements but are widely palatable and often not particularly satisfying to anyone involved. These least-common-denominator solutions to social problems become boilerplate strategies that INGOs turn to time and again. The authority trap catches leading INGOs by encouraging compromise out of necessity. Other INGOs, not weighed down by the same kinds of audience concerns, can really push the boundaries of the status quo, but their voices are rarely heard. Ensnared in the authority trap, they face incentives to join forces with leading INGOs *if* they want to make global change, but this will likely water down their proposals. Some turn away from this and choose to work with a narrow set of audiences at a local or national level. Others shun the pursuit of authority in global politics altogether.

This is a depressing story for those whose hopes for social and political change rest on NGOs. Yet there is reason to think that the authority trap is not inevitable, even if it is likely. The trap ensnares INGOs in their strategic *choices* and provides disincentives to put their reputation on the line or to embrace radical proposals. This does not mean that INGOs cannot move out of the trap. While the authority trap constrains INGO choices, it does not determine them. Some of the reluctance may hinge more on INGOs' perceptions of what audiences want rather than actual audience preferences. At times audience preferences may be either more fluid or more amenable to radical propositions, which can create opportunities for leading INGOs to push further in their policy asks.

Our book argues against popular and academic accounts of INGOs as small, determined social change agents that drive big changes to the status quo. Many leading INGOs themselves reinforce this mythology with their David-and-Goliath origin stories. We have come to expect big things from these little INGOs. Yet some INGOs are big and far from bold. As INGOs have proliferated in number and achieved unprecedented political access, our expectations of INGOs need to change as well. The authority trap highlights the constraints on leading INGOs in choosing how to act and what to demand. Still, vanilla victories are still victories and are much more than other INGOs could achieve, given their lack of authority.

There are some remaining questions regarding the effect of the authority trap. The three preceding empirical chapters explored INGO relations with a wide array of audiences, and we begin this chapter with a synthesis of those insights into how authority shapes INGO strategies. Next, we explore the limits of the authority trap. While the trap is compelling, it is not inescapable. The campaign for an International Criminal Court exemplifies collaborative and confrontational campaigning by leading and other INGOs. It is particularly noteworthy for the scale of INGOs' accomplishment, and it also shows how leading INGOs can creatively exploit different preferences of their many audiences. We then consider how the careful study of the authority of particular actors can improve our understanding of global governance and politics through a short discussion of other nonstate groups that seek authority across multiple audiences. We end the book with an appeal for more attention to the many differences among INGOs, particularly their authority. The authority trap requires more attention from scholars and practitioners interested in INGO effectiveness and influence. Ultimately, those seeking to escape the trap themselves must first acknowledge its existence.

The Authority Trap and Strategies for INGOs

In the previous three chapters, we illustrated a variety of choices faced by leading INGOs and other INGOs. In their relations with states, corporations, and their peers, leading INGOs adopt different strategies than their peers because of their status-maintenance concerns. Below we summarize these strategic choices and highlight the divide between leading INGOs and other INGOs.

INGO status shapes each individual group's choices to collaborate, condemn, and compete. Collaboration requires that actors and their targets share goals and broadly agree on strategies. Competition occurs when actors might share ultimate goals but disagree on the proper means to achieve them. Condemnation arises when an INGO disagrees with its targets' means and ends. While an INGO's tactics on any one issue might be shaped by many factors, authority is an enduring concern that shapes the choices of other INGOs and leading INGOs.

Other INGOs

The strategies of other INGOs largely fit the popular conception of brave little civil society actors. Except for an occasional mention in a newspaper editorial or rare mention by a policymaker, however, their actions go unseen. They are liberated from the constraints faced by leading INGOs, but they are also missed by the spotlight. Below the radar of various global audiences, their scope of action is greater. They do not have to default toward moderate strategies that satisfy multiple audiences. If they are radical, they do not temper their radicalism. The authority trap holds other INGOs back from being heard.

Many INGOs regularly use condemnation and employ a more antagonistic approach toward states, corporations, and leading INGOs. Other INGOs have nothing but their principles, and it is critical that they call out those whose tactics are questionable or who are not true defenders of the principled cause. For example, the People's Movement for Human Rights Learning, a New-York based INGO that has some authority with UN officials, has been particularly vocal in calling for a "worldwide dialogue of transforming the patriarchal world order," a sweeping and provocative condemnation.[1] Other INGOs thus take on "their own" and claim a greater principled legitimacy than leading INGOs have. The value of democratic representation can favor these other INGOs if they have evidence that leading INGOs have ignored their cause (Bell and Coicaud 2006). As the case of the WSF illustrates, however, it is difficult to translate these provocative criticisms into concrete collective action plans that can attract the attention of policymakers and other audiences.

Competition—in the form of different priorities or new rules—may be employed for those other INGOs seeking to offer a new or better approach, but it is rarely viable for those INGOs that exist in obscurity. For example, the UK-based group Karenaid (one of the groups in our random sample) claims to fill a gap left by other actors in providing medical assistance and ophthalmic aid to refugees along the Thai-Burmese border. Occasionally, collective groups of otherwise unknown INGOs can present a substantial challenge to leading INGOs, as in Copenhagen in 2009. The Climate Justice Now! (CJN) group challenged the Climate Action Network (CAN) at the Convention of the Parties for the United Nations Framework for Climate Change (Hadden 2015). The CJN, formed by Friends of the Earth (FoE) and justice-oriented groups, consciously took up more confrontational tactics than the insider strategies traditionally employed by CAN (led by World Wildlife Fund (WWF), Environmental Defense Fund (EDF), and Greenpeace) (Hadden 2014, 10–13). One asset that may have helped this coalition gain attention was the participation of FoE, a leading INGO (see chapter 3). Other INGOs' attempts at competition are inhibited by their low visibility.

Other INGOs can collaborate with states and corporations if they have gotten some attention from their target, but without other supporters, other INGOs might be seen as sellouts, which would make it difficult to move from one close relationship to widespread authority. Other INGOs, for example, cannot challenge the requirements of government funders (Bush 2015), whose large grants are attractive but whose strict reporting requirements limit INGO agency. Multinational corporations get no credit for working with unknown INGOs, so other INGOs are generally left out until the implementation phase of private governance initiatives. When it comes to leading INGOs, other INGOs may envy the attention a few well-known peers enjoy and may be tempted to market their causes to these gatekeepers (Carpenter 2007; Bob 2005). This collaboration comes at a cost, however. In the case of the FTT, the goals of the campaign shifted substantially from a direct challenge to neoliberal capitalism to a small levy raising funds for global development. While collaboration with leading INGOs can open doors, other INGOs' ideas get watered down in the process.

Leading INGOs

In working to draw attention to a particular cause, it is good to be on top. Leading INGOs do not need to *prove* their value to their audience. Still, these INGOs must avoid alienating that audience. Thus, as our case studies show, confrontational condemnation is not a "go to" strategy for leading INGOs. Condemnation can create a reputation for being disagreeable, which can spill over to other audiences. Compared to other civil society activists, leading INGOs use condemnation selectively against states and corporations, and rarely against fellow INGOs. With states and corporations, INGOs that adopt condemnation risk the relationships they have built. The deference that leading INGOs have secured can come with political access or financial support, which reinforces leading INGOs' incentives to collaborate (e.g. Edwards and Hulme 1996). As with other INGOs, leading INGOs that condemn their peers undermine their claim to be working on behalf of shared principles. Because leading INGOs often benefit from the need of states and corporations to listen to "the INGO perspective," condemning other INGOs raises dangerous questions about divisions among INGOs and the representativeness of the big groups. Thus, unless the INGO in question is on the opposite side of a political question (Bob 2012), apathy and ignorance is a safer option than condemning INGO peers.

Leading INGOs collaborate with states and corporations more than their peers do, but not automatically, as their authority also rests on demonstrating some level of independence. One way to manage this tension is to pressure some states while working with middle-power states, as in the FTT, ATT, land mines ban, and cluster munitions campaigns. Leading INGOs working with middle-power states gain access to important decision-making venues but avoid looking like shills for governments. With corporations, leading INGOs are, like all INGOs, split on the desirability of "greenwashing." If most other INGOs favor condemnation and independence, increasing numbers of leading INGOs favor collaboration when they are given the chance, even Greenpeace. The two cases in chapter 5 show that leading INGOs, after launching collaborative efforts at private governance with corporations, then struggled with questions of whether to remain. Leading INGOs have left the TSC and UNGC. Collaboration is also used less frequently in relations between leading INGOs. They seek to differentiate their "products" from those of other INGOs, and they create narrow limits on their collaborative projects. Leading INGOs also need to claim credit for discernible achievements, a need that can impede the construction of robust but flexible networks among INGOs.

Competition is a strategy that leading INGOs adopt most frequently with other INGOs and corporations, but not with states. This has more to do with the environment: the widespread authority of states in rule making, service provision, and enforcement means that these may be tasks that INGOs take on only in the absence of state capacity. As described in the introductory chapter, a leading INGO like MSF has no interest in presenting itself as challenger to states, but rather as an imperfect substitute for effective and equitable state authority. With corporations and other INGOs, leading INGOs are both capable of and interested in private governance, and they introduce initiatives that reinforce their leading status.

In sum, status shapes INGO strategic choices. In some ways, all INGOs face similar obstacles: they are reliant on outside sources of funding, they must fight for access to governance institutions, and they benefit from assumptions of their principled purity. Yet there are pressures that discourage collaboration among INGOs to address these shared concerns. Leading INGOs worry about their reputations, while other INGOs view their peers as overly conciliatory. Instead of laying the foundation for a coherent global civil society, INGOs move in vastly different circles depending on their status. Leading INGOs rub elbows with economic and political elites at the World Economic Forum in Davos, while other INGOs at the WSF struggle for convening spaces in Senegal and have to pay for bottled water in Kenya. Each group ends up privileging the concerns of those whom they court, and the result is fragmentation.

The authority trap determines INGO choices, but not necessarily their influence. This is not a case of building a better mousetrap; leading INGOs might make radical demands and collaborate effectively with other INGOs but still have no guarantee of success. Sometimes, just poor timing dooms these efforts, as in the case of the FTT coalition that announced its launch on the morning of September 11, 2001. Still, if assessments of INGO influence involve looking for both whether change happened as well as the degree of change, the authority trap shows that more authority does not automatically yield greater influence. Structural constraints, whether real or anticipated, shape the behavior of leading INGOs in a profound and consistent way.

Escaping the Authority Trap

The concept of the authority trap explains how agents choose strategies, given structural constraints. It is not a deterministic account of how structure causes outcomes. Some strong tendencies motivate INGOs, but INGOs occasionally avoid the authority trap. There is hope for transformative change from leading INGOs in cases that have proven exceptions to the vanilla victory rule.

Sometimes the authority trap is inactive, and leading INGOs can promote and achieve radical change. The establishment of the International Criminal Court (ICC) is a notable example. The ICC has fundamentally changed international law regarding serious violations of humanitarian norms and human rights. It was also never supposed to emerge, given the vocal opposition of some of the most powerful states in the world (Deitelhoff 2009). The Rome Statute establishing the ICC came into force within four years of its signing in 1998, and there are currently 124 state parties to the statute. This is a sea change in the conflict between norms of noninterference in the domestic affairs of sovereign states and of individual criminal accountability in the case of egregious rights violations (Schabas 2011). While the ICC may be useful in domestic political contests (Simmons and Danner 2010), the court is more than the result of a happy coincidence of interests among member states, and its impact goes far beyond the individual cases prosecuted at the ICC (Helfer and Voeten 2014; Kelley 2007). The fact that states created a global court in which to try individuals is a substantial victory.

The idea of a global tribunal can be dated back to the Nuremberg and Tokyo trials after World War II (Bassiouni 2015), but NGOs played a critical role in the creation of the ICC in the late 1990s. Amnesty International and the World Federalist Movement organized a meeting in early 1995 at which a coalition was founded, with a self-appointed steering committee that also included FIDH (the leading French human rights group), Human Rights Watch, the International Commission of Jurists, and the Lawyers' Committee for Human Rights (today known as Human Rights First) (Glasius 2002; Barrow 2004). These six groups recruited many more members into what became the Coalition for the ICC (CICC),[2] but these six retained a "dominating role" (Glasius 2002, 147) in a coalition that would ultimately grow to 2,500 members.

As in other cases discussed in chapter 4, a coalition formed between INGOs via the CICC and middle and smaller countries (Deitelhoff 2009). INGOs involved themselves in the promotion of the cause of the ICC and later in monitoring the enforcement of those statutes, working so closely with states that personnel were exchanged (Törnquist-Chesnier 2004). For example, the former Amnesty International representative to the United Nations, Andrew Clapham, served as the representative of the Solomon Islands at the Rome Statute negotiations. INGOs also took a front seat in determining some of the key elements of the Rome Statute that established the ICC. The CICC pushed for automatic jurisdiction, gender-related crimes, intervention in civil wars, and at one point universal jurisdiction (Kirsch and Holmes 1999). Amnesty raised the issue of the need for an independent prosecutor to bring cases before the court and argued that the ICC should have jurisdiction over internal conflicts (Struett 2008). The policy recommendations of a 1996 Human Rights Watch paper were all incorporated into the final statute (Struett 2008). Leading INGOs thus played direct roles in shaping the scope and instruments of the ICC, though the additional support of other INGOs was also crucial.

Why were the leading INGOs that campaigned for the ICC able to escape the authority trap? The ICC is a perhaps rare example of loose structural constraints and the convergence of several facilitating conditions. First, widespread public support was not critical for the Rome Statute, though it was helpful in places. For the public audiences that leading INGOs like Amnesty International depend on, the idea of a global criminal tribunal was not a new one. The post–World War II tribunals, the Yugoslavia tribunal, and the recent genocide in Rwanda provided global publics with a basic understanding of the concept and suggested a need for punishing war criminals. A *New York Times* editorial from November 21, 1994, argued simply that it was "time for a Global Criminal

Court." There is little polling data on public attitudes toward the ICC and other international courts (Voeten 2013). Still, the lack of public opposition, combined with stunts like the "lie-in" of thousands of Amnesty International supports outside the Colosseum during the Rome Statute negotiations, may have created the political space for elected state officials to negotiate and sign the ICC, even if ratification remained problematic in some places.[3] Second, the preferences of powerful states were mixed: the United Kingdom was supportive, France was hesitant but ultimately ratified the Rome Statute in 2000, and the United States offered substantial objections to the court (Busby 2010). Leading INGOs could thus use the support of middle-power states and a few powerful states to push an ambitious set of policy proposals. Additionally, leading INGOs, particularly those dependent on deference from US policymakers, were able to exploit political openings within the United States. There was no single preference of the United States toward the ICC; the State and Justice Departments were supportive while the Department of Defense and some powerful senators were opposed (Busby 2010). This created space for leading INGOs. For example, in September 1995, two Human Rights Watch staffers publicly called on President Clinton to endorse the ICC at the coming UN General Assembly meeting.[4] While Clinton avoided the subject at the UN General Assembly, he did seem to endorse the ICC at an October commemoration of the fiftieth anniversary of the Nuremburg trials, a fact that Amnesty International recounted in detail in its 1996 Annual Report.[5] In the Rome negotiations in 1998, the United States was ultimately more concerned about the court's scope than its existence (Scheffer 1999). Finally, the ICC is ambitious but also narrow; it covers a very few (albeit heinous) crimes.

Even in these favorable conditions, however, the CICC could have fallen apart due to competition among leading INGOs, a problem that has plagued many NGO campaigns (Cox 2011). Several analysts attribute the productive and cordial relationships within the CICC to one man, William Pace, head of the World Federalist Movement (Benedetti, Bonneau, and Washburn 2013; Welch and Watkins 2011). The WFM had "a long history" of working on global justice institutions, and Pace and Christopher Hall of Amnesty hosted a "very relaxed" first meeting (Welch and Watkins 2011, 966). Pace's experience, commitment, and "self-effacing nature," combined with the fact that WFM was "perceived as small, neutral, and non-threatening by smaller NGOs, in particular those from 'southern' or 'developing' countries," allowed the coalition to grow and encouraged HRW and Amnesty to cooperate (Welch and Watkins 2011, 969, 976).

In this window, leading INGOs could make big demands that seemed to have little chance of alienating multiple audiences (for a similar claim in the case of the landmines ban, see Shurtman 2008). Leading INGOs did *not* ask for a vanilla victory, and states actually settled on something that went beyond what one might have expected, given resistance from a number of powerful and/or authoritarian countries. In fact, the starting point for the ICC negotiations was more conservative than what became the Rome Statute (Deitelhoff 2009, 36–38). Timing and individual personalities thus help explain leading INGOs' choices. The authority trap can open to allow leading INGOs to use their widespread authority to achieve ambitious policy changes. Other INGOs can help their peers prepare for those moments. But we should be wary of exceptions that rely on timing; timing is rarely on the side of actors seeking change. Similarly, collegial and expert personalities are critical for coalition work, but many campaigners at leading INGOs might lack one or the other on any one particular issue.

The ICC created by the Rome Statute was a thus much stronger institution than the authority trap logic would predict. In practice, the ICC has not yet lived up to its potential for a number of reasons. The United States attempted to circumvent ICC authority under the George W. Bush administration (Birdsall 2010), though it later became more supportive. The ICC is not yet a "court of last resort" (Fairlie 2011), and political balancing between different stakeholders prevents a clear, universal approach to various cases (Roach 2011; Bassiouni 2006). Meanwhile, financial insecurity persists for the court (Hawkins 2008), and it faces ongoing accusations that it is a biased court intent on shaming African leaders.[6] That it is contested is perhaps evidence of its ambition; if it were a vanilla victory, states would offer vague statements of support or would ignore it altogether.

Also important, the ICC case shows that structure is not static or uniform. As we know from agent-structure debates in political science, as much as structure constrains agents, agents play a role in how structure is constructed and perpetuated. What might have seemed impossible may depend less on structure than on audiences seeing mutual gains for taking radical action. We see some evidence in this regard in the strategies pursued by INGOs working on the ATT and FTT: they pursue middle-power states and are more creative in the venues in which they seek policy change. Clearly this is an attempt to work within structural constraints, but in so doing INGOs and their state partners have altered patterns of global treaty negotiations. In the ICC, leading INGOs could have been discouraged by the low public profile of the proposal. Instead of *anticipating* audience disapproval, groups like HRW and Amnesty drew upon their extensive expertise and their political acumen to advance a radical innovation in global justice institutions.

Still, moderation may be part of the organizational makeup and strategy of leading INGOs, particularly as they have grown over time. Many leading

INGOs are complex global conglomerates of national-level sections, each with its own constraints and capabilities. Leading INGOs may face internal incentives to prefer the status quo. A more critical perspective is that leading INGOs have an interest in maintaining the status quo precisely because of their status within the existing establishment (Dauvergne and LeBaron 2014). Depending on where you sit, moderation might be pragmatic or it might be self-interested, or both.

Audience-Based Authority Beyond INGOs

Authority extends well beyond states to the many actors involved in global governance. Our framework draws attention to how authority might be conferred by different audiences with diverse preferences. The authority INGOs enjoy is based on their particular qualities. While we do not claim that authority is conferred on other actors by the exact same audiences and for the same reasons, our claims about the process of authority construction and maintenance apply to other actors.

The authority trap may operate well beyond the INGO world. First, recall that the scope of actor A's authority may be narrow or broad. Actor A may receive deference from audience B, and there may also plausibly be audiences C, D, and E before whom A not have any authority. Second, more authority before more audiences creates more constraints. Compare actor A that has authority before B to an actor X that has authority from B, C, D, and E? Assuming that B, C, D, and E are not carbon copies of one another, the distances among them will limit X if she wants to maintain authority before all of them; this will drive her to move toward some "middle" between all their values and preferences. Authority relationships are specific, but generally speaking, authority boils down to claims to authority by actors and the audiences that defer (or not).

Authority constrains as much as it might enable. This should alter the way scholars study INGOs and many other actors. For example, studies of INGO influence often suffer from selection on the dependent variable by looking at cases where INGOs "get what they want" and then studying the process by which they achieved such a victory. These victories should be considered partial versions of proposals advanced by other INGOs. Authorities, be they INGOs or states or corporations or any other actor in global politics, need to maintain deference from their audiences. The more audiences to which they are known, the bigger the challenge they face. Status as a leading INGO is as much a burden as it is a strength. It takes work to be an authority before a single audience, and much more so when multiple audiences are involved.

The focus on audiences travels beyond INGOs and raises important questions about the limits of power and authority. In international relations, a foundational assumption from Thucydides is that "the strong do what they can and the weak suffer what they must." More material resources increase an actor's influence, an idea that seems commonsense. But these assumptions, even for states, are problematic. A rising state like China suffers from the effects of limited deference. In the summer of 2015, low global investor confidence in Chinese markets led to massive stock market bailouts by the government and private actors.[7] A lack of transparency creates questions about the organizing principles of China's market, which challenges the authority of the Chinese government as capable or legitimate. In security, nuclear arsenals have become a liability as the perception of the utility of nuclear weapons has reversed, and North Korean and Iranian forays into nuclear development have been met with resistance and derision. Neither is seen as commanding more authority as a result of their purported developments.

Great capacity does not necessarily yield great influence. Material resources might give actors the access to audiences they might not otherwise have, but having "more" is not a guarantee of audience deference. In the wrong context, wealth can undermine an actor's authority. Wealthy INGOs with well-compensated managers become suspect as defenders of the public good. Russia used its resources to impersonate peacekeepers, painting their vehicles the same white as those of the United Nations and adopting blue helmets (Hurd 2002). These substantial material resources were not welcomed as contributions to peacekeeping and arguably harmed to Russia's authority. The method used is as important as material capacity.

Of course, extending the authority trap to other actors must be undertaken with care; each actor claims a different basis of authority. For example, some have compared INGOs to domestic interest groups and other political actors (Bloodgood 2011; Naím 2002). For membership organizations like trade unions and the National Rifle Association, their claim to authority rests on a different principle than that of INGOs. Membership organizations primarily serve to represent the preferences of those memberships, though they may couch their demands in language about the greater good. The legitimacy of their participation in politics rests on principles of representation. Most INGOs are not member services organizations. Their authority derives from their claims to first promote "public benefit" activities, even if they also promote member concerns or protect their own self-interest. The authority of any actor in global politics is shaped by social expectations of what that group should be doing. Trade unions are *supposed* to protect laborers. NGOs are *supposed* to protect the public interest. Within these broad social expectations, particular audiences have additional values and preferences that shape how they receive an actor's claims.

To demonstrate the wider potential of our approach, we suggest ways our argument informs current attempts to construct theories of global governance. We then apply our framework to violent nonstate actors.[8]

Global Governance

Global governance is an increasingly preferred term for discussing the outcomes of global politics. Governance "encompasses the activities of governments, but it also includes the many other channels through which 'commands' flow in the form of goals framed, directives issued, and policies pursued" (Rosenau 1995, 14). Because governance is fragmented beyond nation-states, analysts struggle to capture the multiplicity of actors, the factors that facilitate participation, and the norms that shape which nonstate actors participate and how (Castells 2008; Hall and Biersteker 2002; Scholte 2011b; Avant, Finnemore, and Sell 2010; Smith and Wiest 2012; Lake 2010; Weiss and Wilkinson 2014).

Our research offers a few insights toward these efforts. First, global governance may be less crowded than analysts assume. The opportunities for increased participation are not equally distributed. Divisions among Southern and Northern groups exist but may not be the most salient (Smith and Wiest 2005; Smith 2002); status may be more important. As demonstrated in chapter 3, even among the *most likely* to get attention, only a tiny fraction of INGOs do. This should come as some relief to those daunted by the prospect of theory building to capture tens of thousands of INGOs.

Second, this concentration of authority suggests that INGOs are unlikely to correct for the democratic deficit at IGOs or for poor governance by states. Other INGOs are rarely able to reach the powerful, and when they do, leading INGOs take the lead and often moderate their claims. Leading INGOs serve their audiences more than they channel others' grievances. Global governance is designed and maintained by leading states and leading INGOs, and their preferences receive attention at the expense of others.

Third, the strategies global governors employ may be shaped by their own authority traps. Many otherwise excellent treatments of IGO authority equate an increasing scope of IGO work with greater influence (Barnett and Finnemore 2004; Zürn et al. 2012). Our research on INGOs highlights that working across increasing numbers of issues involves relations with more audiences. More audiences can mean less room for organizational-level choices that serve the mission, creating the sort of pathologies that IGO scholars have identified.[9] States, IGOs, corporations, and INGOs may all be inhibited from paying attention to the functional requirements of any one particular issue because of their individual concerns over status maintenance. More optimistically, the need to continually prove relevance may drive these actors to tackle emergent issues and in the process inform their audiences' preferences.

Authority requires deference from audiences and can constrain strategic choices. This framework travels beyond the world of INGOs. Does Canada or Saudi Arabia have authority? With whom do they have it and how it is used? Do Exxon and the North Face have varying levels of authority when they speak about climate-related issues? Even if states and corporations derive their authority in part from their material capacities, we should still consider the same questions that we ask about Amnesty International and the World Future Council.

Violence by Nonstate Actors

Global governance is a broad topic, and many actors involved in global governance seek to reinforce the stability of a system that is run by states and serves Western liberal values. By contrast, violent nonstate actors reject parts or all of such a system. Our conception of audience-based authority is still useful for these very different actors.

Research in political science on terrorism suggests that groups are strategic in their use of violence (Pape 2009). The logic of audiences is inherent in the use of violence as a strategy; terrorists are always trying to appeal to *somebody*, whether their signal is being sent to governments or civilians (Kydd and Walter 2006). Terrorists generally pursue a social or political goal, through violence, that is different from the status quo. Groups that use terror hope to create conditions under which civilian targets begin pressuring their governments to change their policies (Sandler 2011). Terrorists may resort to violence because their positions are so distant from the mainstream that they are unlikely to find support without resorting to techniques that force the issue (Crenshaw 1995). Using this logic, democracies are more vulnerable to domestic terrorism as a method, whether suicide terror (Pape 2003; Wade and Reiter 2007), when there is intergroup competition for government attention (Chenoweth 2010), or as groups compete with one another in an attempt to "outbid" rivals (Bloom 2005). Others have added to this insight, claiming, for example, that terrorist groups in Afghanistan and Pakistan have had to be discriminating in their targeting for fear of losing support from traditional bases of rural support (Johnson 2009). Poor democracies with "inconsistent institutions" also seem susceptible to terrorist activity (Chenoweth 2013), as competing audiences emerge from gaps in governance. In states lacking absolute repression but also lacking resources to govern effectively, officials and citizens constitute two (or more) entirely different audiences for potential terrorists.

For both violent groups like terrorists and nonviolent private groups like INGOs, audiences shape their strategic choices. This pushes back against the tendency to separate nonstate actors that use violence from INGOs. Technically, global groups that use violence are INGOs: they are nonprofit, operate in multiple countries, and serve broader principles. While their strategies and tactics certainly differ, both must construct status as "an authority" in the eyes of one or more audiences, and they may receive instrumental deference from many more. Both violent nonstate actors and INGOs generally lack delegated authority or authority based on an institutional position. Both seek to influence states, but direct state support can undermine their status as an authority. They exist outside conventional political processes, and this independence forms the basis of their legitimacy for many of their supporters. Both types of actors seek affirmation for their activities as well as the tangible benefits of monetary and in-kind support. For INGOs and for violent groups, the public can serve as a recruitment ground.

One objection to the comparison is that violent groups intentionally target members of the public in the process of attaining their goals. But some critics make the same argument about INGOs, that they unintentionally or intentionally disrupt local populations through their work (Simmons 1998; Barber and Bowie 2008). INGOs are not easily held accountable by the populations they serve, and this tension can result in open conflict (Holzer 2015).

Violent international nonstate actors engage at least two audiences—the target government(s) and people in their home society—while affecting the public in the target state. But unlike INGOs, violent nonstate actors are not concerned with deference from those target audiences. Violent groups tend to coerce those audiences, though they select or deselect violence to reshape their audiences' expectations and influence peace negotiations, as was in the case in the Israel-Palestine peace process from 1993 to 2001 (Kydd and Walter 2002). Meanwhile, in the eyes of those who see violent activities as legitimate resistance, violence must still be strategically used rather than adopted as blanket resistance. Any one violent group like ISIS, for example, "seems to tailor attacks for different audiences," as violence in predominantly Muslim nations can endanger the group's legitimacy.[10]

There are important differences between INGOs and violent nonstate actors; to take the comparison too far one way or the other misses the point. Rather than saying INGOs and violent groups are equivalent, the discussion above highlights the shared concerns of nonstate actors that must create and maintain authority.

Our theoretical framework suggests some initial interesting insights beyond INGOs, and others may do much more using our perspective to examine other actors engaged in global governance. This book forges a path toward broader attempts to conceptualize authority in global governance. Like others working in this space, we leave behind the presumption that states are the primary subject and offer a method that may be applied to other kinds of actors engaged in global politics.

INGOs have the potential to become an authority in global politics. A very few have widespread authority in the eyes of many audiences. Yet for INGOs and other actors, authority can constrain as well as enable. The authority trap shapes the type of influence that INGOs achieve and likely does the same for other types of actors as well. Deep and comparative understandings of the authority of various actors should yield new insights into global authority, even if a unifying theory remains elusive. There is no "best practice" for INGOs seeking global political and social influence. Some strategies will easily reach certain audiences and yield minor but real changes. Other strategies might challenge audiences' expectations but reshape the political landscape.

Authoritative INGOs, like all authoritative actors, should be called to account for their choices. Global actors who repeatedly opt for safe, cooperative approaches may disappoint their compatriots and supporters. This also might be the least bad option if such compromise keeps the door open for INGOs at global governance institutions. For those engaged in these battles inside INGOs or within communities of activists, we hope this book hammers home a point while also providing ammunition in those struggles. The authority trap is formidable, but it is not inescapable.

SAMPLING PROCEDURES AND LIST OF INTERVIEWS

This appendix provides more specific information on the data compiled and analyzed in this book. In the first part of the appendix, we provide additional detail on the data from chapter 3. In the second section, we list the interviews we conducted by interview number, organization, and date, and then we separately list the organizations represented in those interviews.

Chapter 3 Data

As explained in chapter 3, we used new and existing data sets to explore the experiences of an "average" NGO and of most likely leading INGOs. In this section, we provide more details on the data employed. First, we explain the construction of the random sample. Second, we provide the specific data on most likely leading INGOs. Third, we list the INGOs in the random samples.

Random Samples

A random sample draw from the global population of INGOs would be of limited use in particular contexts; there is no reason to expect that an INGO working in India, South Africa, and Indonesia would seek authority from the US Congress. To select those organizations likely to seek authority with powerful global audiences, we looked to several places. The random sample referenced in the first half of chapter 3 contains 215 organizations from the United Nations (29), the United States (46), and the United Kingdom (140).

First, we drew a sample from the group of NGOs holding consultative status with the United Nations Economic and Social Council (ECOSOC). Murdie (2014) uses the many levels of UN ECOSOC status as a signal for potential partners and funders of the INGO's underlying motivations. We use it as a signal of an interest in influencing global politics. In September 2010, 171 INGOs held what is called general consultative status. These organizations have sought and received the highest access to the United Nations, which we interpret as explicitly intended to influence global policies. Our UN sample numbers 29 organizations and includes groups such as the Association of Medical Doctors of Asia, CIVICUS, Soroptimist International, and the World Federation of UN Associations.

We also drew random samples of INGOs headquartered in Britain and the United States, and later from Canada (more below). INGOs headquartered in the first two countries accounted for more than 20% of the 55,853 INGOs counted by the Union of International Associations (UIA) in 2010 (Anheier, Kaldor, and Glasius 2012, 20). In 2013, there were more than 8,000 internationally oriented charities in the United States, and more than 3,000 based in the UK.[1]

The data on INGOs is gathered differently in each country. In the UK, the key regulatory agency, the Charity Commission of England and Wales, provided upon request (June 2014) a comprehensive list of all charities (2,794) that operate overseas on issues related to health, poverty alleviation, famine relief, environmental conservation, economic development, and human rights. This number is slightly lower than that reported by the Union of International Associations (UIA); we rely on the national agency rather than the UIA. From this list, we drew a sample of 140 organizations (5%). This is truly random, drawn from multiple sectors and from large and small organizations. The task is more difficult in the United States. The NCCS gathers comparable information on charitable organizations, but a comprehensive list of internationally oriented nonprofits is not publicly available. Instead, we use the charities evaluated by Charity Navigator (CN), a private ratings agency. As of February 2014, CN produced reports on about one-fifth of all charities in the United States (working on both domestic and international issues).[2] It is one of the most prominent charity rating agencies in the United States, and its ratings systems shape broader organizational practices within the charitable sector (Lowell, Trelstad, and Meehan 2005). Charity Navigator only evaluates charities that receive more than $500,000 annually in private donations, so our sample is skewed toward the larger organizations, which are most likely to have the capacity to reach multiple audiences. This sample is helpful in identifying the leading INGOs, but it is biased upwards as a baseline for assessing INGO authority in general. Following the categories used in the UK, we identified 894 organizations rated by Charity Navigator and active in international and environmental affairs. The US tax code does not have a specific category for international environmental charities, but a search of CN yielded a list of environmental charities with international or global activities. Our sample includes 46 organizations (5%).

We constructed the Canadian sample in subsequent iterations of the project, particularly once confronted with the limitations of the UK's historical record of parliamentary proceedings. The Canada Revenue Agency provides information for all registered charities in Canada (more than 80,000). We selected the organizations active in one of ten categories (social structure (B1), infrastructure development (B2), agriculture (B3), medical services (B4), education (B5), disaster/war relief (B6), nature/conservation (G1), species preservation (G2), environmental protection (G3), human rights (H12)), and then selected those organizations conducting overseas activities. From that pool of 743 organizations, we drew a random sample of 37 organizations (5%).

Many INGOs have names that are easily confused with common phrases (for example, the groups named Empower and CARE are difficult to separate from other usages of those words). For these groups, we searched for the name in combination with the word "international." This may undercount the number of mentions for a handful of organizations. Other organizations go by multiple names. Thus, we searched multiple terms for organizations like Human Rights Watch (including HRW and the many regional watch committees that preceded the unified organization name in 1988) and Médecins Sans Frontières (including MSF and Doctors without Borders).

Measuring Standing among Most-Likely Leading INGOs

The values in the table below were used to generate the rankings in table 3.1 and the visualizations in figures 3.1 and 3.2. The numbers need to be interpreted with care. For example, as described in the text, the value of the number provided by Google Trends is meaningless except as a point of comparison; it is standardized and normalized relative to all other Google searches in a particular time period. The financial data should also be interpreted carefully. We selected for the largest INGOs across three sectors, but the average size of a "large" organization is quite different across the sectors and across countries. HRW's income of $67 million USD in 2014 appears negligible beside the relief and development groups, while the French human rights group FIDH suffers by comparison to HRW (with a budget of around $8 million USD). We thus did not choose a numerical cutoff point in selecting "large" INGOs. In addition, some INGOs do not have total counts of their global income. For INGOs that have an asterisk (*) next to the income data, we present their US income only as gathered from their annual financial information reported to tax authorities (IRS 990 forms). Finally, the ranges of each data set are different. For reference, the range of the network data

TABLE A.1 Raw scores for most-likely leading INGOs

NAME	2004–2014 AVERAGE STANDING IN WEEKLY GOOGLE SEARCHES[a]	2010–2012 MENTIONS IN GLOBAL MEDIA[b]	1970–2013 MENTIONS AT US CONGRESS[c]	2001–2013 MENTIONS AT CANADIAN PARLIAMENT[d]	2001–2002 INGO NW[e]	2006/08 MENTIONED AS EFFECTIVE[f]	FOUNDING YEAR[g]	2014 EXPENSES ($USM)[h]
Action Against Hunger	0.00	273	27	1	5	1	1979	108
ActionAid	0.84	1666	25	2	*	2	1972	281
Amnesty International	13.91	14047	3076	838	85	8	1961	291
BRAC	4.77	523	6	0	*	0	1972	612
CAFOD	0.50	470	3	1	28	0	1962	77
CARE International	1.32	4640	159	70	25	16	1945	626
Carter Center	0.63	1099	331	1	*	0	1982	206
Catholic Relief Services (CRS)	0.40	390	608	1	22	10	1943	649
Christian Aid	2.08	1681	3	4	41	1	1945	136
CIVICUS	0.00	49	0	0	51	0	1993	3
Compassion International	1.13	108	10	0	*	1	1952	710
Conservation International	0.18	487	265	0	4	3	1987	130
EarthAction	0.00	21	0	0	121	0	1992	0.1
Environmental Defense Fund	0.07	615	1789	2	3	2	1967	127
FIDH	0.28	183	9	2	36	1	1922	8
Food for the Poor	0.04	205	21	0	0	3	1982	913
Freedom House	1.41	1502	1120	7	6	1	1941	34
Friends of the Earth (FoE)	1.65	5323	1620	55	36	2	1969	6*
Greenpeace	17.42	9202	757	279	27	1	1972	318
Habitat for Humanity	15.47	1857	1378	45	24	3	1976	256

Handicap International	0.80	194	21	4	*	0	1982	146
Heifer International	1.11	349	23	2	*	5	1944	123
Human Rights First (HRF/LCHR)	0.00	368	587	0	15	2	1978	12
Human Rights Watch (HRW)	6.13	13519	3019	148	40	5	1978	67
International Campaign to Ban Landmines (ICBL)	0.00	54	21	3	97	0	1992	4
International Commission of Jurists (ICJ)	0.00	707	137	18	46	0	1952	9
International Committee of the Red Cross (ICRC)	3.24	3457	1998	169	57	5	1863	1201
International Council of Voluntary Agencies (ICVA)	0.00	4	5	1	44	0	1962	2.6
International Institute for Environment and Development (IIED)	0.00	239	35	0	43	0	1971	26
International Planned Parenthood	0.01	2459	187	32	38	1	1952	125
International Rescue Committee	0.30	405	367	1	*	7	1933	553
International Union for Conservation of Nature	2.80	452	216	10	96	0	1948	104
Mercy Corps	0.68	258	171	0	4	6	1979	279

(Continued)

TABLE A.1 (Continued)

NAME	2004–2014 AVERAGE STANDING IN WEEKLY GOOGLE SEARCHES[a]	2010–2012 MENTIONS IN GLOBAL MEDIA[b]	1970–2013 MENTIONS AT US CONGRESS[c]	2001–2013 MENTIONS AT CANADIAN PARLIAMENT[d]	2001–2002 INGO NW[e]	2006/08 MENTIONED AS EFFECTIVE[f]	FOUNDING YEAR[g]	2014 EXPENSES ($SUSM)[h]
MSF/Doctors without Borders	3.06	2383	296	77	24	6	1971	1156
Oxfam	12.49	9803	366	140	128	12	1942	992
Physicians for Human Rights	0.00	465	235	2	7	1	1986	7
Rainforest Action Network	0.00	69	20	1	8	3	1985	5
Reporters with Borders (RWB)	0.18	2557	149	12	8	0	1985	5
Rotary International	2.01	890	81	41	18	3	1905	259
Salvation Army	37.97	8771	2135	246	16	3	1865	3471*
Samaritans Purse	0.54	226	65	13	*	3	1970	476
Save the Children	6.03	8057	474	53	85	8	1919	2000
World Vision	9.32	3417	510	97	*	24	1950	2809
WWF/World Wide Fund for Nature	1.82	3060	853	89	*	6	1952	2359
MAXIMUM VALUE for each indicator	37.97	14047	3076	838	128	24		128

Sources: (a) Google Trends, September 2015; (b) Lexis/Nexis database, last updated January 2016; (c) Proquest Congressional database, October 2015; (d) Parliament of Canada website, www.parl.gc.ca, July 2014; (e) Murdie and Davis 2012a; (f) TNGO Initiative Survey (research supported with funding from NSF Grant SES-0527679, TNGO Initiative, and Moynihan Institute of Global Affairs, Syracuse University) and Mitchell and Stroup 2016; (g) INGO websites; (h) INGO annual reports.

from Murdie and Davis (2012a) is 0 to 185 (for CONGO, the Conference of NGOs in Consultative Relationships with the UN), and the range for the effectiveness mentions data is 0 to 24 (for World Vision). The maximum value for each indicator is shown in the bottom row of table A.1.

INGOs in the Random Samples

UN ECOSOC-registered INGOs

Adventist Development and Relief Agency

Asian Legal Resource Centre

Association of Medical Doctors of Asia

Association for Progressive Communications

Association tunisienne des mères

Centre de recherchés et de promotion pour la sauvegarde des sites et monuments historiques en Afrique

CIVICUS: World Alliance for Citizen Participation

Conference of Non-Governmental Organizations in Consultative Relationship with the UN

Environmental Development Action in the Third World

Foundation for the Support of the United Nations

Friends World Committee for Consultation

Good Neighbors International

International Council on Social Welfare

International Council of Voluntary Agencies

International Higher Education Academy of Sciences

International Planned Parenthood Federation

International Social Security Association

International Trade Union Confederation

Liberal International

New Humanity

Organization of Islamic Capitals and Cities

Oxfam International

Soroptimist International

World Blind Union

World Confederation of Labour

World Confederation of Productivity Science

World Economic Forum

World Federation of United Nations Associations

Youth for Unity and Voluntary Action

US-based INGOs

1000 Friends of Oregon

Absolute Return for Kids US

American Academy in Berlin

American Friends of the Hebrew University

American Technion Society

Amigos de las Américas

As You Sow

Blessings International

Cerge-Ei Foundation

Childcare Worldwide
Clean Ocean Action
Coalition Against Trafficking in
    Women
Direct Relief
Earth Conservation Corps
EMpower
Environmental Defense Fund
Family Legacy Missions
    International
Friends of the Earth
Friends of Women's World
    Banking (FWWB)
Gleaning for the World
Haiti Outreach
Hope for Haiti
IDEX
International Campaign for Tibet
International Institute of Rural
    Reconstruction (IIRR)
International Rivers
KickStart International
The Korea Society
MedShare International

The Mountain Institute
National Strategy Information
    Center
North Cascades Institute
Operation Bootstrap Africa
People for Care and Learning
Public Employees for
    Environmental Responsibility
The Resource Foundation
The Rotary Foundation of Rotary
    International
Sanibel-Captiva Conservation
    Foundation
Soles4Souls, Inc
Torah Schools for Israel
Trailnet
TreePeople
Volunteers for Inter-American
    Development Assistance
Wildlands Network
World Affairs Council of Northern
    California
The Zakat Foundation of America

UK-based INGOs

Achisomoch Aid Company
    Limited
AE Evangelistic Enterprise Ltd
Africa Advocacy Foundation
Africaid
Aid India Forum
Al-Hijrah Trust
Alternative for India's
    Development
Anchor of Hope Christian
    Fellowship
Anglo-Italian Society for the
    Protection of Animals
Ashby Hastings Rotary Club Trust
    Fund

The Ashridge (Bonar Law
    Memorial) Trust
Association for Relief and Medical
    Aid
Avraham Yitzchak Gluck
    Charitable Trust
Bader International Study Centre
The Barretstown Gang Camp Fund
    Limited
The Biochemical Society
Bioproduct Healthcare Foundation
The Bishop Simeon CR Trust
    Incorporating the Living South
    Africa Memorial
Bishopston Kuppam Link

The Blues and Royals Association

Bread of Life Ministries

The Britain—Nepal Otology Service

British Friends of Mifal Chesed Trust

British Friends of Tzidkath Yoseph Naphtali

The British Institute of Archaeology at Ankara

British Lichen Society

The Bubble Foundation UK

Budiriro Trust

The Cadbury Foundation

The Calcutta Tercentenary Trust

Care for the Wild International

Chevras Mo'oz Ladoe

Childaid to Russia and the Republics

Christ Life Mission Church Trust

Church of God (7th Day) Trust

COCOA—Care of China's Orphaned and Abandoned

The Commonwealth Lodges Association Benevolent Fund

Community of St. Mary the Virgin at Wantage

Cosmetic Toiletry and Perfumery Foundation

The Council for British Archaeology

David John Cohen Charitable Trust

The Donald Mackay Trust

Educational Book Exhibits Limited

The Edward Sharp Memorial Trust

The Eldon Charitable Trust

Elijah Tabernacle

The Endangered Wildlife Trust

The English Sector of the Congregation of Working

Sisters of the Holy House of Nazareth

Eurovision Mission to Europe

Eye on the Wild

Fellowship of St. John Trust Association

Francisco Rojas School Trust

The Friends of St Anne's Hospital Liuli

The Friends of Urambo and Mwanhala

Friends in the West International

Gateshead Aid to the Forgotten Children of Chernobyl in Nova Kakhovka

Giving Hope to Children of the World

Griot Foundation Trust

The Handmaids of Mary Trust

The Harrison Zoological Museum Trust

Help My People International

The Holly Hill Charitable Trust

Human Welfare International Charitable Trust

The Huntingdon Foundation Limited

The Hyman Cen Foundation

Imperial Society of Knights Bachelor

Inner Wheel Club of Feltham Benevolent Fund

Intract Charitable Trust

Iraqi Women Association Fund

The Irish Genealogical Research Society

Iris Ministries Limited

ISTD Benevolent Fund

Jamaica Hospitals League of Friends

John and Nathaniel Carter

The Joseph and Mary Hiley Trust
Karen Relief and Development Fund
The Karuna Trust
Kenilworth-Uyogo Friendship Link
The Kenyan Orphan Sponsorship Trust
Kings Church Bolton
The Labone Charitable Trust
Lady Harriet Bentinck Trust Fund
The Leswyn Charitable Trust
Linden Church Trust
The Lodge of Asaph Benevolent Fund
Maluju—South African Artists for Peace
Margaret Hayman Charitable Trust Fund
Martin Shaw King Trust
The Mary Elizabeth Brooke Fund
Medical Missionary News Fund
The Melik Society
Mitsubishi Corporation Fund for Europe and Africa
The National Council for the Conservation of Plants and Gardens
The Nepalese Children's Medical Trust
New Fellowship Trust
New House Trust
The North Nibley Team
The Oliver Charitable Foundation
The Oxford Down Sheep Breeders' Association
Partnership in Action
The Partnership Trust
The Peter Spencer Trust

Revival Life Ministries
Ridgesave Limited
Roman Catholic Purposes in Connexion with the Missionary Convent of the Holy Rosary
The Romanian Aid Fund Limited
Romanian Emergency Aid and Community Help (REACH)
Rotary Club of Bath West Trust Fund
Rotary Club of Coventry Phoenix Charity Fund
Rotary Club of Stokesley Trust Fund
Rotary Club of Streatham Trust Fund
Rotary Club of Welshpool Trust Fund
Royalheath Charitable Trust Limited
The Royal National Lifeboat Institution
The Royal Naval Bird Watching Society
Saiva Munnetta Sangam
Sally and Douglas Shaw Charitable Trust
Saltlic
The Save the Children Fund
Sears Group Trust
Selwyn Trust
The Shipwrecked Fishermen and Mariners' Royal Benevolent Society
Sisters of the Cross and Passion
The Sobell Foundation
The Society for the Protection of Animals Abroad

The Society for the Relief of
Distressed Jews
Somali Welfare Centre
Starlight Children's Foundation
St Giles Trust (Chalfont St Peter)
The Strathspey Charitable
Trust
Tarajni Trust
The Third World Trust

Udichi Shilpi Gosthi
The United Society
Welfare and Relief for Under
Privileged Children in India
Westnell Nursery Society
The William Walton Trust
Women of Praise
World Orthopaedic Concern UK
The Yavari Project

Canadian-based INGOs

Bishop Denis Croteau
Development Foundation
Bracelet of Hope
Camp Uganda Conservation
Education Society
Canada-Mathare Education Trust
(CMET)
Canadian Council of Dr Graham's
Homes
Centre de Nutrition Bon Secours
Bahon
Centre de Solidarité Internationale
Corcovado Inc.
CHF
Chinese International Missions
(Canada)
Cuban Community Relief
Organization
Darfur Diaspora Association
Erdo Foundation
Evangelical Mission to
Ukraine
Extreme Response Canada
Fondation de-la-Salle
Fondation Semafo/Semafo
Foundation
Fontaine Children's Charity
Foundation

Foundation for Open
Development
Foundation for Sustainable
Enterprise and Development/
Fondation pour L'Entreprise et
Le Developpement
Lotus Outreach Society Canada
Machik Canada
Masomo for Children
Nicaragua Children's Foundation
The Ojars Veide Scholarship Fund
Ottawa Valley Aid for Chernobyl
Children
Rayjon Share Care of Sarnia Inc.
Réseau en traide solidarité
monde
ROF—Kingdom Children
Rotary Club of Alliston Charitable
Fund
Schoolbox Inc.
Societe Formons Une Famille Inc
Stand As One Ministry
Touching Tiny Lives Foundation
Tumaini Children's Foundation
Waladi Child Education Fund of
Toronto
Walk Without Fear Foundation
Zerf Productions

Interviews Conducted

Our interview subjects were all offered anonymity. Some chose to be identified and their names appear in the text. The table below provides basic information on the other interviews referred to in the text by interview number. We offer limited information on each subject's organizational experience or background. In the subsequent section, we offer a separate list of the organizations represented by our interview subjects.

TABLE A.2   Interview numbers by organizational experience and date

INTERVIEW NUMBER	EXPERIENCE IN TYPE(S) OF ORGANIZATION	DATE(S) INTERVIEWED
1001	INGO	January 2015
1002	INGO	January 2015
1003	INGO	January 2015
1004	INGO	January 2015
1005	INGO	January 2015
1006	INGO	January 2015
1007	NGO	January 2015
1008	INGO, corporation	February 2015
1009	INGO	February 2015
1010	INGO, corporation	February 2015
1011	INGO	January 2015
1012	INGO	February 2015
1013	Think tank	May 2014
1014	INGO, think tank	May 2014
1015	INGO, think tank	May 2014
1016	INGO, researcher	June 2014
1017	INGO	May 2014
1018	INGO	May 2014
1019	Think tank	February 2014
1020	Government, researcher	November 2013
1021	Researcher	May 2014
1022	INGO	May 2014
1023	Think tank	May 2014
1024	INGO	May 2014
1025	INGO, think tank	March 2014
1026	INGO	January 2012
1027	INGO	August 2014
1028	INGO	May 2014
1029	INGO	January 2014
1030	INGO, researcher	October 2013
1031	INGO	May 2014
1032	INGO	May 2014

INTERVIEW NUMBER	EXPERIENCE IN TYPE(S) OF ORGANIZATION	DATE(S) INTERVIEWED
1033	INGO	February 2014
1034	Researcher	May 2014
1035	INGO	April 2014
1036	INGO	May 2014
1037	INGO	May 2014
1038	INGO, think tank	May 2014
1039	INGO	May 2014
1040	INGO	May 2014
1041	INGO	May 2014
1042	INGO	August 2014
1043	INGO	May 2014
1044	INGO	February 2015
1045	Corporation, INGO, researcher	February 2015
1046	INGO	January 2015
1047	Media	February 2015
1048	INGO	April 2015
1049	Corporation	February 2015
1050	Government	February 2015
1051	INGO	February 2015
1052	INGO	January 2015
1053	Corporation	January 2015
1054	INGO	December 2014
1055	NGO, corporation	February 2015
1056	Corporation	January 2015
1057	INGO	March 2015
1058	INGO	February 2015 (2x)
1059	INGO	March 2015
1060	INGO	April 2015
1061	Corporation	April 2015
1062	Government	June 2015
1063	INGO	June 2015
1064	INGO	August 2014
1065	Government	August 2015
1066	Other	August 2015
1067	INGO	September 2010
1068	INGO	November 2011
1069	INGO	July 2009
1070	INGO, researcher	May 2014
1071	INGO	December 2014
1072	INGO	March 2016
1073	INGO	August 2016
1074	INGO	August 2016
1075	INGO, researcher	September 2016

Organizations Represented by Interview Subjects

350.org
ActionAid
Amnesty International
Article 36
Bridgespan Group
CARE
Catholic Relief Services
Christian Aid
Control Arms Campaign (CAC)
Ecologia
Environmental Defense Fund
Focus on the Global South
Forest Stewardship Council
Freedom House
Future500
Global Public Policy Institute
Global Reporting Initiative
Greenpeace
Human Rights Watch
IANSA
Institute for Development Studies
Institute for Policy Studies
InterAction
International Civil Society Center
INTRAC
Landmine and Cluster Munition
   Monitor
May First/People Link
The Nature Conservancy
Nature Means Business
NOREF (Norwegian Center for
   Conflict Resolution)
Norwegian Foreign Ministry
Overseas Development
   Institute
Oxfam
Plan International
Project Ploughshares
Public Policy Association
Reputation Partners
Save the Children
Seventh Generation
Stamp Out Poverty
The Sustainability Consortium
Transparency International
United Nations Institute for
   Disarmament Research
United States Agency for
   International Development
Walmart
War on Want
WEED
World Economic Forum
WWF

Notes

1. THE AUTHORITY TRAP

1. Nick Paumgarten, "Magic Mountain: What Happens at Davos?" *New Yorker*, March 5, 2012.

2. For a longer discussion of this literature, see Stroup and Wong 2016.

3. For example, the director of CARE was found guilty of grand larceny in the early 1980s, and CARE later restructured to appear less American. "Ex-Chief of CARE Gets Year in Jail," *New York Times*, February 25, 1981; Stroup 2012. Greenpeace came under fire in the Brent Spar case and recently for gross insensitivity to cultural artifacts in Lima. Risse 2010; "Greenpeace Identifies Four Suspects Linked to Protest at Famed Nazca Lines Site," *Guardian*, January 20, 2015.

4. The NGO was formerly named the International Human Rights Law Group. http://www.globalrights.org/indexng.html#, accessed April 7, 2016.

5. Nobel Lecture by James Orbinski, December 10, 1999. Available at http://www.nobelprize.org/nobel_prizes/peace/laureates/1999/msf-lecture.html.

6. Thanks to Patrick Thaddeus Jackson for pointing out the analogy.

7. John Vidal, "From the Amazon to Chicken Nuggets," *Guardian Weekly*, April 14, 2006, 19.

8. Tobias Webb, "Does It Pay to Get into Bed with Business?" *Guardian*, February 25, 2005.

9. Other human rights INGOs have pursued these strategies. Two prominent examples of INGOs that have tried these strategies are Global Rights and the Center for Victims of Torture.

10. http://esango.un.org/civilsociety, accessed April 9, 2016.

11. http://csonet.org/index.php?menu=17, accessed April 9, 2016.

12. Even quiet or limited work is not impact-neutral. The resources and advice that service delivery INGOs supply to recipient countries alter internal political relations.

13. "Embattled Aid Charity Changing Name and Leaving Washington," *Chronicle of Philanthropy*, January 28, 2016.

2. AUTHORITY AND AUDIENCES

1. https://www.theguardian.com/society/2016/mar/03/cholera-haiti-un-experts-chastise-ban-ki-moon, accessed February 13, 2017.

2. This is admittedly circular: status indicates quality, which informs status. This circularity does not pose much of a problem for us; we are not investigating how INGOs achieve high status but rather how differences in authoritative status shape INGO strategy and influence.

3. We also briefly consider public opinion and the media in chapter 3, as they can serve as leverage for INGOs seeking to influence states, firms, and peers.

4. http://www.edf.org/approach/partnerships, accessed September 16, 2014.

5. http://www.npr.org/blogs/goatsandsoda/2014/06/11/321051040/its-all-about-the-girls-is-the-world-listening-to-them, accessed September 16, 2014.

6. http://www.patagonia.com/ca/patagonia.go?assetid=3351, accessed July 29, 2015.

7. We are grateful to David Lake for pointing this out.

8. "A Litmus Test for Kurdistan," *New York Times*, September 30, 2014; "UN to Send Investigators to Iraq over Islamic State 'Atrocities,'" *Guardian*, September 1, 2014. Amnesty has critics, but the fact that its reports get disputed further demonstrates how it commands attention. See NGO Monitor from the right (http://www.ngo-monitor.org/) and critical views from the left (http://www.theguardian.com/commentisfree/2012/nov/11/nick-cohen-is-amnesty-fit-fight), accessed September 18, 2014.

9. See http://www.marcgunther.com/sustainable-business-from-the-bottom-up/ and http://www.rare.org/about#.Vp6S9FMrJR4, accessed January 19, 2016.

3. THE EXCEPTIONAL NATURE OF INGO AUTHORITY

1. http://www.edelman.com/insights/intellectual-property/2014-edelman-trust-barometer/about-trust/executive-summary/, last accessed April 4, 2016.

2. http://www.edelman.com/assets/uploads/2014/03/2001-Edelman-Trust-Barometer.pdf, last accessed April 4, 2016.

3. These policy settings also have global importance, and the relationships between the private and public sectors in these countries may serve as models in other institutional settings. For elaborations of this argument for both for-profit and nonprofit actors, see Farrell and Newman 2010; Reinalda 2015.

4. This follows a frequent distinction in studies of reputation between being known, on one hand, and being known for something or being seen favorably on the other. See Lange, Lee, and Dai 2011.

5. Oxfam's average score was 11.9, WEF was 1.6, and FoE was 1.1. Throughout the search, we used United Nations as an index term to standardize the comparison, as Google Trends only allows users to search five terms at a time.

6. Average score for NGO was 45 during that eleven-year period, and in 2008 it became a more frequent search term than United Nations.

7. The three samples draw from different pools, and the UK sample is a true random sample (see appendix). UK-based INGOs had an average of 59 mentions in global media from 2012, compared to 393 for the UN and US sample. When we reran our analysis excluding the UK, we had fewer organizations with zero mentions but still a skewed distribution of media attention; 10% of the sample received 94% of the mentions.

8. The average age of sample INGOs in 2012 was thirty-seven.

9. Witness appearances among the UN-registered INGOs were rare, only six in the thirty-three-year period covered here. Predictably, US-based INGOs fare better than the UN groups in congressional appearances; the US-based sample had an average number of ninety-four full-text mentions, compared to twenty for the UN sample.

10. There were 169 INGOs in this random sample, which included the original 215 minus the 46 US-based INGOs. The NGO names were searched in the historical Hansard database, which runs up only to 2005. For the years 2005 through 2013, we entered the following into the google search bar: "inurl:cmhansrd site:www.publications.parliament.uk" (for the House of Commons) or "inurl:ldhansrd site:www.publications.parliament.uk" (for the House of Lords), before the organization name in quotes.

11. There were a total of 326 mentions of the 29 INGOs in the random sample.

12. That average was twenty-seven. The Murdie and Davis list does not capture seven of the twenty-nine groups in our random sample.

13. The five sectors are environment, human rights, humanitarian relief, sustainable development, and conflict resolution.

14. "The Transnational NGO Study: Rationale, Sampling and Research Process." *TNGO White Paper*, last updated January 2010 (http://www.maxwell.syr.edu/moynihan/tngo/Data). Many thanks to George Mitchell for help with this data.

15. The entry of so-called B ("benefit") corporations is a recent challenge to the demarcation between principled actors and corporations. See https://www.bcorporation.net/, accessed April 10, 2016.

16. Thirty-seven (5.3%) were mentioned two or three times. The remaining 636 organizations were mentioned only once. O'Connor and Shumate (2014) argue that these are largely local groups.

17. Authors' calculations. Thank you to Michelle Shumate for sharing the original network file.

18. For example, *Foreign Policy* magazine, the *Global Journal*, and *Charity Navigator* have lists of the top ten or one hundred groups, developed according to an often opaque methodology. One frequently used term is "BINGO" (big INGO) to describe these groups. See "BINGOs: The Facts," *New Internationalist* 383 (October 2005).

19. Because norms of appropriateness vary for INGOs across different national settings, the same INGO may receive deference from one audience while being rejected by another. See Tarrow 2005; Busby 2010; Stroup 2012.

20. We drew from INGOs that were founded in the US, UK, and France but now operate globally. The earliest available data comparable across countries comes from 2003 (Stroup 2012). We also included BRAC as the largest INGO based in the Global South.

21. Relief and development groups account for perhaps two-thirds of the total INGO population in the United States, according to the National Center for Charitable Statistics (see appendix).

22. The raw count data we present does not adjust for INGO age. We reordered the INGOs according to mentions/age in 2013, but the results were not substantively different in terms of rankings. A few relatively young organizations do stand out: HRW (86 mentions/age), AI (59), EDF (38), Habitat (37) and FOE (36.8), making their status as established authorities even more impressive. Second, the IRC, IUCN, and Save the Children look less like contenders when controlling for their age. Oxfam is a hard case. Oxfam GB was established in 1942 but Oxfam America was founded in 1970. If we count the later date, Oxfam is still a contender for authority in the eyes of Congress, but a weak one.

23. We risk a tautology here, as we used connectedness to construct the original most-likely leading INGO sample. Only 20% of that sample was chosen because of their high number of incoming ties.

24. The International Union for the Conservation of Nature and IIED were not included in environmental NGOs examined in the study.

25. We lack INGO networking data for WWF and World Vision, but both were reported as effective by US-based peers in the TNGO survey.

4. TARGETING STATES

1. https://www.amnesty.org/en/latest/news/2015/07/india-accountability-still-missing-for-human-rights-violations-in-jammu-and-kashmir/; http://www.environmentalleader.com/2015/07/02/gri-launches-new-tools-services-for-reporting-companies/; "US $374 Million for Fight Against AIDS, TB and Malaria," *Agencia de Informacao de Mocambique* (English), July 1, 2015.

2. See appendix for details about the interview subjects.

3. That group included Argentina, Australia, Costa Rica, Finland, Japan, Kenya, and the UK.

4. https://www.amnesty.org/en/latest/news/2014/12/global-arms-trade-treaty-enters-force/.

5. http://www.ceedweb.org/iirp/camnet.htm.

6. See, for example, a report from a meeting at Friends of the Earth's offices in Washington, DC, in March 1999, https://www.globalpolicy.org/component/content/article/216/46035.html.

7. http://dealbook.nytimes.com/2013/02/06/time-to-revive-the-financial-transaction-tax/?_r=0.

8. http://www.telegraph.co.uk/finance/6522135/US-Treasury-Secretary-Timothy-Geithner-slaps-down-Gordon-Browns-global-tax.html.

9. "FAQs on the Financial Transactions Tax," Institute for Policy Studies, January 2015, available at http://www.ips-dc.org.

10. https://www.oxfam.org/en/pressroom/reactions/hollande-and-merkel-miss-opportunity-robin-hood-tax-need-rethink-path; http://www.reuters.com/article/2015/07/08/eu-axidUSL8N0ZO1YC20150708, all accessed April 26, 2016.

11. https://euobserver.com/economic/131435, accessed April 26, 2016.

12. A search of full-text news publications indexed by LexisNexis, using search terms "currency transactions tax," "financial transactions tax," "Robin Hood tax," and "Tobin tax."

13. http://www.foe.org/news/archives/2013-04-robin-hood-comes-to-congress.

14. "The Arms Trade Treaty: 'Towards Entry into Force'." High-level event, September 25, 2013, UN General Assembly, http://www.mofa.go.jp/policy/page3e_000086.html, accessed July 14, 2015.

15. See Foreign and Commonwealth Office press release, "Arms Treaty Enters into Force," December 24, 2014, https://www.gov.uk/government/news/arms-trade-treaty-enters-into-force, accessed August 20, 2015.

16. http://www.international-alert.org/name-series/biting-bullet, accessed February 11, 2016.

17. See "The UK's Role in the UN Arms Trade Treaty," *Civil Service Quarterly* (blog): https://quarterly.blog.gov.uk/2013/07/12/the-uks-role-in-the-un-arms-trade-treaty-2/, accessed August 20, 2015.

18. For example, see letter from Sens. Jerry Moran and James A. Inhofe to President Barack Obama, September 25, 2014. http://www.moran.senate.gov/public/index.cfm/files/serve?File_id=4ba67ddb-e92b-4863-aebe-30e45e22ad78, accessed August 20, 2015.

19. Larry Elliott, "UK Opposition to Financial Transaction Tax Rejected," theguardian.com, April 30, 2014.

20. George Zornick, "Financial Transactions Tax Introduced Again—Can It Pass This Time?" *The Nation*, February 28, 2013.

21. http://www.ceedweb.org/iirp/camnet.htm, https://www.globalpolicy.org/component/content/article/216/45910.html/.

5. INGOS AND CORPORATIONS

1. http://www.greenpeace.org/international/en/news/features/coca-cola-to-champion-our-cool/; http://www.theguardian.com/sustainable-business/blog/unilever-labour-practices-vietnam-oxfam-report; http://www.theguardian.com/business/2013/may/09/save-the-children-teams-up-glaxosmithkline, all accessed April 26, 2016.

2. After a critical exposé in 2003, the Nature Conservancy restructured its board and developed a conflict-of-interest policy to demonstrate its independence, even though that move reduced its influence with corporations (Bertels, Hoffman, and DeJordy 2014, 27). The Environmental Defense Fund has long worked directly with leading American corporations, but it publicizes that it does not accept funds from its current partners. https://www.edf.org/approach/partnerships/corporate-donation-policy, accessed February 1, 2016.

3. Of course, they might also improve corporate performance; we assume those sorts of efforts need little encouragement from INGOs. See Soule 2009.

4. In fact, all the examples in Yaziji and Doh (2009, 129–35) of benefits for corporations are of leading INGOs, including MSF, WWF, Amnesty, Greenpeace, and FoE.

5. See Edward Alden, "Brands Feel Bite from Protesters," *National Post* [Canada], July 18, 2001. Global Witness also later left the Kimberley scheme in 2011.

6. "African Nations Work Together to Rid Supply Chains of Conflict Materials," *The Guardian*, September 14, 2015.

7. Wageningen University and Nanjing University have since been added as "leading academic institutions" in the TSC. See "The Sustainability Consortium Selects University Partner in China and Appoints China Director," https://www.sustainabili tyconsortium.org/consortium-news/the-sustainability-consortium-selects-university-partner-in-china-and-appoints-china-director/, accessed February 14, 2017.

8. http://www.greenbiz.com/blog/2013/04/15/game-why-walmart-ranking-suppliers-sustainability, accessed March 10, 2015.

9. Christopher Matthews, "Can Walmart (and Other Mega-Corporations) Do Good?" TimeBusiness.com, January 6, 2014, available at http://business.time.com/2014/01/06/walmart-and-the-myth-of-corporate-responsibility/, accessed February 3, 2016.

10. https://www.unglobalcompact.org/AboutTheGC/index.html, accessed March 25, 2015.

11. https://www.unglobalcompact.org/ParticipantsAndStakeholders/index.html, accessed March 25, 2015.

12. https://www.sustainabilityconsortium.org/members/, accessed February 2, 2016.

13. https://www.sustainabilityconsortium.org/consortium-news/the-sustainability-consortium-opens-european-office-appoints-three-new-board-members-including-two-ngos/, accessed October 26, 2016.

14. http://www.care.org/about/partnerships/corporate-partners/our-partners, accessed October 26, 2016.

15. https://www.edf.org/sites/default/files/Product_Sustainability_through_Multistake holder_Engagement_20111129.pdf.

16. See http://corporate.walmart.com/global-responsibility/environmental-sustainabi lity/sustainability-leaders/introducing-the-walmart-sustainability-leaders-shop, accessed March 11, 2015.

17. Bill Karsell, "The Greenwash Tidal Wave: A Call to Action," 2011. Available at http://www.jasongrantconsulting.com/wp-content/uploads/2011/06/Greenwash-Tidal-Wave.pdf.

18. "Business Rallies to UN Ethics Scheme," *Guardian*, July 26, 2000, 12; Joseph Kahn, "Multinationals Sign UN Pact on Rights and Environment," *New York Times*, July 27, 2000, A3.

19. http://www.transparency.org/news/pressrelease/international_corporations_decide_to_add_anti_corruption_principle_to_un_gl, accessed March 25, 2015.

20. Those are Amnesty, HRW, WWF, Human Rights First/LCHR, IUCN, IIED, and World Resources Institute. See chapter 3.

21. Joshua Karliner and Kenny Bruno, "The United Nations Sits in Suspicious Company," *New York Times*, August 10, 2000.

22. Save the Children joined in 2003, and World Vision International became a participant in 2012. Individual chapters of some of these global NGOs joined earlier, including three national chapters of World Vision. Author's search of participant database. https://www.unglobalcompact.org/what-is-gc/participants, last searched February 3, 2016.

23. https://www.icrc.org/eng/resources/documents/statement/2012/privatizaton-war-statement-2012-09-06.htm, accessed October 26, 2016.

24. https://www.globalpolicy.org/component/content/article/177/31749.html; http://3blmedia.com/News/CSR/Oxfam-International-and-United-Nations-Global-Compact-Partner-Poverty-Assessment-Tool; http://www.oxfamnovib.nl/responsibility-to-respect-in-the-global-south.html, all accessed October 26, 2016.

25. https://www.unglobalcompact.org/AboutTheGC/The_Global_Compact_Board/bios.html, accessed March 26, 2015.

26. http://www.transparency.org/whatwedo/publication/un_global_compact_ti_repo rting_guidance_on_the_10th_principle_against_corru, accessed August 25, 2015; for

board members, see minute meetings, https://www.unglobalcompact.org/library/1821, accessed February 3, 2016.

27. http://www.foei.org/press/archive-by-year/press-2012/un-global-compact-turns-a-blind-eye-to-corporate-malpractices; https://www.globalpolicy.org/global-taxes/32267-ngos-criticize-qblue-washingq-by-the-global-compact.html, all accessed August 25, 2015.

28. http://www.ipsnews.net/2000/05/development-ngos-question-un-partnership-with-private-sector-companies/, accessed October 26, 2016.

29. 1,811 local NGOs as of February 4, 2016. Some of these "local" NGOs are arguably international, including InterAction in the United States and national chapters of Plan, World Vision, and CARE.

30. http://www.greenpeace.org/international/en/news/features/gerd-leipold-at-davos/, accessed October 26, 2016.

31. https://www.hrw.org/news/2012/09/17/walmarts-human-trafficking-problem, accessed October 26, 2016.

32. http://www.sigwatch.com/index.php?id=346, accessed October 26, 2016.

33. Wendy Bounds, "Critics Confront a CEO Dedicated to Human Rights," *Wall Street Journal*, February 24, 1997.

34. https://www.hrw.org/report/1997/03/01/corporations-and-human-rights/freedom-association-maquila-guatemala, accessed February 10, 2016.

35. Jim Lobe, "Union Recognition Marks Breakthrough in Maquila Sector," *Inter Press Service*, March 25, 1997.

36. Steven Greenhouse, "Union Criticizes Plant Closing in Guatemala," *New York Times*, February 28, 1999.

37. https://www.oxfam.org/en/campaigns/behind-brands, accessed April 13, 2015.

38. http://www.greenbiz.com/article/growing-trend-towards-certification-best-hope-forests, accessed October 26, 2016.

39. http://www.greenpeace.org/international/en/publications/Campaign-reports/Forests-Reports/FSC-Case-Studies/, accessed August 26, 2015.

40. AccountAbility and Oxfam Novib, "Beyond the Farm Fence," December 2009; Matt Grainger and Kate Geary, "The New Forests Company and its Uganda Plantations," Oxfam Case Study, September 22, 2011.

41. Conroy (2007, 245) observes that the Nature Conservancy and Conservation International were involved in the Sustainable Forestry Board, but Conservation International stepped down. TNC works with both standards but actively promotes FSC certification. http://www.nature.org/ourinitiatives/habitats/forests/howwework/responsible-forest-trade-forest-certification.xml, accessed October 26, 2016.

42. http://www.watchthemed.net/index.php/page/index/12; http://www.refugees-welcome.net/; https://www.kickstarter.com/aidrefugees; http://www.huffingtonpost.com/entry/crowdfunding-aid-is-inspirational-but-has-a-societal-downside_us_561ec4d1e4b050c6c4a42e8b, all accessed March 23, 2016.

6. DEFERENCE FROM INGOS

1. A. Natsios, "NGOs Must Show Results; Promote US or We Will 'Find New Partners,'" www.interaction.org/forum2003/panels.html#Natsios. See also "Howard Tightens Screws on Charities," *Weekend Australian*, August 2, 2003; Jim Lobe, "Bringing the War Home," *Foreign Policy in Focus*, June 13, 2003, http://fpif.org/bringing_the_war_home_right_wing_think_tank_turns_wrath_on_ngos, accessed August 20, 2014. At this time, the American Enterprise Institute, the Federalist Society, and the Australian Institute for Public Affairs hosted a conference to address NGO-government accountability issues and to launch a new website, NGO Watch.

2. CIVICUS, Annual Report 2007, 8, available at www.civicus.org/view/Civicus AnnualReport07.pdf, last accessed October 17, 2016.

3. http://www.greenpeace.org/international/Global/international/planet-2/report/2006/9/ingo-charter.pdf, last accessed October 17, 2016.

4. ICSC, Annual Report 2013, http://icscentre.org/downloads/Annual_Report_2013.pdf.

5. Emphasis in original. http://www.ingoaccountabilitycharter.org/home/what-is-the-charter/, accessed January 11, 2016.

6. http://www.inmotionmagazine.com/global/ogwsf_int.html; https://www.youtube.com/watch?v=IUwelQswa20, last accessed October 17, 2016.

7. http://www.thealliancefordemocracy.org/pdf/AfDJR6114.pdf, last accessed October 17, 2016.

8. chicowhitaker.net/artigo_eng.php?artigo=44, last accessed October 17, 2016.

9. CIVICUS, Annual Report 2007, available at www.civicus.org/view/CivicusAnnualReport07.pdf, last accessed October 17, 2016.

10. http://www.ingoaccountabilitycharter.org/2014/04/letter-from-former-chair-jeremy-hobbs/, last accessed October 17, 2016.

11. With SIDA, the charter has received a €2 million grant to pursue this project. http://www.ingoaccountabilitycharter.org/wpcms/wp-content/uploads/Board-Minutes-April-2015_final.pdf, accessed January 11, 2016.

12. Ken Caldwell, Building Effective Standards for Global NGOs, March 2013, 2. http://www.baobab.org.uk/wp-content/uploads/2013/07/EffectiveStandards03.13.pdf, last accessed October 17, 2016.

13. http://www.ingoaccountabilitycharter.org/wpcms/wp-content/uploads/Board-Minutes-April-2015_final.pdf, last accessed October 17, 2016.

14. http://www.alliancemagazine.org/article/when-is-transparency-a-really-bad-idea/.

15. http://www.carnegiecouncil.org/studio/multimedia/20121108/index.html, last accessed October 17, 2016.

16. https://www.bond.org.uk/about-us/become-a-member, accessed October 14, 2016.

17. Authors' calculations based on INGO Accountability Charter member reports.

18. "Activists Arrested at White House Protesting Keystone Pipeline," *Washington Post*, February 13, 2013.

19. http://www.wsfindia.org/?q=node/3, last accessed October 17, 2016.

20. Randeep Ramesh, "Place in the Sun for Everyone," theguardian.com, January 16, 2004.

21. http://www.ipsnews.net/2011/03/world-social-forum-winning-the-battle-of-ideas/, last accessed October 17, 2016.

22. Authors' calculations. Data available at http://www.weforum.org/events/world-economic-forum-annual-meeting-2013/speakers; http://www.weforum.org/events/world-economic-forum-annual-meeting-2015/speakers; http://www.weforum.org/events/world-economic-forum-annual-meeting-2014/speakers.

23. http://www.memoriafsm.org/bitstream/handle/11398/1475/2004_07.01_Balanco_33.pdf?sequence=1; https://www.travel-impact-newswire.com/2004/01/world-economic-forum-vs-world-social-forum-two-worlds-two-ways/.

24. http://www.ingoaccountabilitycharter.org/, accessed January 11, 2016.

25. The latest list of GRI reporting standards are available at https://www.globalreporting.org/resourcelibrary/GRI-G4-Overview-Tables-G3.1-vs-G4.pdf.

26. http://www.ingoaccountabilitycharter.org/wpcms/wp-content/uploads/CHARTER-REPORTING-GUIDELINES.pdf; http://www.ingoaccountabilitycharter.org/wpcms/wp-content/uploads/Minutes-Board-meeting-22-January-2014_external.pdf.

27. http://www.ingoaccountabilitycharter.org/wpcms/wp-content/uploads/INGO-Accountability-Charter-AGM-2011-minutes.pdf.

28. This campaign was launched by civil society organizations in 2008. Several large INGOs are backers of the campaign, including AC members ActionAid and World Vision.

29. These are Partnership Program Agreements. As of August 2014, ActionAid, Article 19, CARE, Oxfam, Plan, Sightsavers, Transparency International, and World Vision; Islamic Relief does as well but is not a full AC member. Many other official donors engage with IATI. IATI reporting is a requirement for NGO partners of the Dutch foreign affairs ministry. USAID is an IATI signatory but does not yet require NGO partners to report. http://www.nivocer.com/2014/04/roads-to-results-in-iati/; Will McKittrick, "Why Are US NGOs MIA from IATI?" October 2, 2013; http://international.cgdev.org/blog/why-are-us-ingos-mia-iati, last accessed October 17, 2016.

30. This number overstates the number of INGO participants, as several are national chapters of INGO networks (for example, Oxfam Novib and Oxfam GB report separately). http://blog.transparency.org/2013/01/17/my-ceo-will-tear-off-my-head-if-i-suggest-to-him-that-we-implement-iati/; http://www.theguardian.com/global-development-professionals-network/2013/oct/23/plan-usa-iati-aid-transparency, last accessed October 17, 2016.

31. http://www.ingoaccountabilitycharter.org/wpcms/wpcontent/uploads/INGO_CHARTER_web.pdf.

32. Adele Poskitt, "CSO Accountability and the International NGO Accountability Charter," paper prepared for the Foundation for the Future meeting, Tools for Enhancing CSOs' Accountability, May 9–10, 2010 (http://foundationforfuture.org/en/Portals/0/Conferences/Accountability/Presentations/Session%201/Pres-4-CIVICUS_INGO_English.pdf).

33. http://www.ingoaccountabilitycharter.org/2014/04/letter-from-former-chair-jeremy-hobbs/; http://www.ingoaccountabilitycharter.org/wpcms/wp-content/uploads/Minutes-Board-Meeting-3-April-2014_final.pdf.

34. https://www.opendemocracy.net/teivo-teivainen/after-tunis-what-next-for-world-social-forum, last accessed October 17, 2016.

35. https://www.opendemocracy.net/openglobalrights/jamie-k-mccallum-sarah-s-stroup/right-place-for-left-world-social-forum-in-montreal, last accessed October 17, 2016.

36. http://www.civicus.org/index.php/en/about-us-125/brief-history, accessed January 28, 2016.

37. Caty Enders, "Can Sea Shepherd Survive Its Own Success?" theguardian.com, June 5, 2015; Rose Troup Buchanan, "Brighton Beach in EU Migrant Disaster Protest," *The Independent*, April 22, 2015.

38. http://www.forumsocialmundial.org.br/download/WSF_finstrategy_FinalReport_EN.pdf

39. https://electronicintifada.net/blogs/ali-abunimah/oxfam-america-office-refuses-receive-petition-urging-it-dump-scarlett-johansson, accessed April 5, 2016.

40. Like many rising Southern NGOs, Bello's Focus on the Global South receives regular funding from Oxfam.

41. http://www.counterpunch.org/2005/06/17/how-glo-bono-phonies-and-trojan-horse-ngos-sabotage-the-struggle-against-neoliberalism/, accessed April 14, 2016.

42. Maria Tadeo, "Greenpeace Co-Founder Patrick Moore tells US Senate There Is "No Proof" Humans Cause Climate Change," *Independent*, February 28, 2014.

43. Keith Johnston, "Acting Globally—Thinking Globally," unpublished paper, February 2012, on file with author.

7. AUDIENCE-BASED AUTHORITY IN POLITICS

1. http://www.pdhre.org/patriarchy.html, accessed October 2, 2016.

2. Originally, it was called the NGO Coalition for an International Criminal Court.

3. Unlike the FTT, where the finance industry directly attacked the FTT's efficacy as well as its goals, the ICC couldn't be publicly attacked as an unwarranted attack on valid

practices. The scope of the court encompassed a few crimes that are almost universally condemned, but, tellingly, other practices like the death penalty were kept out of the ICC's ambit.

4. Richard Dicker and Juan Mendez, "Letter to the Editor: Why Does U.S. Stall on New World Court?" *New York Times*, September 7, 1995, A26.

5. Amnesty International, *Amnesty International Report 1996*, 55.

6. See, for example, http://www.theguardian.com/world/2016/feb/01/african-union-kenyan-plan-leave-international-criminal-court, accessed March 29, 2016.

7. http://qz.com/646665/chinas-biggest-broker-spent-more-on-bailing-out-the-stock-market-than-it-earned-in-2015/, accessed March 24, 2016.

8. We use this term rather than the more normatively laden term "terrorism." But we do refer to "terrorism" where appropriate if it is germane to existing research on such actors.

9. Perhaps INGOs should follow the lead of some states that sign international agreements and lock themselves into binding commitments or cede their authority.

10. Rukmini Callimachi, "ISIS Seems to Tailor Attacks for Different Audiences," *New York Times*, July 2, 2016.

APPENDIX

1. National Center for Charitable Statistics (US) and the Charity Commission (UK).

2. CN evaluates organizations with annual revenues greater than $1 million that have filed IRS Form 990 for at least seven years. According to the National Center for Charitable Statistics, there were 358,034 charities in December 2013 that filed Form 990; 20% of those had incomes greater than $1 million. This top fifth accounts for 97% of the sector's total revenue. http://blog.charitynavigator.org/2014/02/an-update-on-our-charity-data.html, last accessed October 31, 2016.

References

Abbott, Kenneth W. 2012. "Engaging the Public and the Private in Global Sustainability Governance." *International Affairs* 88 (3): 543–64. doi:10.1111/j.1468-2346. 2012.01088.x.

Abbott, Kenneth W., and Duncan Snidal. 2010. "International Regulation without International Government: Improving IO Performance through Orchestration." *The Review of International Organizations* 5 (3): 315–44. doi:10.1007/s11558-010-9092-3.

Abdelal, Rawi, Mark Blyth, and Craig Parsons. 2010. *Constructing the International Economy.* Ithaca, NY: Cornell University Press.

Ahmed, Shamima, and David M. Potter. 2006. *NGOs in International Politics.* West Hartford, CT: Kumarian Press.

Alcock, Frank. 2008. "Conflicts and Coalitions within and across the ENGO Community." *Global Environmental Politics* 8 (4): 66–91. doi:10.1162/glep.2008.8.4.66.

Aldrich, Howard E., and Jeffrey Pfeffer. 1976. "Environments of Organizations." *Annual Review of Sociology*: 79–105. http://www.jstor.org/stable/2946087.

Álvarez, Rebecca, Erika Gutierrez, Linda Kim, Christine Petit, and Ellen Reese. 2008. "The Contours of Color at the World Social Forum: Reflections on Racialized Politics, Representation, and the Global Justice Movement." *Critical Sociology* 34 (3): 389–407. doi:10.1177/0896920507088165.

Amoore, Louise, and Paul Langley. 2004. "Ambiguities of Global Civil Society." *Review of International Studies* 30 (1): 89–110. doi:/10.1017/S026021050 4005844.

Anderson, Roy, and Eric Hansen. 2003. "Forest Certification: Understanding Ecolabel Usage Requirements." Wood Science & Engineering: Oregon State University. http://www.csagroup.org/documents/testing-and-certification/product_areas/forest_products_marking/Ecolabel_Use.pdf.

Anheier, Helmut. 2007. "Bringing Civility Back In—Reflections on Global Civil Society." *Development Dialogue* 49: 41–49. http://citeseerx.ist.psu.edu/viewdoc/summary?doi=10.1.1.524.3339.

Anheier, Helmut, Mary Kaldor, and Marlies Glasius. 2012. "The Global Civil Society Yearbook: Lessons and Insights 2001–2011." In *Global Civil Society 2012: Ten Years of Critical Reflection,* edited by Mary Kaldor, Henrietta L. Moore, Sabine Selchow, and Tamsin Murray-Leach. New York: Palgrave.

Arendt, Hannah. 1961. *Between Past and Future: Eight Exercises in Political Thought.* New York: Penguin.

Argenti, Paul. 2004. "Collaborating with Activists: How Starbucks Works with NGOs." *California Management Review* 47: 91–116. doi:10.2307/41166288.

Arrington, Celeste L. 2016. *Accidental Activists: Victim Movements and Government Accountability in Japan and South Korea.* Ithaca, NY: Cornell University Press.

Auld, Graeme. 2014. *Constructing Private Governance: The Rise and Evolution of Forest, Coffee, and Fisheries Certification.* New Haven, CT: Yale University Press.

Auld, Graeme, and Benjamin Cashore. 2012. "The Forest Stewardship Council." In *Business Regulation and Non-State Actors: Whose Standards? Whose*

Development, edited by Darryl Reed, Peter Utting, and Ananya Mukherjee-Reed. London: Routledge.

Auld, Graeme, Lars H. Gulbrandsen, and Constance L. McDermott. 2008. "Certification Schemes and the Impacts on Forests and Forestry." *Annual Review of Environment and Resources* 33: 187–211. doi:10.1146/annurev. environ.33.013007.103754.

Auld, Graeme, Stefan Renckens, and Benjamin Cashore. 2015. "Transnational Private Governance between the Logics of Empowerment and Control." *Regulation & Governance* 9 (2): 108–24. doi:10.1111/rego.12075.

Avant, Deborah. 2004. "Conserving Nature in the State of Nature: The Politics of INGO Policy Implementation." *Review of International Studies* 30 (3): 361–82. doi:10.1017/S0260210504006114.

Avant, Deborah D., Martha Finnemore, and Susan K. Sell. 2010. *Who Governs the Globe?* New York: Cambridge University Press.

Baldwin, David A. 2012. "Power and International Relations." In *Handbook of International Relations*, edited by Walter Carlsnaes, Thomas Risse, and Beth Simmons. Thousand Oaks, CA: Sage.

Bandy, Joe, and Jackie Smith. 2005. *Coalitions Across Borders: Transnational Protest and the Neoliberal Order.* Lanham, MD: Rowman & Littlefield.

Banks, Matthew C. 2010. "World Wildlife Fund." In *Good Cop/Bad Cop*, edited by Thomas Lyon. Washington, DC: RFF Press.

Barber, Martin, and Cameron Bowie. 2008. "How International NGOs Could Do Less Harm and More Good." *Development in Practice* 18 (6): 748–54. doi:10.1080/09614520802386520.

Barnett, Michael. 2011. *Empire of Humanity: A History of Humanitarianism.* Ithaca, NY: Cornell University Press.

Barnett, Michael, and Raymond Duvall. 2005. *Power in Global Governance.* New York: Cambridge University Press.

Barnett, Michael, and Martha Finnemore. 2004. *Rules for the World: International Organizations in Global Politics.* Ithaca, NY: Cornell University Press.

Barnett, Michael, and Peter Walker. 2015. "Regime Change for Humanitarian Aid." *Foreign Affairs* 94 (July/August): 130–41.

Barrow, Kristie. 2004. "The Role of NGOs in the Establishment of the International Criminal Court." *Dialogue* 2 (1): 11–22.

Bartley, Tim. 2010. "Transnational Private Regulation in Practice: The Limits of Forest and Labor Standards Certification in Indonesia." *Business and Politics* 12 (3). doi:10.2202/1469-3569.1321.

Bartley, Tim, and Curtis Child. 2014. "Shaming the Corporation: The Social Production of Targets and the Anti-Sweatshop Movement." *American Sociological Review* 79 (4): 653–79. doi:10.1177/0003122414540653.

Bassiouni, M. Cherif. 2015. "Chronology of Efforts to Establish an International Criminal Court." *Revue Internationale de Droit Pénal* 86 (3): 1163–94. http://www.cairn. info/revue-internationale-de-droit-penal-2015-3-page-1163.htm.

——. 2006. "The ICC—Quo Vadis?" *Journal of International Criminal Justice* 4 (3): 421–27. doi:10.1093/jicj/mql022.

Becker, Marc. 2007. "World Social Forum." *Peace & Change* 32 (2): 203–20. doi:10.1111/j.1468-0130.2007.00427.x.

Bell, Daniel A., and Jean-Marc Coicaud. 2006. *Ethics in Action: The Ethical Challenges of International Human Rights Nongovernmental Organizations.* New York: Cambridge University Press.

Benedetti, Fanny, Karine Bonneau, and John L. Washburn. 2013. *Negotiating the International Criminal Court: New York to Rome 1994–1998*. Leiden: Martinus Nijhoff Publishers.

Berliner, Daniel, and Aseem Prakash. 2012. "From Norms to Programs: The United Nations Global Compact and Global Governance." *Regulation & Governance* 6 (2): 149–66. doi:10.1111/j.1748-5991.2012.01130.x.

——. 2015. "'Bluewashing' the Firm? Voluntary Regulations, Program Design, and Member Compliance with the United Nations Global Compact." *Policy Studies Journal* 43 (1): 115–38. doi:10.1111/psj.12085.

Bernstein, Steven F. 2001. *The Compromise of Liberal Environmentalism*. New York: Columbia University Press.

——. 2011. "Legitimacy in Intergovernmental and Non-State Global Governance." *Review of International Political Economy* 18 (1): 17–51. doi:10.1080/096922 90903173087.

Bernstein, Steven, and Benjamin Cashore. 2007. "Can Non-state Global Governance Be Legitimate? An Analytical Framework." *Regulation & Governance* 1 (4): 347–71. doi:10.1111/j.1748-5991.2007.00021.x.

Bertels, Stephanie, Andrew J. Hoffman, and Rich DeJordy. 2014. "The Varied Work of Challenger Movements: Identifying Challenger Roles in the US Environmental Movement." *Organization Studies* 35 (8): 1171–1210. doi:10.1177/0170840613 517601.

Betsill, Michele, and Elisabeth Corell. 2008. *NGO Diplomacy: The Influence of Nongovernmental Organizations in International Environmental Negotiations*. Cambridge, MA: MIT Press.

Betzold, Carola. 2014. "Responsiveness or Influence? Whom to Lobby in International Climate Change Negotiations." *International Negotiation* 19 (1): 35–61. doi:10.1163/ 15718069-12341269.

Bianco, Anthony. 2006. *Wal-Mart: The Bully of Bentonville: How the High Cost of Everyday Low Prices Is Hurting America*. Crown Business.

Bieri, Franziska. 2010. "The Roles of NGOs in the Kimberley Process." *Globality Studies Journal* 20 (November): 1–13. https://gsj.stonybrook.edu/article/the-roles-of-ngos-in-the-kimberley-process/.

Birdsall, Andrea. 2010. "The 'Monster That We Need to Slay'? Global Governance, the United States, and the International Criminal Court." *Global Governance: A Review of Multilateralism and International Organizations* 16 (4): 451–69. http://journals.rienner.com/doi/abs/10.5555/ggov.2010.16.4.451.

Black, Maggie. 1992. *A Cause for Our Times: Oxfam—the First Fifty Years*. Oxford: Oxfam.

Bloodgood, Elizabeth A. 2011. "The Interest Group Analogy: International Non-Governmental Advocacy Organisations in International Politics." *Review of International Studies* 37 (1): 93–120. doi:10.1017/S0260210510001051.

Bloom, Mia. 2005. *Dying to Kill: The Allure of Suicide Terror*. New York: Columbia University Press.

Bob, Clifford. 2005. *The Marketing of Rebellion: Insurgents, Media, and International Activism*. New York: Cambridge University Press.

——. 2012. *The Global Right Wing and the Clash of World Politics*. New York: Cambridge University Press.

Boli, John, and George M. Thomas. 1999. *Constructing World Culture: International Nongovernmental Organizations since 1875*. Stanford, CA: Stanford University Press.

Bolton, Matthew, Héctor Guerra, Ray Acheson, and Oliver Sprague. 2014. "The Road Forward for the Arms Trade Treaty: A Civil Society Practitioner Commentary." *Global Policy* 5 (4): 469–73. doi:10.1111/1758-5899.12172.

Bolton, Matthew, and Thomas Nash. 2010. "The Role of Middle Power—NGO Coalitions in Global Policy: The Case of the Cluster Munitions Ban." *Global Policy* 1 (2): 172–84. doi:10.1111/j.1758-5899.2009.00015.x.

Bolton, Matthew, Eiko Elize Sakamoto, and Hugh Griffiths. 2012. "Globalization and the Kalashnikov: Public-Private Networks in the Trafficking and Control of Small Arms." *Global Policy* 3 (3): 303–13. doi:10.1111/j.1758-5899.2011.00118.x.

BOND. 2005. *The How and Why of Advocacy*. Guidance Notes No 2.1. London: BOND. http://www.innonet.org/resources/files/The_how_and_why_of_advocacy.pdf.

Borton, John, and John Eriksson. 2004. "Lessons from Rwanda: Lessons for Today; Assessment of the Impact and Influence of Joint Evaluation of Emergency Assistance to Rwanda." Danish Ministry of Foreign Affairs.

Bosso, Christopher John. 2005. *Environment, Inc.: From Grassroots to Beltway*. Lawrence: University Press of Kansas.

Boström, Magnus, and Kristina Tamm Hallström. 2010. "NGO Power in Global Social and Environmental Standard-Setting." *Global Environmental Politics* 10 (4): 36–59. doi:10.1162/GLEP_a_00030.

Brassett, James. 2010. *Cosmopolitanism and Global Financial Reform: A Pragmatic Approach to the Tobin Tax*. New York: Routledge.

———. 2012. "Global Justice and/as Global Democracy: The UK Campaign for a Tobin Tax." In *Global Justice Activism and Policy Reform in Europe: Understanding When Change Happens*, edited by Peter Utting, Mario Pianta, and Anne Ellersiek. New York: Routledge.

Brown, L. David. 2008. *Creating Credibility: Legitimacy and Accountability for Transnational Civil Society*. West Hartford, CT: Kumarian Press.

Brown, L. David, Alnoor Ebrahim, and Srilatha Batliwala. 2012. "Governing International Advocacy NGOs." *World Development* 40 (6): 1098–1108. doi:10.1016/j.worlddev.2011.11.006.

Brown, Michael Harold, and John May. 1991. *The Greenpeace Story*. London: Dorling Kindersley.

Bruno, Kenny, and Joshua Karliner. 2000. "Tangled Up in Blue: Corporate Partnerships at the United Nations." CorpWatch. http://www.corpwatch.org/article.php?id=996.

Brysk, Alison. 2009. *Global Good Samaritans: Human Rights as Foreign Policy*. New York: Oxford University Press.

Burger, Ronelle, and Trudy Owens. 2010. "Promoting Transparency in the NGO Sector: Examining the Availability and Reliability of Self-Reported Data." *World Development* 38 (9): 1263–77. doi:10.1016/j.worlddev.2009.12.018.

Burman, Leonard, William Gale, Sarah Gault, Bryan Kim, Jim Nunns, and Steve Rosenthal. 2015. *Financial Transaction Taxes in Theory and Practice*. Washington, DC: Tax Policy Center. https://www.brookings.edu/research/financial-transaction-taxes-in-theory-and-practice-2/.

Burt, Ronald S. 2005. *Brokerage and Closure: An Introduction to Social Capital*. Oxford: Oxford University Press.

Busby, Joshua W. 2010. *Moral Movements and Foreign Policy*. Vol. 116. New York: Cambridge University Press.

Bush, Sarah Sunn. 2015. *The Taming of Democracy Assistance*. New York: Cambridge University Press.

Byrd, Scott C., and Lorien Jasny. 2010. "Transnational Movement Innovation and Collaboration: Analysis of World Social Forum Networks." *Social Movement Studies* 9 (4): 355–72. doi:10.1080/14742837.2010.522305.

Cambridge Policy Consultants. 2012. "Financial Transaction Tax Campaign: Interim Evaluation Report." Oxfam, July. http://policy-practice.oxfam.org.uk/publications/financial-transaction-tax-campaign-evaluation-report-266632.

Campbell, Wallace J. 1990. *The History of CARE: A Personal Account.* New York: Praeger Publishers.

Carpenter, R. Charli. 2007. "Setting the Advocacy Agenda: Theorizing Issue Emergence and Nonemergence in Transnational Advocacy Networks." *International Studies Quarterly* 51 (1): 99–120. doi:10.1111/j.1468-2478.2007.00441.x.

——. 2011. "Vetting the Advocacy Agenda: Network Centrality and the Paradox of Weapons Norms." *International Organization* 65 (1): 69–102. doi:10.1017/S0020818310000329.

——. 2014. *"Lost" Causes: Agenda Vetting in Global Issue Networks and the Shaping of Human Security.* Ithaca, NY: Cornell University Press.

Cashore, Benjamin. 2002. "Legitimacy and the Privatization of Environmental Governance: How Non-State Market-Driven (NSMD) Governance Systems Gain Rule-Making Authority." *Governance* 15 (4): 503–29. doi:10.1111/1468-0491.00199.

Cashore, Benjamin, Graeme Auld, and Deanna Newsom. 2003a. "Forest Certification (eco-Labeling) Programs and Their Policy-Making Authority: Explaining Divergence among North American and European Case Studies." *Forest Policy and Economics* 5 (3): 225–47. doi:10.1016/S1389-9341(02)00060-6.

——. 2003b. "The United States' Race to Certify Sustainable Forestry: Non-State Environmental Governance and the Competition for Policy-Making Authority." *Business and Politics* 5 (3). doi:10.1080/136952042000189393.

——. 2004. *Governing Through Markets: Forest Certification and the Emergence of Non-State Authority.* New Haven, CT: Yale University Press.

Castells, Manuel. 2008. "The New Public Sphere: Global Civil Society, Communication Networks, and Global Governance." *The Annals of the American Academy of Political and Social Science* 616 (1): 78–93. doi:10.1177/0002716207311877.

Chambers, Simone, and Jeffrey Kopstein. 2001. "Bad Civil Society." *Political Theory* 29 (6): 837–65. http://www.jstor.org/stable/3072607?seq=1#page_scan_tab_contents.

Chandler, Geoffrey. 2009. "The Amnesty International UK Business Group: Putting Human Rights on the Corporate Agenda." *The Journal of Corporate Citizenship* 33 (Spring): 29–35.

Chapin, Mac. 2004. "A Challenge to Conservationists." *WORLD• WATCH* (November/December). http://www.worldwatch.org/system/files/EP176A.pdf.

Chapman, Terrence L. 2009. "Audience Beliefs and International Organization Legitimacy." *International Organization* 63 (4): 733–64. doi:10.1017/S0020818309990154.

Chenoweth, Erica. 2010. "Democratic Competition and Terrorist Activity." *The Journal of Politics* 72 (1): 16–30. doi:10.1017/s0022381609990442.

——. 2013. "Terrorism and Democracy." *Annual Review of Political Science* 16: 355–78. doi:10.1146/annurev-polisci-032211-221825.

Chong, Daniel. 2009. "Economic Rights and Extreme Poverty: Moving Towards Subsistence." In *The International Struggle for New Human Rights*, edited by Clifford Bob, 108–29. Philadelphia: University of Pennsylvania Press.

Claessens, Stijn, Michael Keen, and Ceyla Pazarbasioglu. 2010. *Financial Sector Taxation: The IMF's Report to the G-20 and Background Material.* Washington, DC: International Monetary Fund. https://www.imf.org/external/np/seminars/eng/2010/paris/pdf/090110.pdf.

Clark, Ann Marie. 2001. *Diplomacy of Conscience: Amnesty International and Changing Human Rights Norms.* Princeton, NJ: Princeton University Press.

Clark, Michael Rawson, and Joelyn Sarrah Kozar. 2011. "Comparing Sustainable Forest Management Certifications Standards: A Meta-Analysis." *Ecology and Society* 16 (1): 3.

Cochrane, John H. 2013. "Finance: Function Matters, Not Size." *The Journal of Economic Perspectives* 27 (2): 29–50. doi:10.1257/jep.27.2.29.

Coe, J., and J. Majot. 2013. *Monitoring, Evaluation and Learning in NGO Advocacy. Findings from Comparative Policy Advocacy MEL Review Project.* Cambridge: Oxfam America. http://www.alnap.org/resource/19073.aspx.

Collingwood, Vivien, and Louis Logister. 2006. "Non-Governmental Organisations, Power and Legitimacy in International Society." *Review of International Studies* 32 (3): 439–54. doi:10.1017/S0260210506007108.

Commins, Steve. 1997. "World Vision International and Donors: Too Close for Comfort?" In *NGOs, States and Donors; Too Close for Comfort?*, edited by David Hulme and Michael Edwards. New York: Save the Children Fund.

Conner, Alana, and Keith Epstein. 2007. "Harnessing Purity and Pragmatism." *Stanford Social Innovation Review,* Fall.

Conrad, Courtenay R., and Emily Hencken Ritter. 2013. "Treaties, Tenure, and Torture: The Conflicting Domestic Effects of International Law." *The Journal of Politics* 75 (2): 397–409. doi:10.1017/s0022381613000091.

Conroy, Michael E. 2007. *Branded!: How the 'Certification Revolution' Is Transforming Global Corporations.* Gabriola Island, BC: New Society Publishers.

Cooley, Alexander, and James Ron. 2002. "The NGO Scramble: Organizational Insecurity and the Political Economy of Transnational Action." *International Security* 27 (1): 5–39. doi:10.1162/016228802320231217.

Cox, Brendan. 2011. "Campaigning for International Justice. Learning Lessons (1991–2011)." BOND. https://www.bond.org.uk/data/files/Campaigning_for_International_Justice_Brendan_Cox_May_2011.pdf.

Crack, Angela M. 2013. "INGO Accountability Deficits: The Imperatives for Further Reform." *Globalizations* 10 (2): 293–308. doi:10.1080/14747731.2013.786253.

Crawford, Robert, and Craig Smith. 2012. "Walmart: Love, Earth." http://centres.insead.edu/social-innovation/what-we-do/documents/5830-Walmart-LoveEarth-A-CS-EN-0-06-2012-w.pdf.

Crenshaw, Martha. 1995. *Terrorism in Context.* University Park: Pennsylvania State University Press.

Crompton, Tom. 2010. "Common Cause: The Case for Working with Our Cultural Values." Oxfam. http://policy-practice.oxfam.org.uk/publications/common-cause-the-case-for-working-with-our-cultural-values-112367.

Cugelman, Brian, and Eva Otero. 2010. *Evaluation of Oxfam GB's Climate Change Campaign.* Oxford: Lietmotive, AlterSpeak, and Oxfam GB. http://www.mtn forum.org/sites/default/files/publication/files/6393.pdf.

Cutler, Claire, Virginia Haufler, and Tony Porter. 1999. *Private Authority and International Affairs.* Albany: State University of New York Press.

Dauvergne, Peter, and Genevieve LeBaron. 2014. *Protest Inc.: The Corporatization of Activism.* New York: John Wiley & Sons.

Deitelhoff, Nicole. 2009. "The Discursive Process of Legalization: Charting Islands of Persuasion in the ICC Case." *International Organization* 63 (1): 33–65. doi:10.1017/S002081830909002X.

Della Porta, Donatella. 2006. *Globalization from Below: Transnational Activists and Protest Networks.* Minneapolis: University of Minnesota Press.

Deloffre, Maryam Zarnegar. 2010. "NGO Accountability Clubs in the Humanitarian Sector: Social Dimensions of Club Emergence and Design." In *Voluntary Regulation of NGOs and Nonprofits: An Accountability Club Framework,* edited by Mary Kay Gugerty and Aseem Prakash. New York: Cambridge University Press.

DeMars, William E., and Dennis Dijkzeul. 2015. *The NGO Challenge for International Relations Theory.* New York: Routledge.

De Sousa Santos, Boaventura. 2006. *The Rise of the Global Left: The World Social Forum and Beyond.* London: Zed Books.

de Waal, Alex, ed. 2015. *Advocacy in Conflict: Critical Perspectives on Transnational Activism.* London: Zed Books.

DeWinter-Schmitt, Rebecca M. 2007. "Business as Usual? The Mobilization of the Anti-Sweatshop Movement and the Social Construction of Corporate Identity." PhD dissertation, American University.

Dicker, John. 2005. *The United States of Wal-Mart.* New York: Penguin.

Dingwerth, Klaus. 2008. "North-South Parity in Global Governance: The Affirmative Procedures of the Forest Stewardship Council." *Global Governance: A Review of Multilateralism and International Organizations* 14 (1): 53–71. doi:10.5555/ggov.2008.14.1.53.

Doherty, Brian, and Timothy Doyle. 2013. *Environmentalism, Resistance and Solidarity: The Politics of Friends of the Earth International.* New York: Palgrave Macmillan.

Downs, Anthony. 1957. "An Economic Theory of Political Action in a Democracy." *The Journal of Political Economy* 65: 135–50. http://www.jstor.org/stable/1827369?seq=1#page_scan_tab_contents.

Drezner, Daniel W. 2008. *All Politics Is Global.* Princeton, NJ: Princeton University Press.

Dryzek, John S. 2012. "Global Civil Society: The Progress of Post-Westphalian Politics." *Annual Review of Political Science* 15: 101–19. doi:10.1146/annurev-polisci-042010-164946.

Dryzek, John S., and Simon Niemeyer. 2008. "Discursive Representation." *American Political Science Review* 102 (4): 481–93. doi:10.1017/S0003055408080325.

Edwards, Michael, and David Hulme. 1996. *Beyond the Magic Bullet: NGO Performance and Accountability in the Post-Cold War World.* West Hartford, CT: Kumarian Press.

Eilstrup-Sangiovanni, Mette, and Teale N. Phelps Bondaroff. 2014. "From Advocacy to Confrontation: Direct Enforcement by Environmental NGOs." *International Studies Quarterly* 58 (2): 348–61.

EPA. 2006. *Life Cycle Assessment: Principles and Practice.* Reston, VA: United States Environmental Protection Agency. https://cfpub.epa.gov/si/si_public_record_report.cfm?dirEntryId=155087.

Erickson, Jennifer. 2007. "The Arms Trade Treaty: The Politics behind the UN Process." Research Unit European and Atlantic Security, Working Paper FG3-WP09. Berlin: German Institute for International and Security Affairs.

Espach, Ralph. 2006. "When Is Sustainable Forestry Sustainable? The Forest Stewardship Council in Argentina and Brazil." *Global Environmental Politics* 6 (2): 55–84. doi:10.1162/glep.2006.6.2.55.

Fairlie, Megan A. 2011. "The United States and the International Criminal Court Post-Bush: A Beautiful Courtship but an Unlikely Marriage." *Berkeley Journal of International Law* 29: 528–745. doi:10.15779/Z38DW8B.

Farrell, Henry, and Abraham L. Newman. 2010. "Making Global Markets: Historical Institutionalism in International Political Economy." *Review of International Political Economy* 17 (4) (October 1): 609–38. doi:10.1080/09692291003723672.

Feinstein, Andrew, and Alex De Waal. 2015. "Activism and the Arms Trade." In *Advocacy in Conflict*, edited by Alex De Waal. London: Zed Books.

Fernholz, Kathryn, Jim Bowyer, Steve Bratkovich, Matt Frank, Harry Groot, Jeff Howe, John Owen, and Ed Pepke. 2015. "Forest Certification Update: Changes to the SFI and FSC Standards in 2015." Dovetail Partners. http://www.dovetailinc.org/reports/Forest+Certification+Update+Changes+to+the+SFI+and+FSC+Standards+in+2015_n668?prefix=%2Freports.

Finnemore, Martha. 1996. *National Interests in International Society*. Ithaca, NY: Cornell University Press.

Finnemore, Martha, and Kathryn Sikkink. 1998. "International Norm Dynamics and Political Change." *International Organization* 52 (4): 887–917. doi:10.1162/002081898550789.

Fisher, Dana R. 2010. "COP-15 in Copenhagen: How the Merging of Movements Left Civil Society Out in the Cold." *Global Environmental Politics* 10 (2): 11–17. doi:10.1162/glep.2010.10.2.11.

Fisher, Dana R., and Jessica F. Green. 2004. "Understanding Disenfranchisement: Civil Society and Developing Countries' Influence and Participation in Global Governance for Sustainable Development." *Global Environmental Politics* 4 (3): 65–84. doi:10.1162/1526380041748047.

Fisher, William F., and Thomas Ponniah. 2003. *Another World Is Possible: Popular Alternatives to Globalization at the World Social Forum*. London: Zed Books.

Fishman, Charles. 2006. *The Wal-Mart Effect: How the World's Most Powerful Company Really Works—and How It's Transforming the American Economy*. New York: Penguin.

Flathman, Richard E. 1980. *The Practice of Political Authority: Authority and the Authoritative*. Chicago: University of Chicago Press.

Fligstein, Neil, and Doug McAdam. 2011. "Toward a General Theory of Strategic Action Fields." *Sociological Theory* 29 (1): 1–26. doi:10.1111/j.1467-9558.2010.01385.x.

Fombrun, Charles, and Mark Shanley. 1990. "What's in a Name? Reputation Building and Corporate Strategy." *Academy of Management Journal* 33 (2): 233–58. doi:10.2307/256324.

Forsythe, David P. 2005. *The Humanitarians: The International Committee of the Red Cross*. Cambridge: Cambridge University Press.

Fox, Jonathan A., and L. Dave Brown. 1998. *The Struggle for Accountability: The World Bank, NGOs, and Grassroots Movements*. Cambridge, MA: MIT Press.

Freidberg, Susanne. 2015. "It's Complicated: Corporate Sustainability and the Uneasiness of Life Cycle Assessment." *Science as Culture* 24 (2): 157–82. doi:10.1080/09505431.2014.942622.

Friedman, R. B. 1990. "On the Concept of Authority in Political Philosophy." In *Authority*, edited by Joseph Raz, 56–91. Oxford: Basil Blackwell.

Gautney, Heather. 2012. *Protest and Organization in the Alternative Globalization Era: NGOs, Social Movements, and Political Parties*. Basingstoke: Palgrave Macmillan.

Gent, Stephen E., Mark J.C. Crescenzi, Elizabeth J. Menninga, and Lindsay Reid. 2015. "The Reputation Trap of NGO Accountability." *International Theory* 7 (3) (November): 426–63. doi:10.1017/S1752971915000159.

Gereffi, Gary, and Michelle M. Christian. 2009. "The Impacts of Wal-Mart: The Rise and Consequences of the World's Dominant Retailer." *Annual Review of Sociology* 35: 573–91. http://ssrn.com/abstract=1523785.

Glasius, Marlies. 2002. *Expertise in the Cause of Justice: Global Civil Society Influence on the Statute for an International Criminal Court.* New York: Oxford University Press.

Goddard, Stacie E. 2012. "Brokering Peace: Networks, Legitimacy, and the Northern Ireland Peace Process." *International Studies Quarterly* 56 (3): 501–15. doi:10.1111/j.1468-2478.2012.00737.x.

Goetz, Anne Marie, and Rina Sen Gupta. 1996. "Who Takes the Credit? Gender, Power, and Control over Loan Use in Rural Credit Programs in Bangladesh." *World Development* 24 (1): 45–63. doi:10.1016/0305-750X(95)00124-U.

Goodman, James. 2009. "From Global Justice to Climate Justice? Justice Ecologism in an Era of Global Warming." *New Political Science* 31 (4): 499–514. doi:10.1080/07393140903322570.

Goodman, Ryan, and Derek Jinks. 2004. "How to Influence States: Socialization and International Human Rights Law." *Duke Law Journal*: 621–703. doi:http://www.jstor.org/stable/40040439.

Gourevitch, Peter A., David A. Lake, and Janice Gross Stein. 2012. *The Credibility of Transnational NGOs: When Virtue Is Not Enough.* New York: Cambridge University Press.

Grant, Ruth W., and Robert O. Keohane. 2005. "Accountability and Abuses of Power in World Politics." *American Political Science Review* 99 (1): 29–43. http://www.jstor.org/stable/30038917.

Green, Caroline, Deepayan Basu Ray, Claire Mortimer, and Kate Stone. 2013. "Gender-Based Violence and the Arms Trade Treaty: Reflections from a Campaigning and Legal Perspective." *Gender & Development* 21 (3): 551–62. doi:10.1080/13552074.2013.847001.

Green, Duncan, and Anna Macdonald. 2014. "Power and Change: The Arms Trade Treaty." Active Citizenship Case Studies, no. July.

Green, Jessica F. 2013. *Rethinking Private Authority: Agents and Entrepreneurs in Global Environmental Governance.* Princeton, NJ: Princeton University Press.

Grillot, Suzette R., Craig S. Stapley, and Molly E. Hanna. 2006. "Assessing the Small Arms Movement: The Trials and Tribulations of a Transnational Network." *Contemporary Security Policy* 27 (1): 60–84. doi:10.1080/13523260600602354.

Haas, Peter M. 1990. *Saving the Mediterranean: The Politics of International Environmental Cooperation.* New York: Columbia University Press.

——. 1992. "Introduction: Epistemic Communities and International Policy Coordination." *International Organization* 46 (1): 1–35. http://www.jstor.org/stable/2706951.

Hadden, Jennifer. 2014. "Explaining Variation in Transnational Climate Change Activism: The Role of Inter-Movement Spillover." *Global Environmental Politics* 14 (2): 7–25. doi:10.1162/GLEP_a_00225.

——. 2015. *Networks in Contention.* Cambridge: Cambridge University Press.

Hadden, Jennifer, and Sidney Tarrow. 2007. "Spillover or Spillout? The Global Justice Movement in the United States after 9/11." *Mobilization: An International Quarterly* 12 (4): 359–76. http://mobilizationjournal.org/doi/abs/10.17813/maiq.12.4.t221742122771400?journalCode=maiq.

Hafner-Burton, Emilie M. 2008. "Sticks and Stones: Naming and Shaming the Human Rights Enforcement Problem." *International Organization* 62 (4): 689–716. doi:10.1017/S0020818308080247.

Hafner-Burton, Emilie M., Miles Kahler, and Alexander H. Montgomery. 2009. "Network Analysis for International Relations." *International Organization* 63 (3): 559–92. doi:10.1017/S0020818309090195.

Hafner-Burton, Emilie M., and Kiyoteru Tsutsui. 2005. "Human Rights in a Globalizing World: The Paradox of Empty Promises." *American Journal of Sociology* 110 (5): 1373–1411. http://www.jstor.org/stable/10.1086/428442.

Hall, Rodney Bruce, and Thomas J. Biersteker. 2002. *The Emergence of Private Authority in Global Governance*. New York: Cambridge University Press.

Hammad, Lama, and Bill Morton. 2011. "Greater Influence, Greater Responsibility: Are INGOs' Self-Regulatory Accountability Standards Effective?" The North–South Institute. http://www.nsi-ins.ca/english/pdf/INGOFinal.pdf.

Hammond, John L. 2006. "The Possible World and the Actual State: The World Social Forum in Caracas." *Latin American Perspectives*: 122–31. doi:10.1177/0094582X06287868.

Hathaway, Oona A. 2007. "Why Do Countries Commit to Human Rights Treaties?" *Journal of Conflict Resolution* 51 (4): 588–621. http://www.jstor.org/stable/27638567.

Haufler, Virginia. 2009. "The Kimberley Process Certification Scheme: An Innovation in Global Governance and Conflict Prevention." *Journal of Business Ethics* 89 (4): 403–16. http://www.jstor.org/stable/40605378.

Hawkins, Darren. 2008. "Power and Interests at the International Criminal Court." *SAIS Review of International Affairs* 28 (2): 107–19. doi:10.1353/sais.0.0014.

Hawkins, Darren G., David A. Lake, Daniel L. Nielson, and Michael J. Tierney. 2006. *Delegation and Agency in International Organizations*. New York: Cambridge University Press.

Helfer, Laurence R., and Erik Voeten. 2014. "International Courts as Agents of Legal Change: Evidence from LGBT Rights in Europe." *International Organization* 68 (1): 77–110.

Hendrix, Cullen, and Wendy Wong. 2013. "When Is the Pen Truly Mighty? Regime Type and the Efficacy of Naming and Shaming in Curbing Human Rights Abuses." *British Journal of Political Science* 43 (3): 651–72. doi:10.1017/S0007123412000488.

Hillhorst, Dorothea. 2003. *The Real World of NGOs: Discourses, Diversity and Development*. London: Zed Books.

Hoekstra, Rutger, Jan Pieter Smits, Koen Boone, Walter van Everdingen, Fungayi Mawire, Bastian Buck, Anne Beutling, and Katja Kriege. 2014. "Reporting on Sustainable Development at National, Company and Product Levels: The Potential for Alignment of Measurement Systems in a Post-2015 World." Statistics Netherlands, Global Reporting Initiative, and the Sustainability Consortium. http://measurewhatmatters.info/wp-content/uploads/2014/10/Alignment-of-SD-reporting-at-national-company-and-product-levels-CBS-TSC-GRI.pdf.

Hoffman, Andrew, and Stephanie Bertels. 2010. "Who Is Part of the Environmental Movement?" In *Good Cop/Bad Cop: Environmental NGOs and Their Strategies toward Business*, edited by Thomas Lyon. New York: Routledge.

Hoffman, Andrew J. 2009. "Shades of Green." *Stanford Social Innovation Review* 7 (2): 40–49.

Hoffmann, Stanley. 1968. *Gulliver's Troubles: Or, the Setting of American Foreign Policy*. New York: McGraw-Hill.

Holzer, Elizabeth. 2015. *The Concerned Women of Buduburam: Refugee Activists and Humanitarian Dilemmas*. Ithaca, NY: Cornell University Press.

Hopgood, Stephen. 2006. *Keepers of the Flame*. Ithaca, NY: Cornell University Press.

——. 2013. *The Endtimes of Human Rights*. Ithaca, NY: Cornell University Press.

Hoskyns, Teresa. 2014. *The Empty Place: Democracy and Public Space.* Abingdon: Routledge.

Humphreys, David. 2004. "Redefining the Issues: NGO Influence on International Forest Negotiations." *Global Environmental Politics* 4 (2): 51–74. doi:10.1162/152638004323074192.

Hurd, Ian. 1999. "Legitimacy and Authority in International Politics." *International Organization* 53 (2): 379–408. doi:http://www.jstor.org/stable/2601393.

——. 2002. "Legitimacy, Power, and the Symbolic Life of the UN Security Council." *Global Governance* 8 (1): 35–51. doi:http://www.jstor.org/stable/27800326.

——. 2003. "Labour Standards through International Organisations." *Journal of Corporate Citizenship* 2003 (11): 99–111. doi:http://www.jstor.org/stable/27800598.

Huxham, Chris, and Siv Vangen. 2000. "Leadership in the Shaping and Implementation of Collaboration Agendas: How Things Happen in a (Not Quite) Joined-Up World." *Academy of Management Journal* 43 (6): 1159–75. http://www.jstor.org/stable/1556343.

Jackson, Patrick Thaddeus, and Daniel H. Nexon. 2009. "Paradigmatic Faults in International-Relations Theory." *International Studies Quarterly* 53 (4): 907–30. doi:10.1111/j.1468-2478.2009.00562.x.

Johnson, Tana. 2014. *Organizational Progeny: Why Governments Are Losing Control Over the Proliferating Structures of Global Governance.* New York: Oxford University Press.

——. 2016. "Cooperation, Co-optation, Competition, Conflict: International Bureaucracies and Non-Governmental Organizations in an Interdependent World." *Review of International Political Economy.* http://dx.doi.org/10.1080/09692290.2016.1217902.

Johnson, Thomas H. 2009. "Commentary on Mia Bloom, Dying to Kill: The Allure of Suicide Terror." *Critical Studies on Terrorism* 2 (2): 349–52. doi:10.1080/17539150903025002.

Kaneshiro, Matheu, Kirk Lawrence, and Christopher Chase-Dunn. 2012. "Global Environmentalists and Their Movements at the World Social Forums." In *Handbook on World Social Forum Activism,* edited by Jackie Smith et al., 186–205. Boulder, CO: Paradigm Publishers.

Kapstein, Ethan B., and Joshua W. Busby. 2013. *AIDS Drugs for All: Social Movements and Market Transformations.* Cambridge: Cambridge University Press.

Karp, Aaron. 2006. "Escaping Reuterswärd's Shadow." *Contemporary Security Policy* 27 (1): 12–28. doi:10.1080/13523260600602214.

Keane, John. 2003. *Global Civil Society?* New York: Cambridge University Press.

Keck, Margaret E., and Kathryn Sikkink. 1998. *Activists Beyond Borders: Advocacy Networks in International Politics.* Cambridge: Cambridge University Press.

Kelley, Judith. 2007. "Who Keeps International Commitments and Why? The International Criminal Court and Bilateral Nonsurrender Agreements." *American Political Science Review* 101 (3): 573–89. http://www.jstor.org/stable/27644467.

Kell, Georg, and David Levin. 2003. "The Global Compact Network: An Historic Experiment in Learning and Action." *Business and Society Review* 108 (2): 151–81. doi:10.1111/1467-8594.00159.

Keohane, Robert, and Joseph Nye. 1977. *Power and Interdependence: World Politics in Transition.* 2nd ed. Boston: Little, Brown.

Khagram, Sanjeev, James V. Riker, and Kathryn Sikkink, eds. 2002. *Restructuring World Politics: Transnational Movements, Networks, and Norms.* Minneapolis: University of Minnesota Press.

Kindleberger, Charles Poor. 1986. *The World in Depression, 1929–1939*. Berkeley: University of California Press.

Kingston, Lindsey N., and Kathryn R. Stam. 2013. "Online Advocacy: Analysis of Human Rights NGO Websites." *Journal of Human Rights Practice* 5 (1): 75–95. doi:10.1093/jhuman/hus036.

Kirsch, Philippe, and John T. Holmes. 1999. "The Rome Conference on an International Criminal Court: The Negotiating Process." *The American Journal of International Law* 93 (1): 2–12. http://www.jstor.org/stable/2997952.

Klein, Naomi. 2014. *This Changes Everything: Capitalism vs. the Climate*. New York: Simon & Schuster.

Korey, William. 1998. *NGOs and the Universal Declaration of Human Rights*. New York: St. Martin's Press.

Krain, Matthew. 2012. "J'accuse! Does Naming and Shaming Perpetrators Reduce the Severity of Genocides or Politicides?" *International Studies Quarterly* 56 (3): 574–89. doi:10.1111/j.1468-2478.2012.00732.x.

Krasner, Stephen D. 1976. "State Power and the Structure of International Trade." *World Politics* 28 (3): 317–47. doi:10.2307/2009974.

Krause, Keith. 2002. "Multilateral Diplomacy, Norm Building, and UN Conferences: The Case of Small Arms and Light Weapons." *Global Governance* 8: 247–58.

Krause, Monika. 2014. *The Good Project: Humanitarian Relief NGOs and the Fragmentation of Reason*. Chicago: University of Chicago Press.

Krebs, Ronald R., and Patrick Thaddeus Jackson. 2007. "Twisting Tongues and Twisting Arms: The Power of Political Rhetoric." *European Journal of International Relations* 13 (1): 35–66. doi:10.1177/1354066107074284.

Kydd, Andrew H. 2005. *Trust and Mistrust in International Relations*. Princeton, NJ: Princeton University Press.

Kydd, Andrew H., and Barbara F. Walter. 2002. "Sabotaging the Peace: The Politics of Extremist Violence." *International Organization* 56 (2): 263–96. http://www.jstor.org/stable/3078606.

——. 2006. "The Strategies of Terrorism." *International Security* 31 (1): 49–80. http://www.jstor.org/stable/4137539.

Lake, David A. 2009. "Relational Authority and Legitimacy in International Relations." *American Behavioral Scientist* 53 (3): 331–53. doi:10.1177/0002764209338796.

——. 2010. "Rightful Rules: Authority, Order, and the Foundations of Global Governance." *International Studies Quarterly* 54 (3): 587–613. http://www.jstor.org/stable/40931128.

——. "Globalizing Authority." Unpublished manuscript, last modified 2012.

Lake, David A., and Wendy Wong. 2009. "The Politics of Networks: Interests, Power, and Human Rights Norms." In *Networked Politics: Agency, Power, and Governance*, edited by Miles Kahler. Ithaca, NY: Cornell University Press.

Landau, Jean-Pierre. 2004. *Les Nouvelles Contributions Financières Internationales*. La Documentation Française. Rapport au President de la République. http://www.ladocumentationfrancaise.fr/var/storage/rapports-publics/044000440.pdf.

Lang, Sabine. 2013. *NGOs, Civil Society, and the Public Sphere*. Cambridge: Cambridge University Press.

Lange, Donald, Peggy M. Lee, and Ye Dai. 2011. "Organizational Reputation: A Review." *Journal of Management* 37 (1): 153–84. doi:10.1177/0149206310390963.

Larkin, Amy. 2013. *Environmental Debt: The Hidden Costs of a Changing Global Economy*. London: Macmillan Publishers.

Laurance, Edward J. 2013. "The Small Arms Problem As Arms Control." In *Controlling Small Arms: Consolidation, Innovation and Relevance in Research and Policy*, edited by Peter Batchelor and Kai Michael Kenkel. New York: Routledge.

Lenox, Michael J., and Charles E. Eesley. 2009. "Private Environmental Activism and the Selection and Response of Firm Targets." *Journal of Economics & Management Strategy* 18 (1): 45–73. doi:10.1111/j.1530-9134.2009.00207.x.

Levy, David L., Halina Szejnwald Brown, and Martin De Jong. 2010. "The Contested Politics of Corporate Governance the Case of the Global Reporting Initiative." *Business & Society* 49 (1): 88–115. doi:10.1177/0007650309345420.

Lindenberg, Marc, and Coralie Bryant. 2001. *Going Global: Transforming Relief and Development NGOs*. Bloomfield, CT: Kumarian Press.

Linden, Eugene. 1976. *The Alms Race: The Impact of American Voluntary Aid Abroad*. New York: Random House.

Lipschutz, Ronnie D. 1992. "Reconstructing World Politics: The Emergence of Global Civil Society." *Millennium—Journal of International Studies* 21 (3): 389–420. doi:10.1177/03058298920210031001.

Lloyd, Robert, Virginia Calvo, and Christina Laybourn. 2010. "Ensuring Credibility and Effectiveness: Designing Compliance Systems in CSO Self-Regulation." *One World Trust Briefing Paper* 127: 1–18.

Lowell, Stephanie, Brian Trelstad, and Bill Meehan. 2005. "The Ratings Game." *Stanford Social Innovation Review* 3: 38–45.

Lyon, Thomas. 2010. *Good Cop/Bad Cop: Environmental NGOs and Their Strategies toward Business*. Abingdon: Taylor & Francis.

Mack, Daniel, and Brian Wood. 2009. "Civil Society and the Drive Towards an Arms Trade Treaty." United Nations Institute for Disarmament Research (UNIDIR). http://www.unidir.org/files/medias/pdfs/civil-society-and-the-drive-towards-an-arms-trade-treaty-eng-0-418.pdf.

Mansfield, Edward D. 1993. "Concentration, Polarity, and the Distribution of Power." *International Studies Quarterly* 37 (1): 105–28. http://www.jstor.org/stable/2600833.

Marx, Axel, and Dieter Cuypers. 2010. "Forest Certification as a Global Environmental Governance Tool: What Is the Macro-effectiveness of the Forest Stewardship Council?" *Regulation & Governance* 4 (4): 408–34. doi:10.1111/j.1748-5991.2010.01088.x.

Massengill, Rebekah Peeples. 2013. *Wal-Mart Wars: Moral Populism in the Twenty-First Century*. New York: New York University Press.

Mattli, Walter, and Tim Büthe. 2005. "Accountability in Accounting? The Politics of Private Rule-Making in the Public Interest." *Governance* 18 (3): 399–429. doi:10.1111/j.1468-0491.2005.00282.x.

McEntire, Kyla Jo, Michele Leiby, and Matthew Krain. 2015. "Human Rights Organizations as Agents of Change: An Experimental Examination of Framing and Micromobilization." *American Political Science Review* 109 (3): 407–26. doi:10.1017/S0003055415000295.

Mearsheimer, John J. 2001. *The Tragedy of Great Power Politics*. W. W. Norton & Company.

Meeks, Margot, and Rachel Chen. 2011. "Can Walmart Integrate Values with Value?: From Sustainability to Sustainable Business." *Journal of Sustainable Development* 4 (5) (October): 62–66.

Mertes, Tom, and Walden F. Bello. 2004. *A Movement of Movements: Is Another World Really Possible?* New York: Verso.

Merton, Robert K. 1968. "The Matthew Effect in Science." *Science* 159 (3810): 56–63. doi:10.1126/science.159.3810.56.

Mitchell, George E. 2015. "The Strategic Orientations of US-Based NGOs." *Voluntas* 26 (5): 1874–93. doi:10.1007/s11266-014-9507-5.

Mitchell, George E., and Sarah S. Stroup. 2016. "The Reputations of NGOs: Peer Evaluations of Effectiveness." *The Review of International Organizations.* doi:10.1007/s11558-016-9259-7.

Mitchell, Stacy. 2013. "Walmart's Assault on the Climate: The Truth Behind One of the Biggest Climate Polluters and Slickest Greenwashers in America." Institute for Local Self-Reliance. http://ilsr.org/wp-content/uploads/2013/10/ILSR-_Report_WalmartClimateChange.pdf.

Morena, Edouard. 2012. "Campaign or 'Movement of Movements'? Attac France and the Currency of Transaction Tax." In *Global Justice Activism and Policy Reform in Europe: Understanding When Change Happens,* edited by Peter Utting, Mario Pianta, and Anne Ellersiek, 273–96. Abingdon: Routledge.

Moreton, Bethany. 2009. *To Serve God and Wal-Mart: The Making of Christian Free Enterprise.* Cambridge, MA: Harvard University Press.

Mühle, Ursula. 2010. *The Politics of Corporate Social Responsibility: The Rise of a Global Business Norm.* New York: Campus Verlag.

Mulley, Clare. 2009. *The Woman Who Saved the Children: A Biography of Eglantyne Jebb: Founder of Save the Children.* Oxford: Oneworld Publications.

Murdie, Amanda. 2014. *Help or Harm: The Human Security Effects of International NGOs.* Stanford, CA: Stanford University Press.

Murdie, Amanda, and David R. Davis. 2012a. "Looking in the Mirror: Comparing INGO Networks Across Issue Areas." *The Review of International Organizations* 7 (2): 177–202. doi:10.1007/s11558-011-9134-5.

——. 2012b. "Shaming and Blaming: Using Events Data to Assess the Impact of Human Rights INGOs." *International Studies Quarterly* 56 (1): 1–16. doi:10.1111/j.1468-2478.2011.00694.x.

Murdie, Amanda, and Johannes Urpelainen. 2015. "Why Pick On Us? Environmental INGOs and State Shaming as a Strategic Substitute." *Political Studies* 63 (2): 353–72.

Mwangi, Wagaki, Lothar Rieth, and Hans Peter Schmitz. 2011. "Encouraging Greater Compliance: Local Networks and the United Nations Global Compact." In *The Persistent Power of Human Rights: From Commitment to Compliance,* edited by Thomas Risse, Stephen C. Ropp, and Kathryn Sikkink. Cambridge: Cambridge University Press.

Naidoo, Kumi. 2009. "Global Civil Society Forums and Poverty." In *Global Civil Society Yearbook 2009: Poverty and Activism,* edited by Ashwani Kumar, Jan Aart Scholte, Mary Kaldor, Marlies Glasius, Hakan Seckinelgin, and Helmut K Anheier. London: Sage Publications.

Naidoo, Kumi, and Rajesh Tandon. 1999. *Civil Society at the Millennium.* West Hartford, CT: Kumarian Press. http://www.jstor.org/stable/20097573.

Naím, Moises. 2002. "Al Qaeda, the NGO: After Floundering During the 1990s, Can Political Parties Learn a Few Lessons from Nongovernmental Organizations? (Missing Links)." *Foreign Policy* 129 (March–April): 99–100.

Nelson, Paul. 2002. "New Agendas and New Patterns of International NGO Political Action." *Voluntas: International Journal of Voluntary and Nonprofit Organizations* 13 (4): 377–92. doi:10.1023/A:1022062010375.

Nelson, Paul J., and Ellen Dorsey. 2008. *New Rights Advocacy: Changing Strategies of Development and Human Rights NGOs.* Washington, DC: Georgetown University Press.

Neumann, Iver B., and Ole Jacob Sending. 2010. *Governing the Global Polity: Practice, Mentality, Rationality*. Ann Arbor: University of Michigan Press.

Newman, Abraham L. 2008. *Protectors of Privacy: Regulating Personal Data in the Global Economy*. Ithaca, NY: Cornell University Press.

Nielson, Daniel L., and Michael J. Tierney. 2003. "Delegation to International Organizations: Agency Theory and World Bank Environmental Reform." *International Organization* 57 (2): 241–76. doi:10.1017/S0020818303572010.

Nye, Joseph S. 2008. "Public Diplomacy and Soft Power." *The Annals of the American Academy of Political and Social Science* 616 (1): 94–109. doi:10.1177/000271620 7311699.

———. 2004. *Soft Power: The Means to Success in World Politics*. New York: PublicAffairs Books.

O'Connor, Amy, and Michelle Shumate. 2014. "Differences Among NGOs in the Business-NGO Cooperative Network." *Business & Society* 53 (1) (January 1): 105–33. doi:10.1177/0007650311418195.

O'Rourke, Dara. 2014. "The Science of Sustainable Supply Chains." *Science* 344 (6188): 1124–27. doi:10.1126/science.1248526.

Overdevest, Christine. 2010. "Comparing Forest Certification Schemes: The Case of Ratcheting Standards in the Forest Sector." *Socio-Economic Review* 8 (1): 47–76. doi:10.1093/ser/mwp028.

Overdevest, Christine, and Mark G. Rickenbach. 2006. "Forest Certification and Institutional Governance: An Empirical Study of Forest Stewardship Council Certificate Holders in the United States." *Forest Policy and Economics* 9 (1): 93–102. doi:10.1016/j.forpol.2005.03.014.

Padgett, John F., and Christopher K. Ansell. 1993. "Robust Action and the Rise of the Medici, 1400–1434." *American Journal of Sociology* 98 (6): 1259–1319. http://www.jstor.org/stable/2781822.

Pallas, Christopher L., and Anders Uhlin. 2014. "Civil Society Influence on International Organizations: Theorizing the State Channel." *Journal of Civil Society* 10 (2): 184–203. doi:10.1080/17448689.2014.921102.

Pape, Robert A. 2003. "The Strategic Logic of Suicide Terrorism." *American Political Science Review* 97 (3): 343–61. doi:10.1017/S000305540300073X.

———. 2009. "Introduction: What Is New About Research on Terrorism." *Security Studies* 18 (4): 643–50. doi:10.1080/09636410903369100.

Patomäki, Heikki. 2009. "The Tobin Tax and Global Civil Society Organisations: The Aftermath of the 2008–9 Financial Crisis." *Ritsumeikan Annual Review of International Studies* 8 (1): 1–18. http://www.ritsumei.ac.jp/acd/cg/ir/college/bulletin/e-vol.8/01_Hekki.pdf.

Paul, Thaza Varkey, Deborah Welch Larson, and William C. Wohlforth. 2014. *Status in World Politics*. Cambridge: Cambridge University Press.

Pelc, Krzysztof J. 2013. "Googling the WTO: What Search-Engine Data Tell Us About the Political Economy of Institutions." *International Organization* 67 (3): 629–55. doi:10.1017/S0020818313000179.

Penrose, Angela, and John Seaman. 1996. "The Save the Children Fund and Nutrition for Refugees." In *The Conscience of the World: The Influence of Non-Governmental Organisations in the UN System*, edited by Peter Willetts. London: C. Hurst & Co. Publishers.

Percy, Sarah V. 2007. "Mercenaries: Strong Norm, Weak Law." *International Organization* 61 (2): 367–97. doi:10.1017/S0020818307070130.

Pew Research Center. 2003. *Views of a Changing World*. Global Attitudes Project. Washington, DC: Pew Research Center. http://www.people-press.org/files/legacy-pdf/185.pdf.

Pinsky, Marian. 2010. "From Reactive to Proactive: The World Social Forum and the Anti-/Alter-Globalization Movement." *McGill Sociological Review* 1: 3–28. https://www.mcgill.ca/msr/volume1/article1.

Plambeck, Erica L., and Lyn Denend. 2008. "The Greening of Wal-Mart." *Stanford Social Innovation Review* 6 (2): 53–59. http://ssir.org/articles/entry/the_greening_of_wal_mart.

Pleyers, Geoffrey. 2012. "A Decade of World Social Forums." In *Global Civil Society 2012: Ten Years of Critical Reflection*, edited by Mary Kaldor, Henrietta L. Moore, and Sabine Selchow. New York: Palgrave Macmillan.

Podolny, Joel M. 2010. *Status Signals: A Sociological Study of Market Competition.* Princeton, NJ: Princeton University Press.

Poe, Steven C., C. Neal Tate, and Linda Camp Keith. 1999. "Repression of the Human Right to Personal Integrity Revisited: A Global Cross-National Study Covering the Years 1976–1993." *International Studies Quarterly* 43 (2): 291–313. http://www.jstor.org/stable/2600757.

Polman, Linda. 2010. *The Crisis Caravan: What's Wrong with Humanitarian Aid?* New York: Macmillan Publishers.

Post, James E. 2012. "The United Nations Global Compact: A CSR Milestone." *Business & Society.* doi:10.1177/0007650312459926.

Potoski, Matthew, and Aseem Prakash. 2005. "Green Clubs and Voluntary Governance: ISO 14001 and Firms' Regulatory Compliance." *American Journal of Political Science* 49 (2): 235–48. doi:10.1111/j.0092-5853.2005.00120.x.

Prakash, Aseem, and Mary Kay Gugerty. 2010. *Advocacy Organizations and Collective Action.* Cambridge: Cambridge University Press.

Prakash, Aseem, and Matthew Potoski. 2012. "Voluntary Environmental Programs: A Comparative Perspective." *Journal of Policy Analysis and Management* 31 (1): 123–38. doi:10.1002/pam.20617.

Price, Richard. 1998. "Reversing the Gun Sights: Transnational Civil Society Targets Land Mines." *International Organization* 52 (3): 613–44. http://www.jstor.org/stable/2601403.

———. 2003. "Transnational Civil Society and Advocacy in World Politics." *World Politics* 55 (4): 579–606. http://www.jstor.org/stable/25054239.

Quinn, Bill. 2012. *How Walmart Is Destroying America and the World: And What You Can Do About It.* 3rd ed. Berkeley, CA: Ten Speed Press.

Rao, Hayagreeva, Gerald F. Davis, and Andrew Ward. 2000. "Embeddedness, Social Identity and Mobility: Why Firms Leave the NASDAQ and Join the New York Stock Exchange." *Administrative Science Quarterly* 45 (2): 268–92. doi:10.2307/2667072.

Rasche, Andreas. 2009. "'A Necessary Supplement.' What the United Nations Global Compact Is and Is Not." *Business & Society* 48 (4): 511–37. doi:10.1177/0007650309332378.

Raz, Joseph. 1986. *The Morality of Freedom.* Oxford: Oxford University Press.

Redfield, Peter. 2013. *Life in Crisis: The Ethical Journey of Doctors without Borders.* Oakland: University of California Press.

Reimann, Kim D. 2006. "A View from the Top: International Politics, Norms and the Worldwide Growth of NGOs." *International Studies Quarterly* 50 (1): 45–68. http://scholarworks.gsu.edu/political_science_facpub/4.

Reinalda, Bob. 2015. "The Co-Evolution of Non-Governmental and Intergovernmental Organizations in Historical Perspective." In *The NGO Challenge for International Relations Theory*, edited by William E. DeMars and Dennis Dijkzeul. New York: Routledge.

Reitan, Ruth. 2007. *Global Activism*. New York: Routledge.

——. 2009. "The Global Anti-War Movement Within and Beyond the World Social Forum." *Globalizations* 6 (4): 509–23. doi:10.1080/14747730903298892.

Reitan, Ruth, and Shannon Gibson. 2012. "Climate Change or Social Change? Environmental and Leftist Praxis and Participatory Action Research." *Globalizations* 9 (3): 395–410. doi:10.1080/14747731.2012.680735.

Rickenbach, Mark, and Christine Overdevest. 2006. "More than Markets: Assessing Forest Stewardship Council (FSC) Certification as a Policy Tool." *Journal of Forestry* 104 (3): 143–47. http://www.ingentaconnect.com/content/saf/jof/2006/00000104/00000003/art00008.

Risse, Thomas. 2000. "'Let's Argue!': Communicative Action in World Politics." *International Organization* 54 (1): 1–39. http://www.jstor.org/stable/2601316.

——. 2010. "Rethinking Advocacy Organizations? A Critical Comment." In *Advocacy Organizations and Collective Action*, edited by Aseem Prakash and Mary Kay Gugerty. New York: Cambridge University Press.

Risse, Thomas, Stephen C. Ropp, and Kathryn Sikkink. 1999. *The Power of Human Rights International Norms and Domestic Change*. Vol. 66. Cambridge: Cambridge University Press.

Roach, Steven C. 2011. "The Turbulent Politics of the International Criminal Court." *Peace Review* 23 (4): 546–51. doi:10.1080/10402659.2011.625870.

Roberts, J. Timmons, Bradley C. Parks, and Alexis A. Vásquez. 2004. "Who Ratifies Environmental Treaties and Why? Institutionalism, Structuralism and Participation by 192 Nations in 22 Treaties." *Global Environmental Politics* 4 (3): 22–64. doi:10.1162/1526380041748029.

Ron, James, Howard Ramos, and Kathleen Rodgers. 2005. "Transnational Information Politics: NGO Human Rights Reporting, 1986–2000." *International Studies Quarterly* 49 (3): 557–88. doi:10.1111/j.1468-2478.2005.00377.x.

Rosenau, James N. 1995. "Governance in the Twenty-First Century." *Global Governance* 1 (1): 13–43. http://www.jstor.org/stable/27800099.

Rubenstein, Jennifer C. 2014. "The Misuse of Power, Not Bad Representation: Why It Is Beside the Point That No One Elected Oxfam." *Journal of Political Philosophy* 22 (2): 204–30. doi:10.1111/jopp.12020.

Rucht, Dieter. 2012. "Social Fora as Public Stage and Infrastructure of Global Justice Movements." In *A Handbook on World Social Forum Activism*, edited by Jackie Smith, S. Byrd, E. Reese, and E. Smythe. Boulder, CO: Paradigm Publishers.

Ruggie, John Gerard. 2001. "The Global Compact as Learning Network." *Global Governance* 7 (4): 371–78. http://www.jstor.org/stable/27800311.

——. 2004. "Reconstituting the Global Public Domain—Issues, Actors, and Practices." *European Journal of International Relations* 10 (4): 499–531. doi:10.1177/1354066104047847.

——. 2013. *Just Business: Multinational Corporations and Human Rights*. Norton Global Ethics Series. New York: W. W. Norton & Company.

Rutherford, Ken, Stefan Brem, and Richard Anthony Matthew. 2003. *Reframing the Agenda: The Impact of NGO and Middle Power Cooperation in International Security Policy*. Westport, CT: Greenwood Publishing Group.

Sandler, Todd. 2011. "New Frontiers of Terrorism Research: An Introduction." *Journal of Peace Research* 48 (3): 279–86. doi:10.1177/0022343311399131.

Sasser, Erika N., Aseem Prakash, Benjamin Cashore, and Graeme Auld. 2006. "Direct Targeting as an NGO Political Strategy: Examining Private Authority Regimes in the Forestry Sector." *Business and Politics* 8 (3). doi:10.2202/1469-3569.1163.

Scerri, Andy. 2013. "The World Social Forum: Another World Might Be Possible." *Social Movement Studies* 12 (1): 111–20. doi:10.1080/14742837.2012.711522.

Schabas, William A. 2011. *An Introduction to the International Criminal Court.* 4th ed. Cambridge: Cambridge University Press.

Scheffer, David J. 1999. "The United States and the International Criminal Court." *The American Journal of International Law* 93 (1): 12–22. http://www.jstor.org/stable/2997953.

Schepers, Donald H. 2010. "Challenges to Legitimacy at the Forest Stewardship Council." *Journal of Business Ethics* 92 (2): 279–90. doi:10.1007/s10551-009-0154-5.

Scholte, Jan Aart. 2002. "Civil Society and Democracy in Global Governance." *Global Governance* 8 (3): 281–304. http://www.jstor.org/stable/27800346.

——. 2011a. *Building Global Democracy? Civil Society and Accountable Global Governance.* Cambridge: Cambridge University Press.

——. 2011b. "Towards Greater Legitimacy in Global Governance." *Review of International Political Economy* 18 (1): 110–20. doi:10.1080/09692290.2011.545215.

Scott, Esther, and L. David Brown. 2004. *Oxfam America: Becoming a Global Campaigning Organization.* Kennedy School of Government Case Program. Harvard Business Publishing. http://case.hks.harvard.edu/oxfam-america-becoming-a-global-campaigning-organization/.

Seabrooke, Leonard, and Duncan Wigan. 2015. "How Activists Use Benchmarks: Reformist and Revolutionary Benchmarks for Global Economic Justice." *Review of International Studies* 41 (5): 887–904. doi:10.1017/S0260210515000376.

Sell, Susan K. 2002. "TRIPS and the Access to Medicines Campaign." *Wisconsin International Law Journal* 20 (3): 481–595. http://heinonline.org/HOL/LandingPage?handle=hein.journals/wisint20&div=24&id=&page=.

Sending, Ole Jacob. 2015. *The Politics of Expertise: Competing for Authority in Global Governance.* Ann Arbor: University of Michigan Press.

Sethi, S. Prakash, and Donald H. Schepers. 2014. "United Nations Global Compact: The Promise-Performance Gap." *Journal of Business Ethics* 122 (2): 193–208. doi:10.1007/s10551-013-1629-y.

Shawki, Noha. 2010. "Organizational Structure and Strength and Transnational Campaign Outcomes: A Comparison of Two Transnational Advocacy Networks." *Global Networks* 11 (1): 97–117. doi:10.1111/j.1471-0374.2011.00309.x.

Shumate, Michelle, and Amy O'Connor. 2010. "Corporate Reporting of Cross-Sector Alliances: The Portfolio of NGO Partners Communicated on Corporate Websites." *Communication Monographs* 77 (2): 207–30. doi:10.1080/03637751003758201.

Shurtman, Monica. 2008. "The Challenges of Evaluating NGO 'Success' in Cross-Border Rights Initiatives." In *Progress in International Law,* edited by Russell Miller and Rebecca M. Bratspies, 357–80. Boston: Martinus Nijhoff Publishers.

Siméant, Johanna. 2013. "Committing to Internationalisation: Careers of African Participants at the World Social Forum." *Social Movement Studies* 12 (3): 245–63. doi:10.1080/14742837.2012.714125.

Simmons, Beth A., and Allison Danner. 2010. "Credible Commitments and the International Criminal Court." *International Organization* 64 (2): 225–56. doi:10.1017/S0020818310000044.

Simmons, Peter J. 1998. "Learning to Live with NGOs." *Foreign Policy* 112: 82–96. http://carnegieendowment.org/1998/10/01/learning-to-live-with-ngos.

Smith, Jackie. 2002. "Bridging Global Divides? Strategic Framing and Solidarity in Transnational Social Movement Organizations." *International Sociology* 17 (4): 505–28. doi:10.1177/0268580902017004003.

——. 2004. "The World Social Forum and the Challenges of Global Democracy." *Global Networks* 4 (4): 413–21. doi:10.1111/j.1471-0374.2004.00102.x.

Smith, Jackie, and Dawn Wiest. 2005. "The Uneven Geography of Global Civil Society: National and Global Influences on Transnational Association." *Social Forces* 84 (2): 621–52. doi:10.1353/sof.2006.0036.

——. 2012. "Social Movements in the World-System: The Politics of Crisis and Transformation." Russell Sage Foundation. http://www.jstor.org/stable/10.7758/9781610447775.

Snow, David A., and Sarah A. Soule. 2010. *A Primer on Social Movements*. New York: W.W. Norton & Company.

Soule, Sarah A. 2009. *Contention and Corporate Social Responsibility*. New York: Cambridge University Press.

Spar, Debora L., and James Dail. 2002. "Of Measurement and Mission: Accounting for Performance in Non-Governmental Organizations." *Chicago Journal of International Law* 3 (1): 171–74. http://chicagounbound.uchicago.edu/cjil/vol3/iss1/15.

Spar, Debora L., and Lane T. La Mure. 2003. "The Power of Activism: Assessing the Impact of NGOs on Global Business." *California Management Review* 45 (3): 78–101. doi:10.2307/41166177.

Stalker, Chris, and Steve Tibbett. 2012. *Oxfam International Arms Trade Treaty/Control Arms Campaign Independent Review*. Oxford: Oxfam.

Stavrianakis, Anna. 2012. "Missing the Target: NGOs, Global Civil Society and the Arms Trade." *Journal of International Relations and Development* 15 (2): 224–49. doi:10.1057/jird.2011.22.

Stecher, Heinz, and Michael Bailey. 1999. "Time for a Tobin Tax? Some Practical and Political Arguments." *Policy Paper*. http://policy-practice.oxfam.org.uk/publications/time-for-a-tobin-tax-some-practical-and-political-arguments-114052.

Steger, Manfred B., and Erin K. Wilson. "Anti-Globalization or Alter-Globalization? Mapping the Political Ideology of the Global Justice Movement 1." *International Studies Quarterly* 56 (3) (2012): 439–54. doi:10.1111/j.1468-2478.2012.00740.x.

Stein, Janice Gross. 2008. "Humanitarian Organizations: Accountable—Why, to Whom, for What, and How?" In *Humanitarianism in Question: Politics, Power, Ethics*, edited by Michael Barnett and Thomas Weiss. Ithaca, NY: Cornell University Press.

Stoddard, Abby. 2006. *Humanitarian Alert: NGO Information and Its Impact on US Foreign Policy*. Bloomfield: Kumarian Press.

Stohl, Rachel. 2015. "A Year On, States Aren't Enforcing the Landmark Arms Trade Treaty." *World Politics Review* (December 29). http://www.worldpoliticsreview.com/articles/17563/a-year-on-states-aren-t-enforcing-the-landmark-arms-trade-treaty.

Stroup, Sarah S. 2012. *Borders Among Activists: International NGOs in the United States, Britain, and France*. Ithaca, NY: Cornell University Press. http://www.jstor.org/stable/10.7591/j.ctt7z7j1.

——. 2016. "Robbing from the Rich: NGO Power in the Financial Transactions Tax Campaign." Paper prepared for the annual meeting of the International Studies Association, Atlanta, GA, March 16–19.

Stroup, Sarah S., and Wendy H. Wong. 2013. "Come Together? Different Pathways to International NGO Centralization." *International Studies Review* 15 (2): 163–84. doi:10.1111/misr.12022.

——. 2016. "The Agency and Authority of International NGOs." *Perspectives on Politics* 14 (1): 138–44. doi:10.1017/S153759271500328X.

Struett, Michael J. 2008. *The Politics of Constructing the International Criminal Court*. New York: Palgrave Macmillan.

Subramanian, Vairavan, Wesley Ingwersen, Connie Hensler, and Heather Collie. 2012. "Comparing Product Category Rules from Different Programs: Learned Outcomes Towards Global Alignment." *The International Journal of Life Cycle Assessment* 17 (7): 892–903. doi:10.1007/s11367-012-0419-6.

Swidler, Ann. 2006. "Syncretism and Subversion in AIDS Governance: How Locals Cope with Global Demands." *International Affairs* 82 (2): 269–84. doi:10.1111/j.1468-2346.2006.00530.x.

Synnott, Timothy. 2005. "Some Notes on the Early Years of FSC." November. https://ic.fsc.org/preview.notes-on-the-early-years-of-fsc.a-798.pdf.

Tallberg, Jonas, Thomas Sommerer, Theresa Squatrito, and Christer Jönsson. 2013. *The Opening Up of International Organizations: Transnational Access in Global Governance*. Cambridge: Cambridge University Press.

Tarrow, Sidney. 2005. *The New Transnational Activism*. Cambridge Studies in Contentious Politics. Cambridge: Cambridge University Press.

Thérien, Jean-Philippe, and Vincent Pouliot. "The Global Compact: Shifting the Politics of International Development?" *Global Governance: A Review of Multilateralism and International Organizations* 12 (1): 55–75. http://www.jstor.org/stable/27800598.

Thrall, Trevor, Dominik Stecula, and Diana Sweet. 2014. "May We Have Your Attention Please? Human-Rights NGOs and the Problem of Global Communication." *The International Journal of Press/Politics*. doi:10.1177/1940161213519132.

Törnquist-Chesnier, Marie. 2004. "NGOs and International Law." *Journal of Human Rights* 3 (2): 253–63. doi:10.1080/1475483042000210766.

Ul Haq, Mahbub, Inge Kaul, and Isabelle Grunberg. 1996. *The Tobin Tax: Coping with Financial Volatility*. Oxford: Oxford University Press.

Voeten, Erik. 2013. "Public Opinion and Legitimacy of International Courts." *Theoretical Inquiries in Law* 14 (2): 411–36.

Vogel, David. 2005. *The Market for Virtue. The Potential and Limits of Corporate Social Responsibility*. Washington, DC: Brookings Institution Press.

———. 2008. "Private Global Business Regulation." *Annual Review of Political Science* 11: 261–82. doi:10.1146/annurev.polisci.11.053106.141706.

Vollenweider, Jürg. 2013. "The Effectiveness of International Environmental Agreements." *International Environmental Agreements: Politics, Law and Economics* 13 (3): 343–67. doi:10.1007/s10784-012-9193-y.

Wade, Sara Jackson, and Dan Reiter. 2007. "Does Democracy Matter? Regime Type and Suicide Terrorism." *Journal of Conflict Resolution* 51 (2): 329–48. doi:10.1177/0022002706298137.

Wahl, Peter. 2014. "The European Civil Society Campaign on the Financial Transaction Tax." Global Labour University Working Paper. http://EconPapers.repec.org/RePEc:ilo:ilowps:484767.

Wallace, Tina. 2009. "NGO Dilemmas: Trojan Horses for Global Neoliberalism?" *Socialist Register* 40: 202–19. http://socialistregister.com/index.php/srv/article/viewArticle/5818#.V_Kmynpmps5.

Waltz, Susan. 2014. "Arms Transfers and the Human Rights Agenda." In *The Uses and Misuses of Human Rights: A Critical Approach to Advocacy*, edited by George Andreopoulos and Zehra F. Kabasakal Arat. New York: Palgrave Macmillan.

Wapner, Paul. 1996. *Environmental Activism and World Civic Politics*. Albany: State University of New York Press.

Warleigh, Alex. 2000. "The Hustle: Citizenship Practice, NGOs and 'Policy Coalitions' in the European Union—the Cases of Auto Oil, Drinking Water and Unit Pricing." *Journal of European Public Policy* 7 (2): 229–43. doi:10.1080/135017600343179.

Watkins, Susan Cotts, Ann Swidler, and Thomas Hannan. 2012. "Outsourcing Social Transformation: Development NGOs as Organizations." *Sociology* 38: 289–315. doi:10.1146/annurev-soc-071811-145516.

Weaver, Catherine. 2008. *Hypocrisy Trap: The World Bank and the Poverty of Reform.* Princeton, NJ: Princeton University Press.

Weaver, James H., Randall Dodd, and Jamie Baker. 2003. *Debating the Tobin Tax: New Rules for Global Finance.* Washington, DC: New Rules for Global Finance Coalition.

Weiss, Thomas George, and Leon Gordenker. 1996. *NGOs, the UN, and Global Governance.* Boulder, CO: Lynne Rienner.

Weiss, Thomas G., and Rorden Wilkinson. 2014. "Rethinking Global Governance? Complexity, Authority, Power, Change." *International Studies Quarterly* 58 (1): 207–15. doi:10.1111/isqu.12082.

Welch, Claude E. 2001. *NGOs and Human Rights: Promise and Performance.* Philadelphia: University of Pennsylvania Press.

Welch, Claude E., and Ashley F. Watkins. 2011. "Extending Enforcement: The Coalition for the International Criminal Court." *Human Rights Quarterly* 33 (4): 927–1031.

Williams, Oliver F. 2004. "The UN Global Compact: The Challenge and the Promise." *Business Ethics Quarterly* 14 (4): 755–74. doi:10.5840/beq200414432.

——. 2014. "The United Nations Global Compact: What Did It Promise?" *Journal of Business Ethics* 122 (2): 241–51. doi:10.1007/s10551-014-2219-3.

Wong, Wendy H. 2011. "Is Trafficking Slavery? Anti-Slavery International in the Twenty-First Century." *Human Rights Review* 12 (3): 315–28.

——. 2012. *Internal Affairs: How the Structure of NGOs Transforms Human Rights.* Ithaca, NY: Cornell University Press.

Yanacopulos, Helen. 2015. *International NGO Engagement, Advocacy, Activism: The Faces and Spaces of Change.* Basingstoke: Palgrave Macmillan.

Yang, Guobin. 2005. "Environmental NGOs and Institutional Dynamics in China." *The China Quarterly* 181 (1): 44–66. doi:10.1017/S0305741005000032.

Yaziji, Michael, and Jonathan Doh. 2009. *NGOs and Corporations: Conflict and Collaboration.* Cambridge: Cambridge University Press.

Zelko, Frank. 2013. *Make It a Green Peace!: The Rise of Countercultural Environmentalism.* New York: Oxford University Press.

Zürn, Michael. 1998. "The Rise of International Environmental Politics: A Review of Current Research." *World Politics* 50 (4): 617–49. http://www.jstor.org/stable/25054058.

——. 2017. "From Constitutional Rule to Loosely Coupled Spheres of Liquid Authority: A Reflexive Approach." *International Theory* FirstView. http://dx.doi.org/10.1017/S1752971916000270.

Zürn, Michael, Martin Binder, and Matthias Ecker-Ehrhardt. 2012. "International Authority and Its Politicization." *International Theory* 4 (1): 69–106. doi:10.1017/S1752971912000012.

Index

Page numbers followed by t refer to tables.